C000098394

Therapeutic Action

Therapeutic Action

A GUIDE TO PSYCHOANALYTIC THERAPY

ENRICO E. JONES, PH.D.

JASON ARONSON INC.
Northvale, New Jersey
London

Production Editor: Elaine Lindenblatt

This book was printed and bound by Book-mart Press, Inc. of North Bergen, NJ.

Library of Congress Cataloging-in-Publication Data

Jones, Enrico E., 1947–
    Therapeutic action : a guide to psychoanalytic therapy / by Enrico E. Jones.
        p. cm.
    Includes bibliographical references and index.
    ISBN 0-7657-0243-6
    1. Psychodynamic psychotherapy.   2. Psychoanalysis.   3. Psychotherapist and patient.   I. Title.
    [DNLM: 1. Psychoanalytic Therapy—methods. WM 460.6 J76t 2000]
  RC489.P72 J66 2000
  616.89'17—dc21
                                                                    99-044464

Printed in the United States of America on acid-free paper. For information and catalog write to Jason Aronson Inc., 230 Livingston Street, Northvale, NJ 07647-1726, or visit our website: www.aronson.com

To Marta Port Jones,
who taught me to understand others
and the value of independent thought,
with love and gratitude

Contents

Preface

A Guide to Psychoanalytic Therapy

This book clarifies approaches to intervention that are derived from a psychoanalytic perspective and have, in many instances, found their way into the broad culture of psychotherapy. Many therapists may not be fully aware of the psychoanalytic theory behind these approaches. The detailed descriptions of process in psychoanalytic psychotherapy contained in this book will aid clinical practitioners who want to learn more about effective intervention and the theoretical bases and scientific foundations for their techniques.

This book is grounded in empirically derived descriptions of the therapy process in recorded analytic treatments. These illustrations are accompanied by explanations of presumed change mechanisms, all framed in such a way as to advise therapists how treatments might be effectively conducted. Recordings, whether audio- or videotaped, of the dialogue between patient and therapist are rare because of the need to safeguard patient confidentiality. As a consequence, therapists in training rarely have the opportunity to directly observe the methods of experienced therapists. This book provides verbatim illustrations of different interventions and types of interactions between patient and therapist.

Verbatim dialogue from therapy sessions is, of course, open to alternate interpretations or formulations. After reviewing the segments that are provided throughout this volume, the reader may come to conclusions that differ from those of the author. Such differences in interpretation of clinical material are reasonable given the theoretical differences among psychoanalytically oriented clinicians. Differences in interpretation also arise due to an absence of simple methods to verify or validate formulations. Verbatim illustrations offer the advantage of making open and available the data from which alternative formulations might be derived. It is hoped that these illustrations will stimulate thought and discussion.

This book advances a theory about how patients change in therapy, that is, the nature of therapeutic action. The means by which analytic therapies promote patient change is currently one of the most debated topics in the field. A new model of *interaction structure* attempts to bridge those theories of therapeutic action that focus on insight and those that emphasize the therapy relationship. Interaction structures allow consideration of both the intrapsychic and interpersonal interaction by recognizing the intrapsychic as an important basis for what becomes manifest in the interactive field.

This book is also a guide to psychoanalytic therapy. There has been an increasing interest among psychotherapists, and the mental health world in general, in research on the effectiveness of psychological treatments and on how they work. Treatment manuals have become popular. They can serve to guide the training of therapists and, in studies of psychotherapy, to measure therapists' conformity with the intended treatments. The origin of this book is in the need for a description of psychoanalytic psychotherapy.

The exposition of psychoanalytic therapy in a manual format presents complex challenges. It is more difficult to design a manual for psychoanalytic psychotherapies—in which the therapist's actions are guided by a dynamic conceptualization of the patient's problems after the patient has been listened to and presumably understood—than for treatments that are more strongly prescriptive, such as cognitive-behavioral or drug addiction counseling modalities. Proficiency in the conduct of psychoanalytic therapy can be achieved only through the combination of didactic teaching, closely supervised clinical practice, and development of the clinician's self-reflective capacities. This book can serve as a foundation for the training of therapists and a useful reference for more experienced therapists.

Therapy manuals are usually based on a combination of theory and clinical experience. Recommendations for therapist technique rely mostly on clinical vignettes. However, empirical data verifying the nature of the therapy process are usually not available. Although manuals attempt to specify what, in theory, should occur in the treatment, they do not describe what actually occurs in psychotherapies. In contrast, this book is grounded in descriptions of the therapy process in real treatments. The Berkeley Psychotherapy Research Project undertook the intensive study of videotapes and verbatim transcripts of hundreds of treatment sessions from brief and long-term psychotherapies and psychoanalyses conducted by experienced therapists and psychoanalysts. The nature and evolution of the treatment process in these therapies were described using a measure called the Psychotherapy Process Q-set (PQS) (see Chapters 7 and 8). This measure generated a rich set of descriptors of the range of techniques and intervention styles applied in these treatments, as well as of the nature of the patient–therapist interaction and transference–countertransference reactions. These empirically derived descriptions are the foundation for this book. Descriptions of therapy process as it naturally occurs demonstrate, in concrete and specific terms, how therapists conduct effective treatments. The reader is also able to see how clinical and theoretical principles are brought to bear on clinical case material in straightforward and vivid language. This more empirical approach to constructing a manual stands in contrast to the usual statements about treatments that rely on one theorist's articulation of a particular approach to therapy.

Theoretical Point of View

The model of psychoanalytic therapy presented here emphasizes that there are two persons in the therapy relationship, and that the unconscious psychological processes of each influence the other. Conventional conceptions about therapy assume that therapist actions or techniques promote patient change. Influence is presumed to flow principally in one direction—from therapist to patient. Conventional approaches to diagnosis, and manuals that attempt to tailor treatments to particular diagnostic categories, underemphasize, indeed overlook, a conception of process that is attentive to the role of the therapist's interaction with the patient in the change process. An interactional perspective recognizes more explicitly the influence of patient characteristics and behavior on the therapist, on the therapy relationship, and on the development of the therapeutic process. It emphasizes an appreciation of mutual influence processes in psychotherapy.

Contemporary Freudian and modern Kleinian perspectives also strongly inform this work. The ideas developed here by no means derive from an exclusively relational or intersubjective point of view. Indeed, the point of view espoused here does not fit easily into a theoretical "box." The focus is on therapeutic *process*, not a theoretical school. The perspective on diagnosis, technique, and therapeutic action that is assumed is relevant to the several theories within psychoanalysis. This "pantheoretical" perspective is in keeping with the empirical basis of this book, and with the research methods used to arrive at key constructs. The notion of *interaction structures* will be discussed more fully in later chapters as a central component of therapeutic action. It is derived from the research application of the PQS, which was constructed to be a theoretically inclusive instrument for describing and quantifying analytic therapy process.

Interaction Structures

The two principal lines of thought about the nature of therapeutic action have been organized around the mutative effects of (1) interpretation and (2) interpersonal interaction. Those who emphasize the importance of interpretation view as decisive the patient's self-knowledge, understanding, and insight. Interactive models, in turn, emphasize interpersonal and relationship factors, such as empathy, a sense of safety, the containment of feelings, the holding environment, and therapeutic alliance. Interaction-oriented theorists stress the possibilities offered by a new object relationship to permit the resumption of developmental processes that are hypothesized to have been arrested by trauma or deficiencies in early interpersonal relations. These ideas parallel the debate concerning the usefulness of a one-person as opposed to a two-person psychology for conceptualizing therapeutic and analytic process.

The efforts of the Berkeley project led to the development of a theory of therapeutic action that bridges the therapeutic effects of insight and the effects of the therapist–patient relationship. It brings together these polarities in a new framework that emphasizes the presence and meaning of repetitive patterns of interaction in the ongoing therapeutic process. This theory has as its central postulate *interaction structures*, that is, repeated, mutually influencing interactions between analyst and patient that are a fundamental aspect of therapeutic action. Interaction structures provide a way of formulating and operationalizing those aspects of analytic therapy process that have come to be termed intersubjectivity, transference–countertransference enactments, and role responsiveness. In this model, insight and relationship have complementary roles, since psychological knowledge of the self can develop only in the context of a relationship where the therapist endeavors to understand the mind of the patient through the medium of their interaction.

It bears repeating that the interaction structure construct, though influenced by contemporary relational and intersubjective theory in psychoanalysis, is not specific to this theoretical perspective. It is compatible with ego psychological and drive/structural perspectives as well as an object relations, intersubjective, or relational point of view. Patient and therapist interact in repetitive ways. These slow-to-change patterns of interaction likely reflect the psychological structure of both patient and therapist. Interaction structures are the manifest, behavioral, and emotionally experienced aspect of the transference-countertransference. These interaction patterns are observable, and hence accessible for exploration. The experience, interpretation, and comprehension of the meaning of such repetitive interactions constitute a major component of therapeutic action in analytically informed therapies. Interaction structure is a bridging construct in the debate about the nature of therapeutic action, linking the mutative effects of interpretation and psychological knowledge with those of interpersonal interaction.

The Research Background

The PQS is the means for empirically grounding descriptions of therapy process. It is a measure that provides a basic language for the description of the therapy process. The PQS consists of

100 items that are closely bound not to particular theoretical concepts, but rather to notions of therapy process. The influence of observers' theory on their descriptions of the nature of process is controlled within the flexible but stabilizing framework provided by the Q-set. The items are conceptualized at clinically meaningful levels and anchored, as far as possible, to concrete behavioral and verbal cues that can be identified in recordings of therapy hours. Here are some examples of Q-items: "The therapist is sensitive to the patient's feelings; attuned to the patient; empathic." "The patient experiences ambivalent or conflicted feelings about the therapist." "The therapist's own emotional conflicts intrude into the relationship." The appendix of this book contains the 100 Q-items along with examples of their application. It also specifies the rules governing the use of inference in making Q-ratings. An entire session is the time frame rated, allowing a greater opportunity to capture events of importance. After studying the record of a therapy session, clinical judges order the 100 items. The rating procedure permits judges to form hypotheses and study the material for confirmation or alternative formulations.

Hundreds of hours of verbatim transcripts and video recordings of psychoanalytic psychotherapy and psychoanalysis were rated with the PQS by experienced clinicians. Those sessions judged to contain particularly clear or strong examples of certain kinds of processes or therapist technique were then reviewed, and illustrations were extracted from the record of the treatment hour and are reported verbatim as "in vivo" demonstrations. Psychotherapists rely on the thinking, experience, and wisdom accumulated by generations of clinical practitioners to guide their work. This volume adds to that store of clinical understanding by empirically grounding key aspects of the psychotherapy process. The research on which this volume is based establishes with greater certainty the premises of clinical technique through careful description of effective therapeutic processes. Therapist interventions such as transference interpretation are illustrated with compelling verbatim examples. This strategy furthers the reader's understanding of such frequently used terms as *interpretation, interaction, confrontation, clarification, transference,* and *countertransference* by providing a range of illustrations of intervention strategies and interactions in the context of actual treatments.

It has been argued by some that clinical data from the consulting room cannot be used effectively in research aimed at verifying or falsifying psychoanalytic ideas about how and why patients change. I believe that clinical data, or data derived from the therapy process itself, are essential for the study of psychoanalytic hypotheses because they provide an ecologically valid context for inquiry. The extensive research that provides the underpinning for this book demonstrates that process of psychoanalytic therapies can be studied in formal, quantifiable ways.

Topics Covered

Chapter 1 provides a full clinical and theoretical discussion of interaction structure, a construct that provides a lens through which to view different ways of thinking about what promotes patient change in therapy. It also provides the vantage point from which later chapters consider important topics in contemporary psychoanalytic theory, including the debate about one-person versus two-person psychology; the issues of therapist neutrality and anonymity, self-disclosure, and the therapist's subjectivity; and the distinction between expressive and supportive approaches to treatment. Chapter 1 considers how patients change from the perspective of interaction structures, which are the behavioral and emotionally experienced aspect of the transference-countertransference.

Chapter 2 discusses the evaluation of patients for therapy. It advocates an approach to assessment based on the premise that a patient's problems and pathology, as well as his or her psychological strengths and capacities, are in fact more adequately understood through the process of treatment. Treatment manuals are customarily specified for a particular diagnostic category, such as anxiety or depression. Such manualized treatments attempt to articulate the congruence between a particular pathology, such as borderline personality disorder or anxiety disorder, and the treatment parameters, for example, format of treatment, strategies and techniques, and focus of the sessions.

This book is not specifically linked to any diagnostic category, but rather takes the position that theories of therapeutic action and approaches to intervention derived from such theories must be linked to psychological processes, not to diagnostic categories or symptom clusters. All psychoanalytic theories of therapeutic action are in fact linked to psychological processes, such as conflicts, defenses, mental representations, and transferences. Diagnostic categories do not necessarily, or even usually, imply specific pathological processes. Even if the diagnostic similarity between two patients did imply related psychological processes, it would not necessarily suggest that the same intervention strategy will be equally effective with both patients. So even if patients meet the criteria for a particular diagnosis, they may require different interventions.

Treatment response in patients involves factors such as motivation for change, capacity for relationship, and psychological mindedness, all of which are fairly remote from diagnostic criteria. No matter what diagnosis is applied to the patient, the therapist cannot know ahead of time how a patient might respond to an analytic therapy. This kind of evaluation usually requires more than one session, but can be accomplished in a few. This approach has the advantage of linking assessment directly and immediately to therapy.

Chapter 3 discusses basic techniques for developing patients' capacity to perceive their experience, and express and reflect on it in ways that facilitate change. It takes up, as well, the question of to what extent psychotherapists need to make links between the patient's present difficulties and their past history, and why.

Chapter 4 discusses how therapists can help bring patients' reliance on defensive maneuvers, designed to limit their range of experience, into greater awareness. It illustrates how to observe and identify defensive maneuvers, and provides suggestions about when and how to interpret unconscious or warded-off feelings and ideas. The therapist does not assume a privileged position as the one who knows what is going on in the patient's mind. Instead, therapists introduce interpretations with a collaborative attitude, inviting an exchange, and encouraging patients to modify or verify how they understand their experience. This strategy will likely increase the accuracy of the therapists' formulation, as well as help patients accept interpretations.

Chapter 5 takes up the central topic of transference and countertransference and discusses the uses, and potential abuses, of the therapist's subjectivity. A neutral stance on the part of the therapist, and the accompanying abstinence and anonymity, is today no longer considered attainable by many analytic therapists, and is in fact considered undesirable by some. How do contemporary ideas about subjectivity translate into working with patients, particularly in terms of interpreting the transference? Therapists can observe and understand their countertransference with the help of close attention to repetitive patterns in the interaction with the patient.

Contemporary relational theories within psychoanalysis have had the effect of blurring the distinction between supportive and more analytic approaches to treatment, leaving many clinicians uncertain as to whether this is a meaningful distinction. Chapter 6 discusses the nature of supportive interventions, and when they might be useful. It demonstrates how therapist countertransference reactions are often hidden in supportive efforts.

Chapter 7 describes how analytic therapies can be studied empirically in ways that remain useful and meaningful to clinicians, and Chapter 8 reports three examples of such research case studies. This research investigated therapy process as well as treatment outcomes in terms of both structural change and reduction of symptoms. These chapters fill out the research background for the book, and point the direction toward meaningful future research on the process and outcome of psychoanalytic therapy.

Acknowledgments

It is a pleasure to acknowledge those who have helped me with this book. The past and present members of the Berkeley Psychotherapy Research Project have especially sustained me during the several years of research and writing that this work represents. Among those whose contributions are most important are Stuart Ablon, Mary Coombs, Meg Jay, William Lamb, Ann O'Crowley, Pauline Price, Wendi Robbins, Zenobia Saphia, Celeste Schneider, and Wendy Weil.

Charlie Garfield provided inspiration and generous support and advice about the book project, from its inception to its final form. Mel Schupack and Marshall Greene offered constructive criticism, and Cindy Spring provided helpful commentary.

I would also like to express deep appreciation to the patients and their therapists whose treatments provided the many examples throughout the book. This work would not have been possible without their courageous contribution.

One person deserves special mention. As the book unfolded, my wife, Cheryl Goodrich, read and reread every word, and offered encouragement, insight, and invaluable help.

1

Modes of Therapeutic Action

In psychoanalytic thinking there has been a tension between two theoretical points of view on what brings about patient change. One perspective emphasizes the effect of interpretation and psychological knowledge in therapeutic change, and the other emphasizes the role of interpersonal interaction. This dialectic has had important implications for clinical technique. This chapter summarizes these alternative points of view about the nature of therapeutic action, and introduces a new empirically derived "interaction structure" model that attempts to bridge therapeutic action by insight and by relationship. Interaction structure is a way of formulating those aspects of therapeutic and analytic process that have been termed intersubjectivity, transference–countertransference enactments, and role responsiveness. The concept operationalizes important aspects of interpersonal interaction, and can help specify the two-person patterns that emerge in psychotherapy.

Patient and therapist interact in repetitive ways. These interaction patterns are the manifest part of the transference-countertransference. They are behavioral, and emotionally experienced, and hence more accessible to direct observation. These slow-to-change patterns of interaction likely reflect the psychological structure of both patient and therapist. Therapeutic action is located in the experience, recognition, and understanding by patient and therapist of these repetitive interactions. Interaction structures stress the importance of the intrapsychic as a basis for what becomes manifest in the interactive field.

Interaction structures can be routinely observed in clinical practice. It is also possible to empirically demonstrate their presence and role in patient change. The interaction structure construct has much in common with already familiar theoretical and technical terms such as analyzing the transference in the *here and now*, and *working through*. It also provides an empirical base for aspects of these concepts. Moreover, it includes the two-person, intersubjective component of therapeutic action. It refers not only to how the patient's conflicts are represented in the transference, but also to the therapist's reactions to these conflicts.

An Illustration: Ms. L

A 35-year-old woman who had been divorced for about 10 years, Ms. L sought an analysis because of her ongoing difficulties in maintaining a loving relationship with a man. When she did not have a boyfriend, she longed to have a man in her life. When she did have a boyfriend, she filled her hours with complaints about men, how irresponsible and uncaring they were, and how they only wished to dominate and exploit women. During the first year of her treatment with a female analyst, Ms. L repeatedly threatened to reduce the frequency of her analytic sessions or to terminate. These threats occurred about once a month, and sometimes corresponded with her ending a relationship with a man she was dating. They were sometimes also linked to an action on the part of the analyst. For example, when the analyst once arrived late for an hour, Ms. L interpreted this to mean the analyst didn't think she needed treatment. Ms. L also declared she wished to terminate the day her analyst returned from vacation and when, on another occasion, she was charged for a missed appointment. Ms. L treated the analyst coolly during her sessions, and usually acted as if she had no awareness of the relationship implications of these abrupt threats to leave. Ms. L's threats to terminate kept the analyst off balance, and she felt anxious and angry. The analyst had to contend with her countertransference, particularly her own narcissistic vulnerability to rejection. The analyst realized that she was wondering defensively if she should simply let Ms. L quit, particularly since she had a waiting list that included some individuals who were likely to be more rewarding than Ms. L. The analyst felt as if she were being provoked into rejecting Ms. L by the patient's continual preemptive threats to reject her. Paradoxically, when the analyst energetically interpreted the patient's wish to leave, and sometimes even heatedly advised against it, the patient always seemed pleased and gratified.

Despite these intense provocations, the analyst slowly began to understand the meaning of this repetitive interaction. She began to address the patient's angry and destructive reaction to what Ms. L felt were the inequities in the relationship, feelings that paralleled her longstanding problems with men. Ms. L felt the analyst did not need her, and retaliated by demonstrating she didn't need the analyst; she expected and indeed provoked rejection. She attempted to redress her experience of inequity by a kind of reversal, by becoming the superior, rejecting person. At the same time, she could not reflect on what she was doing or gain any understanding unless she was able to see the therapist as not succumbing to her rejection. Still, the threat of rejection had to be experienced as real by both, and Ms. L needed to see the analyst as worried, a state of mind she was able to evoke with great effectiveness.

This illustration captures an interaction structure. It is clearly an interpersonal interaction that both analyst and patient could identify as repetitive and recurring. The mutually influencing quality of this interaction structure can be seen in the manner in which the patient's transference evokes in the analyst her own countertransference reaction. Interaction structures are the manifest part of the transference-countertransference. They are the behavioral and emotionally experienced aspects that are more directly observable, and hence accessible. Patient change is the result of quite specific repetitive interactions that facilitate the psychological processes required to experience and represent certain mental states together with the knowledge of one's own intentionality. The experience, interpretation, and comprehension of the meaning of such repetitive interactions constitute a major component of therapeutic action in analytically informed therapies.

In this theory of patient change, interaction is seen as more than suggestive influence, just as interpretation contains elements of interaction. The interaction structure construct includes important aspects of the change process by linking interaction, interpretation, and the patient's growing capacity for self-knowledge. Interaction structure is a bridging construct in the debate about the nature of therapeutic action, linking the mutative effects of interpretation and psychological knowledge with those of interpersonal interaction.

Interpretation and Interaction

The long-standing scientific and clinical debate concerning the nature of mutative or change factors in analytic treatments has been renewed in recent years. The two principal lines of thought about the nature of therapeutic action have been organized around the mutative effects of (1) interpretation and (2) interpersonal interaction. These ideas parallel the debate concerning the usefulness of a one-person versus a two-person psychology for conceptualizing analytic and therapeutic process. The question here is whether change processes can be thought of as within the mind of an individual, or whether primary attention should be given to an individual's experience of the external, particularly of the therapist. The interaction structure construct brings together these polarities in a framework that emphasizes the presence and meaning of repetitive patterns of interaction. It postulates repeated, mutually influencing interactions between therapist and patient as a fundamental aspect of therapeutic action. The interaction structure construct is derived from the longitudinal study of longer-term analytic therapies and psychoanalyses. In this model insight and relationship are inseparable. Psychological knowledge of the self can develop only in the context of a relationship where the therapist endeavors to understand the mind of the patient through the medium of their interaction.

Interpretation, as it is used here, is not simply the translation of the meaning of a symptom or behavior into words, or even the broadening or enhancing of the meaning given to the patient's speech. The term most importantly refers to providing knowledge of the content of the mind and the processes by which these contents are both avoided and expressed. Much of this knowledge may be acquired through the patient's experience of the actual and fantasy relationship with the therapist. Nevertheless, those who emphasize the importance of interpretation view as decisive the patient's self-knowledge, understanding, and insight. Interactive models, in turn, emphasize interpersonal and relationship factors, such as empathy, a sense of safety, the containment of feelings, the holding environment, and therapeutic alliance. Interaction-oriented theorists stress the possibilities offered by a new relationship, including the resumption of developmental processes that are hypothesized to have been arrested by trauma or deficiencies in early interpersonal relations.

The tension between the importance placed upon uncovering psychological meaning and that attributed to interaction has existed from the beginning of psychoanalytic theorizing. Interaction was thought to be a process similar to interpersonal influence or indirect suggestion. Since Freud's early experiments influencing hypnotized patients through explicit suggestion, the predominant trend in psychoanalytic thinking has been to view as nonanalytic those psychotherapy models that rely on interpersonal influence and the therapist's use of authority. In nonanalytic therapies the therapist purposefully influences the patient in a manner that is outside of the patient's explicit awareness, and in a way that involves a deflection from the contents of the patient's mind. One of the criticisms of the use of suggestive influence, derived from the early experience with hypnosis, was that patient change achieved under such conditions was temporary and vulnerable to relapse once the therapist's authority to help suppress conflicts ended. Nevertheless, clinical and theoretical interest in the therapeutic effect of a benevolent relationship continued, albeit as a minority point of view (e.g., Ferenczi 1932).

Newer theoretical contributions and the findings of psychoanalytically informed developmental research have kept alive the tension between conceptualizations of therapeutic action that emphasize interpretation and those that give primacy to interaction. These contributions raise the question of whether interaction is necessarily, or at least exclusively, indirect suggestion. Clinical psychoanalytic theorizing (Kohut 1984, Winnicott 1965) has helped to explain how interpersonal interaction effects change beyond what has often been considered suggestive influence. Inferences drawn from developmental research (Main 1993) and research on child analysis (Fonagy and Target 1996) have led to theories suggesting that increases in patients' subjective sense of themselves as the source of wishes, feelings, and intentions, and their capacity for self-reflection, depend strongly on interaction with the therapist. This perspective has also received support from philosophers of the mind who argue that the mind is inherently intersubjective (Cavell 1993). The mind cannot develop without interaction; by extension, a patient's mind cannot change without meaningful interaction.

Therapeutic Action: Suggestion, Influence, and Psychological Knowledge

Freud (1921) considered suggestibility, or the tendency to be influenced without adequate rational foundation, to be an irreducible, fundamental fact in mental life. It was at base an expression of an emotional tie—love, libido, sexual instinct. As Freud more fully understood the phenomenon of transference, psychoanalytic theorists took a position in strong opposition to the use of hypnosis, and have since been cautious about the purposeful or unwitting use of the

therapist's authority to influence patients. In his paper on
the therapeutic effect of inexact interpretation, Glover
(1931) advanced a theory of suggestive influence to explain
how nonanalytic therapies could effect behavior change.
He classified suggestive procedures according to the
amount and means of deflection from psychological truth.
A related means of symptom relief without psychological
knowledge or insight can occur when the therapist makes
some fairly accurate explanations about the nature of the
patient's difficulties. These are nevertheless sufficiently
inexact to serve a defensive function; that is, they help to
ward off knowledge about some threatening mental content. Glover's formulation anticipated Strachey's (1934)
view of the nature of therapeutic action in considering
suggestion therapies to function by allowing the sharing
of the patient's guilt with the therapist. This permits the
patient to rely on the therapist's superego or moral authority, and to accept a new, more adaptive substitution
for the symptom.

The early approach to interpretation focused on symptoms and was based on the topographical model: unconscious → preconscious → conscious. The aim of interpretation was to make the unconscious conscious. It involved
attempting to correctly infer and articulate the unconscious
meaning of a symptomatic behavior. This early form of
interpretation analysis evolved into resistance analysis, as
the structural model of mental functioning, or id–ego–
superego, became the dominant theoretical paradigm. In
the structural model, symptoms are understood to be compromises between a threatening desire and the need to feel
safe. The function of neurotic symptoms was to defend
against an unconscious trend of thought that was unacceptable, while at the same time providing some gratification.
The earlier model assumed that if the unconscious trend

were discovered and the patient made aware of it (making the unconscious conscious) there would be no further need for the symptom and it would then disappear. However, it was soon observed that most patients resisted discovering unconscious mental content. Even if the patient were made fully aware of the unconscious, it might remain an intellectual awareness, and the symptom would persist. The emphasis then shifted to analyzing or interpreting resistances or defenses, and less on investigating unconscious mental content. Interpreting resistance consisted of "confirming its presence, finding out its purpose, and co-ordinating its form with those past experiences of the patient out of which it originates" (Fenichel 1941, p. 106).

As the early form of interpretation analysis, where the aim was to make the unconscious conscious, evolved into resistance or defense analysis, there was a greater attentiveness to the role of relational aspects. Freud (1926a) stated his understanding of this aspect of therapeutic action: "Personal influence is our most powerful dynamic weapon. . . . The neurotic sets to work because he has faith in the analyst, and he believes him because he acquires a special emotional attitude towards the figure of the analyst. . . . We make use of this particularly large 'suggestive' influence. Not for suppressing symptoms . . . but as a motive force to induce the patient to overcome his resistances" (pp. 224–225). There was more interest in how the analytic atmosphere of tolerance allows patients to be less fearful about experiencing threatening ideas and feelings.

Strachey (1934) proposed a formal role for relationship factors. In his view patient change is made possible as a consequence of the therapist's suggestion that the patient become more tolerant of threatening mental contents. "Mutative interpretations" effected change partially by means of the therapist's influence as a more tolerant moral authority or auxiliary superego. The patient is given permission to consciously experience some threatening emotion or idea ("You can allow yourself to experience your hostility and hatred"). Here, then, the role of the therapist's suggestive influence is an important factor in the change process, though applied in a limited, articulated, and self-conscious way. Some modern defense analysis–oriented theorists such as Gray (1994) argue that this means of influence, though still widely practiced, relies too much on indirect suggestion and the use of positive transferences to an authority. He notes that in Strachey's conceptualization, an important element of therapeutic action is the gradual replacement of the harsh, underdeveloped moral sense (or primitive superego) by the internalization of the more benevolent attitude of the therapist. The problem, in his view, is that these processes occur outside the patient's awareness. In serving as an affectionate, approving, and protective authority, the therapist can help relieve anxiety and conflict, but at the cost of participating in an illusion of safety from criticism, punishment, and loss of love. Gray instead emphasizes the importance of helping patients develop the capacity for self-observation. He focuses on those mental processes, such as defensive ways of avoiding knowing about troubling mental contents, that can be consciously and directly observed by both therapist and patient.

Therapeutic Action: Models of Interpersonal Interaction

Recent reemphasis on the role of trauma and the experience of the early parent–child relationship in the etiology of mental problems has led to a greater emphasis on the emotional climate in which treatment takes place. Psychoanalytic developmental research and infant observation may support models of therapeutic action that parallel those of normal development. The interpersonal-interaction models assume a strong developmental point of view in which the parent–infant caregiving relationship has replaced the doctor and patient as the central metaphor for the therapy relationship (Mayes and Spence 1994). These models construct an analogy of the interpersonal, empathic bond between therapist and patient for that between parent and child, and assert that uninterpreted aspects of interaction are equally, or even more, mutative than achieving psychological knowledge through the interpretive process. Particularly influential in this regard have been Ferenczi's (1932) ideas about the importance of the environment, of trauma-induced paralysis of thought, and of the psychological functioning of the mother and her containment capacity.

Many believe that the relational approach derives primarily from object relations theory. There are in fact several theories within the psychoanalytic frame that emphasize interpersonal interaction or relationship as the mode of therapeutic action, and they derive both from conventional ego psychology or modern structural theory (e.g., Weiss and Sampson 1986) as well as object relations theory (Mitchell 1993, Modell 1976). As a consequence, there are several points of view within interactional or intersubjective approaches. While all these theories emphasize the therapeutic effect of interaction, they differ in their explanation of the nature of the psychological processes by which a new kind of interpersonal experience causes change.

Loewald (1960), for example, thought of therapeutic action as a process that was parallel to psychic development, particularly early identification through introjection, or taking in the mother's image of the child. He held that if therapy was to be a process leading to personality change (or change in mental structure), interactions of comparable nature would have to take place. There is little concern in his writing with the putative problems of suggestion or with the limitations of an unanalyzed positive transference to an approving and protective authority. Positive transference keeps alive the potential of a new object relationship, creating new possibilities for being oneself. Ogden (1994) argues that a crucial interactive mutative force lies in the therapist's capacity to tolerate the patient's projections, to capture them in words and images, and to interpret the motives for the projections: "The subject cannot create itself; the development of subjectivity requires experiences of specific forms of intersubjectivity" (p. 60). He assumes that interpretation is a form of object relationship, and that object relationship is a form of interpretation in the sense that every interaction conveys an aspect of the therapist's understanding of the patient (interpretive action). Therapeutic action lies not so much in psychological knowledge as in developing a sense of subjectivity.

In models whose mode of therapeutic action is hypothesized to lie in interaction, the therapeutic relationship is seen as the "message" as well as the "medium" (Schlesinger 1988). Such models have not addressed, however, the potential for suggestive influence, compliance with authority, idealization of the therapist, and strengthening of repression and other defenses relative to attempts to promote change through interaction. It is the concern about suggestive influence, and the constant effort to minimize its effects, that in part lies behind the psychoanalytic tradition of neutrality and caution about self-disclosure. Experienced therapists are well aware of the inclination, either as a result of their own motives or in response to the patient's attempts to draw them into certain role relationships

(Sandler 1976), to assume the position of expert authority who knows what lies behind the patient's problems and what ought to be done.

There are also limitations to reasoning by analogy from mother–infant interactions to therapist–patient interaction (e.g., Wolff 1996). The problem lies in the plausibility of attributing to the mental states of infants that which observers can only assume about the adult patient's experience of early childhood. The presence of what are presumed to be primitive modes of mental functioning in adults tends to be regarded, for example, as evidence of the persistence of pathogenic experiences during development, or of regression to such experiences. However, there is some question as to whether such mental processes (e.g., splitting) are in fact representative of early forms of cognitive activity. It is also possible that their emergence in adult mental functioning might be linked to later or cumulative trauma (Westen 1990).

Interactional models have been criticized for placing too much emphasis on the role of external influences, and for conceptualizing motivation, intent, and instrumentality as having primarily external sources. Many relational thinkers view both the transference and resistance as the creation of the interaction between patient and therapist rather than as located within the patient (Sugarman and Wilson 1995). It is assumed, for example, that defensive processes are catalyzed by failures in the therapist's empathy or by some misunderstanding by the therapist. Human motivation has its source primarily in reaction to important people. "The patient is granted instrumentality only in the realm of fairly passive and benign object-seeking. ... Deviation from this benign object-seeking is seen as stemming from the failure of an external object;

during development, it is the relational or empathic failure of the mother; during treatment, it is the failure of the analyst" (Murray 1995, p. 34). It has been argued that this approach may encourage selective expression particularly of anxiety-relieving, protection-seeking transferences to an authority figure perceived as benign, affectionate, and approving. The exploration by patient and therapist of a need for the therapist's constant empathic mirroring or containment of troublesome affect may be avoided, and aggressive, hateful, or sadomasochistic transferences may be suppressed.

Interaction Structures in Therapy

Newer theoretical and research contributions have set the groundwork for models of therapeutic action that address the complementary roles of interpretation and interaction. One way of conceptualizing the change process is that an understanding of specific and repetitive patterns of interaction between the therapist and patient can contribute to patients' capacity for reflection and self-understanding. Interaction structure provides a way of formulating and operationalizing empirically those aspects of the therapeutic or analytic process that have been termed role responsiveness, transference–countertransference enactments, and intersubjectivity. Role responsiveness refers to the intrapsychic role relationship both therapist and patient impose on each other (Sandler 1976). It is the role in which the patient casts him- or herself in relation to the therapist, and the complementary role that the patient prompts the therapist to assume. Enactments can be defined as symbolic interactions between therapist and patient, often experienced by either as a consequence of the behavior of the other, that have unconscious meaning to both (Chused 1991, McLaughlin 1991). The intersubjective perspective can be contrasted to the view that the therapist can objectively recognize and interpret what occurs in therapy. Instead, the shared emotional experience is emphasized, and is thought to be created by both participants. The interaction-structure construct is a way of formulating these related ideas. The construct allows the consideration of both the intrapsychic and interpersonal interaction by recognizing the intrapsychic (ideas, emotion-laden fantasies) as an important basis for what becomes manifest in the interpersonal or interactive field. The interpersonally observable, or the enacted dimension of the therapeutic process, is not the same as what is dynamically unconscious. It represents some aspect of the unconscious of both patient and therapist that has come alive in the interaction.

Our research on therapeutic and analytic process (see Chapter 8) has demonstrated the presence of repetitive patterns (structures) of interaction across treatment sessions. In other words, patient and therapist interacted in repetitive ways over the course of therapy. These slow-to-change patterns likely reflect the psychological structure (character structure and defenses) of both patient and therapist. Changes in these patterns of interaction were related to changes in patients' psychological structure, as well as to symptom improvement. A given patient–therapist interaction can be considered as one of a sequence of interactions that extend over time. In this model of patient change, causal influences are not assumed to flow only from the direction of therapist to patient. The impact of the patient's characteristics and behavior on the therapist and on the emerging patterns of relationship are taken into account, along with the manner in which the therapist's interventions mobilize patient change.

This provides a framework in which reciprocal influence processes between patient and analyst can be considered.

Illustration: The Case of Mr. S

Therapeutic action in the case of Mr. S, whose first treatment was a psychotherapy, and who subsequently undertook a psychoanalysis with me, will be considered from three contrasting standpoints: the mutative roles of (1) interpersonal influence, (2) interpretation and self-knowledge, and (3) interaction structures. This illustration shows how these different approaches to formulating clinical material influence the way a therapist might work.

Interpersonal Influence

Mr. S, a man in his early 50s, grew up an only child in a middle-class household. Mr. S vividly recalled his father's unpredictable, angry outbursts. Father was a dominating force in the family, and Mr. S described his mother as abjectly submissive to his father, though often inciting his father to anger. He attributed many of his difficulties to his alcoholic mother; he claimed that he hated his mother and never got along with her. She died in an auto accident when Mr. S was 12 years old.

Years later Mr. S became seriously depressed and began an intensive therapy with Dr. H twice or three times weekly. Mr. S adored Dr. H, and thought he was the most wonderful, most intelligent man he had ever met. He felt that Dr. H was enormously helpful to him; he experienced a warmth, security, and emotional acceptance with Dr. H that he never felt with his father. Nevertheless, there was a long period in his therapy during

which he did not agree with Dr. H in the slightest, and
was very angry and recalcitrant. At one point, Dr. H told
him that if he didn't want to work, they should stop.
Mr. S described this as the turning point in the treatment.

Mr. S felt he would never have been able to marry
or gain admission to law school without Dr. H. However, within a few months after terminating because he
was relocating to a distant city, he reported that many
of the gains he had made seemed to evaporate; in particular, he began to have sexual difficulties, and he was
troubled by a sense of confusion and uncertainty. Finally, frustrated and despairing, he returned to Dr. H
for a consultation. To the patient's surprise, Dr. H told
him they hadn't finished, and recommended an analysis. He was willing to accept any suggestion from Dr. H.
Nevertheless, a very formidable resistance was to orga-
nize itself around his experience of the collapse of the
achievements of his therapy. He was suspicious of any
sense of optimism, or expectation for improvement in
the analysis, since he felt it would constitute an illusory
hope, and that any change would be a false cure. He
described the Dr. H experience in this way: "I felt on
top of the world; then it all disappeared, like it was a
bad joke on me."

Much of the considerable benefit Mr. S received from
this treatment was evidently unstable, and the nature of
therapeutic action in this treatment is a striking example
of a powerful transference love to a charismatic therapist
who relied a great deal on suggestive influence. Mr. S was
particularly impressed with Dr. H's analysis of his slips,
other parapraxes, and his dreams. It seemed to him a particularly persuasive demonstration of the power of "psychoanalysis." Dr. H repeatedly reminded Mr. S that, although

he felt only hatred and contempt for his mother, she must have loved him. Dr. H attempted to persuade an unconvinced Mr. S that his depression must be related to her loss. He urged Mr. S to try to stay on better terms with his father. Dr. H not only provided advice and encouragement, but also exhorted the patient to make a greater effort in his studies and in finding a suitable wife: "There are lots of nice women who could love you, if you look for them." Mr. S's tenacious efforts to avoid looking at himself and knowing more about the contents of his thoughts were not taken up, discussed, or understood. Instead, such resistances were overcome through Dr. H's use of his authority and power: "I want to help those who can work with me; if you can't, we should recognize that and end the treatment." As a consequence, Mr. S achieved little insight into his conflicts or their origins.

It could be argued that therapeutic action in this treatment primarily lay not in suggestive influence, but in the analyst's empathic containment of Mr. S's painful frustration, agitation, and suffering. This allowed Mr. S to rely on internalized images of the therapist's authority and capacity to tolerate his attacks in order to cope with frightening feelings of hate and destructive urges. In other words, therapeutic action could be said to lie in the therapist's containment of Mr. S's rage, hatred, and envy in the treatment relationship, and the disavowal and attribution to others of dangerous aspects of himself. Mr. S's transference to Dr. H remained largely outside of conscious psychological knowledge, yet the patient clearly derived benefit from the treatment. The question the case poses is the extent to which the intrapsychic can become more adaptively organized through interaction alone, with little psychological knowledge or insight.

Interpretation and Self-Knowledge

In the period before an initial consultation with me for what was to become a seven-year analysis, Mr. S engaged in several dangerous and frightening sexual escapades. He connected this with beginning the analysis, noting that he had not been able to discuss a very significant problem of sexual perversion with Dr. H, something he later speculated was related to his relapse. Mr. S had very little sex with his wife, and was plagued by violent sexual fantasies. He initially insisted that his sexual difficulties could be solved if he found a woman who was provocatively sexy. Through my persistent interpretation of this adamant defensive externalization ("You want to blame your wife for your sexual difficulties; it is painful and humiliating to look at your part in this"), he was gradually able to more fully accept his sadistic feelings toward women.

In this early phase of treatment, Mr. S had little sense of himself as the author of his thoughts and feelings, accusing either me or the process of putting ideas into him. He experienced both his thoughts and his feelings, which were characterized by immediacy and intensity, as forces or objects. He had difficulty reflecting on his emotional reactions; his thoughts tended to be constricted, and he could not represent much of his mental content. Others tended to be experienced as objects, and as a consequence he had a restricted appreciation of their emotional states.

Mr. S reported that treatment with me was quite different from that with Dr. H, who was an impressive and charismatic father figure. In poor contrast, I was slow and ineffectual in providing him immediate relief from his suffering. He complained bitterly when I refrained from advising him about how to live his life. Mr. S routinely attacked me and psychoanalysis, claiming there was no scientific evidence that analysis worked. When I asked him why, if that were true, he wanted an analysis, he replied that he was desperate for help. An important current in Mr. S's sadomasochistic transference was his insistent wish that I save him from his deeply troubling and frightening fantasies and feelings. His passivity, sense of resignation, and lack of curiosity about himself constituted a formidable resistance. My attempts to explore Mr. S's fear of pursuing his thoughts frequently ground to a halt in the patient's fear of being disillusioned if his ideas turned out to be false, as well as in his fear of his own thoughts and the madness to which they might lead.

Interpretations in this phase of the treatment were met with angry indignation, derision, and defensive rationalization. Mr. S felt insulted and humiliated by my observations, and in turn attacked my ideas, especially interpretations that attempted to draw connections between problems in the analytic relationship and problems occurring in his relations with his wife or employers. These reactions sometimes escalated into violently angry outbursts in which he yelled that he hated me. I felt demeaned and assaulted, and sometimes found myself in tense wrangles with the patient as a way to avoid feeling dominated and controlled. I also felt angry at Mr. S's attempts to bully me. More often I felt a sense of despair and hopelessness, wondering if I would be able to help him. Mr. S insisted that it would be a mistake for him to like me. The thought of being close to me made him suspicious, since he didn't want to be duped into liking someone, just to wake up a few months later to discover his true feelings. He explained that he was stubborn, recalcitrant, and argumentative out of fear of repeating the "Dr. H experience." On more than one occasion I wondered whether Mr. S was analyzable and gave serious consideration to terminating the analysis. I felt I was being prompted to a destructive, sadistic attack on our analytic effort by having my good intentions and capacity to know and to think repeatedly denigrated, attacked, and defeated.

Interaction Structures

Conceptualizing therapeutic action in terms of interaction structures provides a means for linking both interpretation and insight, and the emotionally charged interactions between analyst and patient, to Mr. S's slowly growing capacity for self-reflection during the course of the analysis. An example of a repetitive interaction was termed by Mr. S as "A state of not knowing." This interaction pattern was characterized by Mr. S's destroying the meaning of both his thoughts and words as well as my own, leaving both of us with a sense of hopelessness and futility. Mr. S would make provocative statements or engage in actions that he expected would provoke an attack from me, followed by a denial that his words or actions had any particular intention. For example, without warning he would fail to appear for a session, and then at his next session declare that "psychoanalysis" would surely claim that he was angry, but he was not at all sure about that; his absence had no meaning at all. Any attempt to interpret meaning directly ("You didn't come as a way of retaliating for feeling humiliated by me at our last meeting") would be met with scornful attacks on my ideas ("There is no evidence of that; it could mean anything"). Mr. S would report a dream that seemed very meaningful, or reveal perverse fantasies or behavior

that seemed potentially useful clinically, and then declare
that he hesitated to mention these thoughts for fear that
some incorrect implications would be drawn from them. In
other words, neither he nor I were allowed to think about
the contents of his mind.

This kind of repetitive interaction, which contained
powerful and often only partially understood transferences
and countertransferences, constitutes an interaction structure. In an analytic treatment, reflective capacity may be
acquired through the shared experience of mental states
between patient and analyst (Fonagy et al. 1993a) that can
occur within interaction structures of this kind. Mr. S's
paranoia and anxiety compromised his capacity to consider
either his own motives and intentions or those of the analyst. Consistent interpretation of interactions of this kind
(the mutual "state of not knowing") required Mr. S to focus on his mental state as well as how he imagined I was
thinking about him. Through a repeated sharing of mental states (e.g., not knowing) between the patient and the
analyst, the analyst captures, represents, and extends an understanding of the patient's feeling states, conflicts, thought
processes, and defensive deflections. I would, for example,
show Mr. S how he could understand the meaning of an
action and then explain it away, just as he could take my
thoughts about him and critique them with what he called
"sophistry" and "argument for argument's sake" in such a
way as to destroy them and render them useless. Then neither of us could know or understand anything about him
or his problems. He would then claim he did this out of
anger because neither his efforts at understanding himself
nor my ideas brought any relief of his pain and suffering.

When I then confronted him with the fact that he believed his rageful reactions were perfectly justifiable, he began to see how he used his anger defensively. As his angry

attacks on his and my capacity to know gradually diminished, the insights we arrived at became more meaningful to him. The experience, identification, and gradually understood meaning of this interaction structure allowed Mr. S to develop a sense of himself as initiator of thoughts and feelings that can be known and understood, and to gain a new capacity for relationship in the face of previously too disruptive upsurges of rage.

What becomes manifest in the interpersonal or interactive field as interaction structures represents the internal world of both analyst and patient. It is likely that every treatment contains interactions structures. In Mr. S's therapy with Dr. H, a repetitive interaction was also organized around a state of not knowing. Dr. H responded to "not knowing" by assuming a fatherly role, explaining to Mr. S what must be in his mind, and instructing him how to behave. Mr. S, in turn, protected Dr. H as a good object through his idealization and compliance. Dr. H also inspired an important sense of hope that analysis could help Mr. S. However, this interaction structure was enacted rather than understood by analyst and patient, leaving its defensive function intact and the results of the therapy unstable.

Support from a Psychoanalytic Case

The construct of interaction structure was empirically derived from a series of intensive studies of process in psychoanalysis and analytic therapy. One such study was the case of Mrs. C, a by now frequently studied psychoanalysis for which verbatim transcripts were available (Jones and Windholz 1990, Spence et al. 1993, Weiss and Sampson 1986).

Mrs. C was an attractive, married social worker in her late twenties who complained of lack of sexual responsiveness, difficulty experiencing pleasurable feelings, and low self-esteem. Her father was a professional man, her mother a housewife, and she was the second of four children. She had been married less than two years to a successful businessman when the analysis was begun.

Her chief complaint concerned her sex life. She did not enjoy sex, did not have orgasms, and indeed was reluctant to have intercourse. She sought treatment at the insistence of her husband, who had threatened to divorce her if she did not overcome her sexual difficulties. There were other complaints as well: she was unable to relax and enjoy herself, and felt tense and driven at work and at home. She was very self-critical, and worried whenever she made even a minor mistake. Mrs. C experienced herself as emotionally constricted, and inhibited and fearful in her behavior. She felt she was unable to hold her own opinions, that she did not have the strength of her own convictions; especially difficult was disagreeing either with her parents or her husband. She was uncomfortable with her co-workers and her clients, especially her male clients, with whom she believed herself to be overly strict and impatient (Jones and Windholz 1990).

The analysis was conducted over a six-year period, or for approximately 1,100 hours; its outcome was considered to be very good by both analyst and patient. All of the analytic hours were audio-recorded and transcribed. A sample of seventy sessions was rated with the Psychotherapy Process Q-set, a 100-item instrument constructed to provide a basic language and rating procedure for the comprehensive description of the analytic process in a form suitable for quantitative comparison and analysis (see Chapter 7 and Appendix). The Q-set provides a means for rendering reliable the impressions and formulations derived from a substantial amount of clinical data while at the same time summarizing the data through the ordering of a set of statements that describe various aspects of the analytic process. Transcripts of the analytic hours were independently Q-sorted in completely random order by at least two clinically experienced judges, and interrater reliabilities were good (see Jones and Windholz 1990 for details about the study method).

The Q-ratings of each of the analytic hours were subjected to a statistical procedure, an exploratory factor analysis, in an attempt to determine the presence of interaction structures. The procedure yielded four clusters of items, some of which were interpreted as capturing interaction structures. One factor will be discussed here to illustrate how the construct operationalizes aspects of the interaction that are central to the change process. This factor comprised the following Q-items, which are ordered in terms of their importance (factor loadings) in defining the cluster: "Sexual feelings and experiences are discussed"; "Love or romantic relationships are discussed"; "Analyst suggests the meaning of the behavior of others (e.g., family members)"; "Patient has difficulty understanding the analyst's comments"; "Patient does not feel understood by the analyst"; "There is an erotic quality to the analytic relationship"; "Real as opposed to fantasized meanings of experiences are differentiated"; and "Patient's dreams and fantasies are discussed."

The analyst had a term for this interaction structure: playing stupid. In this repetitive interaction, the patient's thoughts became muddled and confused when she talked about sexual feelings and her wish to arouse men. The analyst found himself talking more than usual in an effort to explain matters. An excerpt from a transcript of a session during the fifth year of the analysis provides a clinical illustration of the interaction that the Q-factor captures. At the beginning of the hour, the patient notes she has been feeling angry all weekend because she wanted the analyst to say something during the previous session, but she is unsure specifically what she wanted him to say.

Patient: I don't know, it just seems rather strange to me, because it isn't as if I really don't have any idea of what I'm thinking about. But then I muddle it all up, so I can't think about it in any kind of a straight way.

Analyst: Well, you know, what you've just been describing is really a very good description of the way you have sounded the past weeks here. You've been feeling—and all last week it's true you wanted me to say something—but you were sounding as though you were feeling terribly confused, you couldn't put anything together, and it all started with your husband saying you were playing stupid. And I think that's a pretty good description. The week before you had talked about what does an IQ number mean? You can't be that stupid.

The point I'm trying to get at, it's as though all week, what you have been doing—for I think, a very particular reason—is muddling up your thoughts. You said, when I did say some things that I was trying to put together to help point you in a certain direction, you find yourself not thinking about them, ignoring them. As though you were trying to maintain this very state you were just describing—feeling muddled, confused. And not because you didn't know something. Quite the contrary.

Now, you see, I think what really started this was when you made love Sunday afternoon with your husband during your daughter's nap. I think it's been since then that increasingly you've found it necessary to be in this frame of mind, where you're sort of pseudo-stupid. Playing stupid, confusing yourself, muddling things.

The analyst goes on, in a lengthy interpretation, to connect this state of mind with a memory the patient had reported: When she was a little girl, she was supposed to be taking a nap one day, but wasn't, and she saw something that troubled her. What she saw was never clarified. She was supposed to be sleeping, so she had to play dumb, to hide what she knew. The patient had trouble understanding what the analyst was saying, demonstrating in the interaction what the analyst has been interpreting. Recall the Q-items that define this repetitive interaction, e.g., "Sexual feelings and experiences are discussed"; "Patient has difficulty understanding the analyst's comments"; "Patient does not feel understood by the analyst"; and so on. In fact, the analyst is induced to repeat the interpretation later in the hour.

P: And I don't know, somehow, getting into my curiosity, if I keep thinking, well, are you implying that the seeing the rabbits, and then pretending that I didn't see it, well I don't know, somehow it, I keep thinking, well it must be from what you are saying. And I know I've lost something you've said, the fact that I know something that I don't want to admit I know. And then I don't know, then I think, well I don't know what that is.

A: It's true you don't know what makes it hard for you to try to get at what it is. Is this playing stupid? All last week, everything I said you sort of heard it, and then dropped it. And you even commented on how you hadn't dealt with the things I had said I thought were related in some way. . . . You're finding it necessary to be stupid, to stay in this state, to not know.

P: (*silence*) Mm, it's not that I'm getting anywhere, and maybe I am. But I was just thinking of the fact that in not letting myself know—because I feel as if that's what I'm doing right now, too—and not understanding in the way I know I should, what you've just said. Or not just this last time, but before. Because I did understand what you said, and it just reminds me of this tension that I had all weekend.

This illustration captures an interaction structure. It is clearly an interaction that both analyst and patient identify as repetitive and recurring. The reciprocal, mutually influencing quality of these repetitive patterns can be seen in how the patient's stance evokes in the analyst his own countertransference reaction. His interpretations are lengthy, carefully explanatory, and contain some exasperation. Interaction structures are the manifest part of the transference-countertransference. They do not, of course, express all of what is dynamically unconscious. They are the behavioral and emotionally experienced and enacted aspects that are more directly accessible to therapist and patient. Therapeutic action is located in the recognition and understanding of these interaction structures by both therapist and patient. Patient change is the result of quite specific repetitive patterns that facilitate the psychological processes required to experience and represent certain mental states together with the knowledge of one's own intentionality. It is the experience, interpretation, and comprehension of the meaning of such of interactive patterns that constitute a major component of therapeutic action.

Therapeutic Change and Interaction Structures

In this view of therapeutic action, psychological knowledge gained through interpretation and interpersonal interaction are complementary. There is further research directly linking interaction structures to patient change. In a study of recorded cases of analytic therapy (see Chapter 8 for a full discussion of this research), statistical analysis of treatment hours rated with the Psychotherapy Process Q-set yielded clearly identifiable interaction patterns. There was evidence that the reduction in frequency and intensity of interaction patterns of this type, through their interpretation and mutual understanding by therapist and patient, promotes patient change.

The first case was that of a young woman, whose complaints included severe depression and problems in intimate relationships. One important interaction pattern with this patient was labeled "wish for rescue." This interaction structure was captured by the following Q-items: "Silences occur during the hour"; "Patient does not initiate topics; is passive"; "Patient feels shy and embarrassed"; "Patient has difficulty beginning the hour"; "Patient feels sad and depressed"; "Patient feels inadequate and inferior"; and "Patient relies upon therapist to solve her problems." This repetitive interaction was characterized by the patient's passivity and lengthy silences accompanied by feelings of depression, a strong sense of inadequacy and inferiority, and a wish to rely on the therapist to solve her problems. There was a strong implicit, and often explicit, demand on the therapist to fill the painful silences and to deliver transformative explanations. The therapist, on his part, often felt ineffective, and was prompted to become more active in drawing the patient out and rescuing them both from her tortured silences. The therapist was nevertheless able to interpret this pattern as, among other meanings, a way of avoiding the pain associated with talking about herself, reflecting on past traumas, and the fear of making herself vulnerable by revealing herself. This interaction structure also represented an unconscious effort by the patient to prompt the therapist into pursuing her, which repeated in the transference the traumatic sexual abuse the patient had experienced in childhood and early adolescence. The data suggested that the slow decline in frequency and intensity of this interactive pattern predicted the patient's improvement in both her depression and her daily functioning.

A second case demonstrated very modest symptom change after more than two years of twice-weekly psychotherapy. One interaction structure was labeled "angry interaction." This interaction structure was captured by the following Q-items: "Patient does not feel understood"; "Therapist is distant, aloof"; "Patient rejects therapist's comments and observations"; "Therapist is tactless"; "Patient is controlling"; "There is a competitive quality to the relationship"; "Therapist's own emotional conflicts intrude into the relationship"(or countertransference); and "Discussion centers on cognitive themes." These interactions were tense, competitive, and intellectualized exchanges in which the patient attempted to control the therapist, and in which the patient did not feel understood and rejected the therapist's attempts to help. The therapist, in turn, was inclined to be distant or aloof, less tactful, and had to struggle with angry, contemptuous countertransference feelings. Statistical analysis demonstrated that the severity of the patient's depression, anxiety, and other symptoms predicted the frequency and intensity of angry interactions. These interaction structures were insufficiently interpreted and understood, and we conclude that this unanalyzed, and relatively unchanging, interaction pattern was associated with the fact that the patient reported only very modest improvement at termination (see Chapter 8).

Change in Mental Structure

What, then, is the relationship between interaction structures and the patient's overall mental structure? A goal of analytic therapies is long-term symptom relief coupled with enduring change in personality processes or psychological structure. Psychological structure has been defined in a variety of ways and has been used to refer to the structural model of the mind, impulse-defense configurations, a grouping and organization of functions that regulate a sense of self and relationships, unconscious fantasy and wishes (i.e., structures of meaning), and core conflicts. My use of the term follows Kernberg's (1980) integration of drive/structural and object relations concepts. Mental structure and unconscious mental life are determined by fantasied and real interpersonal interactions that are internalized as a world of self and object representations. Conflict within this world of self and object representations is more than simply conflict between wishes and desires (i.e., impulse) and the anxious avoidance and control of such feelings (i.e., defense). More accurately, it is the conflict between incompatible types or sets of self and object representations that have specific emotional meanings. Pathology is associated both with (1) undifferentiated, disorganized, and unintegrated mental structures; and (2) inhibitions of the capacity to think and otherwise represent experience.

Interaction structures animate, in the interactive field, aspects of both the patient's and the therapist's mental structure. The experience, identification, and understanding of interaction structures is mutative by way of two overlapping modes, which can be termed integrative and developmental (Abrams 1990). The integrative mode focuses on tolerating and raising to awareness threatening ideas and feelings. The consequence is integration of these usually primitive, disowned, and unconscious self-other representations, which express specific wishes and fears, with more differentiated and conscious mental structures. The recognition of interaction patterns permits changes in mental representations by providing an opportunity to bring these to a conscious state and to systematically explore the mental representations expressed in the interaction. In this way, mental representations acquire greater internal cohesion. Links are fostered between old mental representations and new representations of both internal states and the perceptions of the therapist and others. Integration of previously isolated or conflicted ideas of self and other permits the achievement of an integrated self concept and a greater harmony of the representational world.

The developmental mode fosters mental processes that have been arrested or inhibited, particularly the capacity to represent experience and reflect on mental states. Recognition of repetitive interactions can promote previously inhibited mental processes by mobilizing them in the therapist–patient interaction. Interpretation of an interaction structure invites the patient to conceive of the therapist's mind, that is, how the therapist is experiencing and thinking about the patient. The patient uses these experiences of understanding the therapist's mental state to explore his own mind, and to develop a clearer representation of his own mental states. The patient develops a greater capacity to represent ideas and meanings and a greater sense of subjectivity (Fonagy et al. 1993a,b).

Subsequent chapters will discuss how particular thera-peutic strategies and interventions foster the integration of mental representations of self and other and the capacity to represent and reflect on experience. But first we must turn to the complicated question of determining which patients might benefit from an analytic treatment. Chapter 2 describes an approach to evaluating patients for treatment that uses the intervention process itself to reach a more complete understanding of the nature and mean-ing of the patient's symptoms and to gauge whether an ana-lytic treatment might be effective for the patient. It makes the link between clinical evaluation and theories about how patients change—the nature and mode of therapeutic action.

2

Intervention as Assessment

Evaluating Patients for Psychotherapy

This chapter discusses patient assessment, and the relationship of diagnosis to treatment, from the standpoint of psychoanalytic theory and therapy. Conventional approaches to diagnosis are overly narrow and static in their focus on pretreatment or untreated features. The rationale of conventional treatment manuals is that they design a treatment for a specified diagnostic category, such as depression or panic disorder. Such manuals describe the congruence between a particular patient pathology (e.g., depression or anxiety disorder) and the treatment parameters (e.g., format of treatment, strategies and techniques, and focus of the sessions). A formal diagnosis is central to the application of the treatment guidelines contained in the manual. In actuality, however, the implications of static, symptom-oriented, pretreatment diagnoses for treatment planning are often unclear, and such assessments offer very limited psychological understanding to the patient.

An alternative approach to assessment is advocated based on the premise that patients' psychopathology, as well their psychological strengths, are in fact better understood through the actual process of treatment. Treatment response in patients involves factors such as self-reflective capacity, and nature of initial transferences, as well as the therapist's countertransference, none of which are described in a static diagnosis. It is impossible to know whether or not an individual can benefit from a psychoanalytic approach until the therapist works with the patient for a brief period. This approach to assessment usually requires a few sessions, and has the advantage of linking patient evaluation directly to intervention.

Static and Process-Oriented Approaches to Evaluation

What kinds of individuals, suffering from what kinds of problems, will benefit from analytic therapy and psychoanalysis? This question has come into sharp focus as a result of the increasing influence of psychiatric diagnostic systems such as the *Diagnostic and Statistical Manual of Mental Disorders* (*DSM-III, III-R,* and *IV*; American Psychiatric Association 1980, 1987, 1994). A good deal of recent research has been aimed at determining whether a patient with a symptom picture conforming to a particular *DSM* category is more likely to benefit from one or another kind of therapeutic intervention. In response to these developments, clinicians are under increasing pressure from insurance companies, hospitals, government agencies, and their own colleagues to sum up the individuals in their care with a diagnostic phrase and a numerical category. This trend has pressed psychotherapists to consider how such diagnostic designations fit with psychoanalytic thinking about symptoms and psychological disorder. Among psychoanalytically oriented clinicians there has been a long-standing debate about the validity of *DSM* psychiatric diagnosis, and a good deal of uncertainty regarding its usefulness. Many argue that a thorough assessment of patients' psychopathology as well as their psychological strengths requires knowledge about character structure, the nature of the relationship and the transferences that are likely to develop with the therapist, and capacity to experience affect. In short, attention to the manner in which the patient engages the treatment, and how the treatment process evolves, are essential in forming a diagnostic and psychological understanding of the patient.

This approach to evaluation, in contrast to a static, pretreatment diagnostic categorization of a patient, can be termed a process-oriented assessment. It links patient evaluation more directly to the treatment. From the very first contact, patient and therapist enter into a relationship, and much that is of diagnostic value for the treatment can be learned in the context of that relationship. A good deal may be inferred, for example, from the patient's response to an intervention, such as a trial interpretation, a mild confrontation, or the proposal of a particular frequency of therapy sessions. The patient's reaction helps in evaluating the capacity for insight, the rigidity of defenses, the severity of anxiety, and the capacity for a relationship. The therapist can, over several sessions, achieve a sufficient understanding of a patient to make a more informed decision about whether to offer a consultation only, a brief therapy, a more intensive therapy or psychoanalysis, or a referral for another form of treatment.

This strategy for assessment is closely linked to the topic of how to introduce patients to psychotherapy in a way that will begin to foster a therapeutic process. Many prospective patients come with vague and often inaccurate ideas about psychotherapy. They often assume, or hope, that their problems will be alleviated in only a few sessions. Or they wonder whether another kind of treatment may be more effective, or if they should be taking medication. The extent to which a therapeutic process can begin early on is helpful for evaluating whether the patient will benefit from psychoanalytic therapy. This chapter presents approaches to informing and educating patients about psychotherapy in a manner that engages them in the therapy process.

Complications in Diagnosis and Evaluation

Anxiety and depression are two of the most common patient complaints, and several treatments have been developed for these disorders. A discussion of the diagnosis of these symptom clusters will highlight some of the problems surrounding diagnosis in general, and its problematic link to treatment. When faced with an individual seeking help for feelings of anxiety and depression, clinicians encounter a perplexing array of concepts, categories, and terms. In the area of depression, there is major and minor depression, unipolar and bipolar depression, cyclothymia, mood disorder, affective disorder, subaffective disorder, dysthymic disorder, depressive symptoms, depressive character, depressive illness, depressive position, anaclitic and introjective depression, and pathological bereavement. In the area of anxiety there is signal anxiety, generalized anxiety disorder, panic attacks, agoraphobia, social phobia (and other specific phobias), separation anxiety, and castration anxiety. In addition, anxiety and depression can be conceptualized from several standpoints and with varying levels of specificity. Etiologic conceptualizations can be either biological or genetic (e.g., endogenous depression), primarily social or environmental (e.g., social phobia, reactive depression), or predominantly psychological or interpersonal (e.g., panic attack, depression as a symptomatic expression of underlying personality difficulties). Yet another perspective, often termed the phenomenological, conceptualizes anxiety and depression primarily in terms of behavioral descriptions (e.g., for anxiety: restlessness, difficulty concentrating, muscle tension, and sleep disturbance; for depression: sleeplessness, weight loss, and chronicity).

It is understandable that the clinician is often uncertain how to use this formidable array of approaches as an aid in understanding anxious and depressed patients, developing treatment plans, and assessing patient improvement. This perplexity reflects real conceptual and theoretical ambiguities. Indeed, it is questionable whether current diagnostic and nosological categories clarify clinical phenomena in a way that is useful for treatment. A central problem is whether anxiety or depression is more appropriately conceptualized as a distinct category of disorder, or as a continuum of disordered mood and affect. The limits of current taxonomic approaches are often minimized or disregarded in favor of the seeming reassurance offered by the suggestion that psychopathologies have been definitively understood when, in fact, they have not.

Static Pretreatment Approaches to Diagnosis

In the last few decades the *DSM* has become the standard model for the diagnosis of mental disorder, and clinicians must grapple with its advantages and limitations. The fundamental goal of the *DSM* is to formulate an atheoretical and reliable set of diagnostic criteria for mental disorders. Before the advent of the *DSM*, psychiatric diagnosis was based in a broad psychosocial conceptual framework informed by psychoanalysis, sociology, and, later, biological knowledge (the "biopsychosocial" model). There were significant limitations inherent in the biopsychosocial approach to diagnosis. Diagnosis was famously unreliable;

the diverse conceptualizations and overlapping categories of psychopathology made it difficult to achieve consensus among clinicians. The 1970s saw an enormous increase in the use of medication for an ever wider-range of mental disorders, with heightened concern about the unreliable nature of diagnosis. More explicit criteria that allowed reliable diagnosis and the selection of homogeneous research samples were important for clinical trials of anxiolytics and antidepressant medication, and for their effective use. Although the development of the *DSM* was motivated by a wish to develop a more empirically based psychiatry, the resulting classification system represents a politically tinged consensus of committees. And although they were in a sense intended as hypotheses to be tested, *DSM-III* and *-IV* have in fact become textbooks in psychopathology (Wilson 1993). Discontent about the scientific status of *DSM* and discomfort with its great influence have come from several quarters. Even some within biological psychiatry have found the *DSM* nosologic categories inadequate.

In the *DSM* taxonomic system anxiety and depression are conceptualized as distinct categories of mental disorder. However, as this discussion has already implied, they may be more appropriately represented by a dimensional model rather than a categorical model. That is, they may be more usefully conceptualized as the extremes of a continuum of normal traits and behavior. Studies of personality disorder in clinical and general populations do not find discontinuities. There is in fact a continuum across most diagnostic categories and many individuals drawn from nonclinical populations fall into the clinical distribution on measures of psychological functioning. This suggests that a class or category model does not accurately represent pathological phenomena.

A series of conceptual conundrums in the *DSM* diagnosis of anxiety and depression underscores these problems with its categorical approach: (1) the presence of long-term, trait-like depressive and anxious tendencies in certain individuals; (2) the difficulty in differentiating anxiety and depression; and (3) the high frequency of comorbid diagnosis among individuals meeting criteria for the two categories. The *DSM* treats depressive and anxious symptoms as largely independent of personality, but these are sometimes related to a type of enduring character or temperament. The concept of the depressive personality, for example, as opposed to depressive symptomatology, has been used by clinicians for decades. Depressive personality, or a variant of this construct (depressive neurosis, neurotic depression), is included in the international psychiatric diagnostic system (International Classification of Diseases, ICD-10; World Health Organization 1989). Similar diagnoses (depressive neurosis, cyclothymic and affective personality) were listed in the first and second editions of the *DSM*. The category "depressive neurosis" was dropped from *DSM-III* and *-III-R* and was reconceptualized as an affective disorder. The elimination of depressive neurosis was one of the most controversial changes in *DSM-III*, and since then many clinical theorists and researchers have argued for including an axis II category for depressive personality.

Clinicians have long been well aware of the common difficulty in making clear distinctions between anxiety and mood disorders. Depressive affects and anxiety are often present in the same individual, a routine observation reflected in the terms *agitated depression* and *anxious depression* and in the high comorbidity rates for diagnoses of the two disorders. Measures that assess depression and anxiety, especially self-report measures, are so highly correlated in both clinical and nonclinical samples that almost no meaningful discrimination between the two can be made using such assessment techniques. Longitudinal research suggests that there is significant clinical overlap between depression and anxiety; 40 to 80 percent of panic disorder patients have been shown to have experienced a major depressive episode, whereas 25 percent of depressed patients have lifetime history of panic disorder.

In addition, there is often a nonspecific drug response in both disorders; that is, depression can be alleviated by anxiolytics and anxiety by antidepressants. Given the *DSM*'s premise that anxiety and depression are distinct disorders, with presumably different underlying etiologic factors, this frequent problem in clearly distinguishing the clinical features of anxiety and depression creates conceptual and diagnostic confusion. Another complication lies in the problem of comorbidity, that is, an additional diagnosis on axis I or a coinciding axis II diagnosis. The frequency of comorbid diagnosis in psychiatric patients generally is as high as 50 percent. Among depressed patients comorbidity rates are particularly high in relation to axis II personality disorders, ranging from 23 to 95 percent. These several important conceptual problems unfortunately do not allow the *DSM* to bring real clarity to diagnoses or elucidate underlying processes. And, as we shall see, *DSM* is of only limited help in guiding intervention. The pursuit of diagnostic clarity using only symptom features can be a dead end for the treating clinician because many nonsymptom factors can give rise to similar symptom pictures.

Limitations of Pretreatment Diagnoses

The *DSM* leaves unaddressed practical clinical problems. *DSM*-derived diagnoses of anxiety and depression are not, for example, intended to reliably distinguish between those individuals who may be successfully treated through psychotherapy and those who require medication. Nor are such diagnoses particularly helpful in identifying individuals who are at risk for relapse or chronic, recurrent problems. One of the problems is that a diagnosis of depression or anxiety disorder is sometimes mistakenly equated with a disease entity, and a specific etiology or genetic vulnerability, which in turn suggests a specific kind of intervention (Millon 1991). Treatment research has not given us much reason to presume we will find this kind of specific effect, for example, that depression will respond specifically to particular treatments. The National Institute of Mental Health (NIMH) Treatment of Depression Collaborative Research Program's controlled clinical trial comparing antidepressant medication, interpersonal psychotherapy, and cognitive-behavioral treatment for major depression demonstrated that psychotherapy and medication were generally equally effective (Elkin et al. 1989). Similarly, medication for anxiety disorders has not been demonstrated to be consistently superior to psychosocial interventions.

Formal diagnosis has no relationship to processes of change, and is rarely helpful in anticipating the events of the treatment. Treatment response in patients always involves factors that are fairly remote from the core diagnostic criteria for *DSM* disorders. Indeed, many psychoanalytic clinicians consider diagnoses derived from the *DSM* to be superficial descriptors, groupings of symptoms and behavioral traits that are mostly irrelevant to those aspects of the person pertinent to treatment. They view diagnoses as unessential in identifying those patients who might benefit from psychotherapy, since they do not bear upon patient characteristics—such as motivation, conflicts, flexibility of defenses, capacity to experience affect and use insight, and the nature of the transferences likely to develop with the therapist—that many consider in assessing suitability for psychotherapy. Moreover, diagnosis seems to emphasize symptomatic improvement, and gives little consideration to how improvements in functioning and in interpersonal relatedness might require more than a focus on obvious symptoms.

Few psychoanalytically oriented clinicians would minimize the importance of symptom improvement, or a general sense of well-being. However, a goal in many psychoanalytic treatments is the achievement of more enduring change, change in what might be termed "psychological structure," that is, long-term symptom relief coupled with significant shifts in psychological processes, such as habitual ways of thinking, the capacity to tolerate strong feelings, or the ability to sustain intimate relationships. Psychological structure has been used to refer to the structural model of mind; as impulse-defense configurations; as a grouping and organization of functions that lead to object and self-constancy; as unconscious fantasy, wishes, and structures of meaning; and as the organization of internalized object relations. Assessments oriented around these kinds of conceptualizations move away from static, pretreatment diagnoses and use the process of intervention itself as a means of understanding the patients' mental life and the nature of the disorder.

Psychoanalytic Views of Anxiety and Depression

Psychoanalytic views of psychopathology offer an understanding of the meaning of symptoms such as anxiety and depression. Freud (1917), in his paper on mourning and melancholia, stated that depression has diverse clinical appearances, and noted his uncertainty about whether it can be considered a single entity. He conceptualized depression as an affective expression of object loss that has been kept out of conscious awareness. Through identification with the lost object, the self is altered and associated painful feelings are partially warded-off. Depression results from punishing the abandoning object, now part of the self. The criticism and rebuke that would have been directed at the lost object is now aimed at the self, because the self has identified with the object. The loss of the object is thereby partially denied, since the object lives on through the identification, and the need to rebuke the object can simultaneously be expressed. Loss is broadly defined, and potentially includes feeling slighted, neglected, or disappointed.

One of the most important modern conceptualizations of depression is Brenner's (1974, 1982). Using Freud's model of anxiety as "signal," he argues that the content of thoughts associated with depressed affect differs in different individuals, and that there is no consistent ideational content. He advances the view that the presence of depression implies nothing about etiology and dynamics. Instead, depression tends to be a response to the often unconscious memory of a childhood disaster and to the unconscious fantasy or conviction that a similar disaster has occurred in the present. He argues that while depression may be an important symptomatic category, it is not a useful diagnostic category. He postulates that depression, like anxiety, is an unpleasurable affect associated with frustration, disappointment, and loneliness. Depression, however, is a response to a disaster that is thought to have already occurred. "Depressive affect has as its ideational content a calamity or calamities that exist in the present ... while anxiety has as its ideational content a future calamity" (1982, p. 164).

Freud's (1926b) theory of anxiety, briefly summarized, is that anxiety is caused by a traumatic situation, defined as the experience of helplessness in the face of overwhelming excitation of either internal or external origin. Anxiety is a response to impending trauma. Situations of threat and danger most commonly involve separation from or loss of a loved object, or the loss of its love, evoking a sense of helplessness. Anxiety functions as a signal to monitor danger in the internal or external world. The signal model of anxiety has been extended to other affects, such as guilt, anger, shame, and hate.

Contributions to the theory of depression and anxiety have also been made from the object relations perspective, which underscores the impairments in object representations and efforts to maintain contact with objects. Object relations theorists have in particular emphasized the role of self and object representations in generating and regulating affective states. Human interaction, and the mental representations they both create and invoke, are essential in the experience of affective states.

Melanie Klein (1935) postulated that depression is a response to "the persecutions and demands of bad internalized objects; the attacks of such objects upon one another ... the urgent necessity to fulfill the very strict demands of the 'good objects' and to protect and placate them within the ego, with the resultant hatred of the id; the constant uncertainty as to the 'goodness' of the good object, which causes it so readily to become transformed into a bad one" (p. 151). Depression is related to the anxious fear that rage has destroyed, or will destroy, loving objects or deplete their love. Depression is the affective experience of worry and regret, and often engenders a wish to restore and repair. Klein also redefined anxiety as signals of dangers in the relationship with the inner maternal object, as responses to real or imagined failures of the actual maternal object to protect and serve the infantile self. Anxiety signals the potential destruction of the vital parts of one's internal world.

One of the difficulties with much of psychoanalytic theorizing about anxiety and depression is that it attempts to specify too systematically and precisely the nature of the mental contents that are associated with these affects. These theories often fail to distinguish psychological processes (e.g., identifications, signals of danger) from specific mental contents (unconscious hostility, fear of abandonment). The variety of human experience that can reach an end point in the experience of depression or anxiety is enormous. As a consequence it is problematic to claim exclusive validity of one or another theory of depression or anxiety based on a specific mental content. Theories such as Brenner's (1982) that emphasize mental processes rather than contents avoid this difficulty. Contemporary relational theory is also organized around processes rather than contents. For example, Spezzano (1993) holds that anxiety serves not only as a signal of danger, but also as a way to communicate to others our sense of being in danger. Anxious states originate and are regulated intersubjectively. Relational theorists emphasize the importance of parent–infant reciprocity in affective development generally, and more specifically in the individual's modes of regulating and expressing anxiety. The extent to which a child's constitutional anxiety level will evolve into anxieties about specific mental contents (e.g., object loss, loss of the object's love, castration, or superego attacks) is largely determined by early experiences in relationships.

Alternative Strategies for Evaluation: Ms. M

The limitations of static pretreatment approaches to diagnosis are considerable. An alternative strategy for assessing a patient and evaluating the possible effectiveness of a psychoanalytic treatment will now be illustrated by way of assessments conducted as part of the psychotherapy of Ms. M, who was diagnosed, using the *DSM*, as suffering from major depressive disorder. Her treatment was a twice-weekly, two-and-a-half-year psychodynamic psychotherapy conducted as part of an investigation of longer-term therapies for depression.

> Ms. M was 35 years old at the beginning of treatment. She had divorced some ten years ago, and had three children by that marriage. She and her children were currently living with a man whom she married during the course of the therapy. Her presenting complaint was that she had gone into an emotional tailspin when her eldest son, age 16, expressed the desire to live with his father, her former husband. Ms. M's first episode of severe depression occurred six years earlier when, in the course of one year, she underwent two abortions. She was treated by a psychiatrist through a regimen of antidepressant medication and some psychotherapy. She reported that the medication alleviated her symptoms of sleeplessness and loss of appetite, but that this therapy did not seem to be helpful.
>
> Ms. M's father was a successful business entrepreneur whom she, as a child, adored. She remembered never

being very close to her mother, who was a housewife. Ms. M had one sibling, a half-brother who was nine years older, whom she greatly admired and looked up to. This was her mother's son by a previous marriage; Ms. M felt her father had always been disappointed in not having a son of his own. When Ms. M was 7 years old, her brother was killed in a swimming accident. Ms. M's mother, who was described as once very energetic, outgoing, and vivacious, went into a severe and prolonged depression, and functioned well enough only to manage basic household activates. The patient believed her mother never really recovered from her brother's death. Ms. M felt that her father then deserted both her and her mother, and she felt excruciatingly lonely. Her mother became increasingly passive, and her father, who was eventually himself treated for an emotional disorder, drank excessively and became mean and aggressively domineering. Nevertheless, Ms. M did well in school and was popular among her classmates. Her parents' increasingly acrimonious marriage eventually ended in divorce. Ms. M married after her freshman year in college. She had her first child at 21, and worked as a teacher; she ended her nine-year marriage largely because of her husband's problems with alcohol.

Constructing a Case Formulation for Ms. M

A thorough evaluation of the patient might include, in addition to an assessment of the patient's symptoms, a formulation or hypothesis about the potential meanings of symptomatic behavior, the patient's goals in therapy, the relationship of current difficulties to past experiences, and how the patient is likely to use the therapist in the work of the treatment. This approach to evaluation integrates diagnosis and a formulation of the patient's psychology, in which an attempt is made to understand the complexity of the individual patient and what factors might maintain the symptoms of depression. A group of five psychoanalytically oriented clinicians viewed the 90-minute intake interview for Ms. M and were asked to then independently write formulations of the case. They had no other information about Ms. M beyond that contained in the intake interview. Each of the clinical judges developed formulations using Horowitz and Rosenberg's (1994) consensual response formulation method, which were combined into a final consensual formulation. (There are several methods for developing reliable case formulations, including Luborsky and Crits-Christoph's [1998] core conflictual relationship theme method, Weiss's [1993] plan diagnosis method, and McWilliams's [1998] relationally sensitive diagnosis.)

The consensual formulation, which has the advantage of capturing agreement among a number of clinical judges, is represented by the following narrative description. Ms. M's depression was characterized by agitation, weight loss, sleeplessness, and feelings of becoming crazy. She gave some evidence of affective mood swings during her lifetime. Ms. M's history gives the impression of a relatively benign early childhood, with a typical oedipal constellation marred by the death of her older brother. She then felt abandoned by both parents, neither of whom successfully mourned the death of her brother. The patient probably felt responsible for her brother's death and hence guilty. She seemed to repeat a pattern of achieving success, and then destroying it at its peak. There was agreement about her unresolved grief, and her use of isolation and manic defenses to ward off her grief. Following her abortions there may have been a collapse of her defenses against depressive affect. Her grief seemed to stem from her repeated abortions and conflicted wishes to be free of her children, which recalled likely early murderous wishes toward her brother. The judges considered such clinically relevant features as nature of defenses, likely transferences, and possible difficulties that might arise in the treatment. They emphasized that Ms. M was intelligent, articulate, and self-reflective, and had achieved a good deal. However, they also noted that she had a great capacity for denial of her depression, a great need to be in control, and little tolerance for dependence. In a defensive manic flight she might deny her guilt, depression, and need for treatment. Another potential problem was that the patient's guilt about achieving happiness might lead her to defeat the therapist. Ms. M had self-punitive, attacking, controlling introjects. There was agreement that the treatment's success might hinge on how well the therapist responded to a negative maternal transference stemming from her hatred of her mother and her anger about her mother's unavailability.

Evaluating Patients through Response to Treatment

Including a formulation allows the integration of a diagnosis with a more thoroughgoing understanding of Ms. M and with treatment considerations. This assessment permits consideration of the functional components of *her* depression and how they can be addressed in order to modify her conflicts and troubling mental representations. The patient's response to the therapist, and the earliest phase of the treatment, can also yield information about the patient that contributes to the evaluation. In fact, understandings about the patient gained through the therapist–patient interaction are of the most immediate use in terms of assessing an individual's likelihood of benefiting from treatment. The following dialogue takes place during Ms. M's second therapy session. She reports a long history of depression, noting she has not been helped much by different forms of treatment. Moreover, despite her previous therapies, she doesn't seem to know how to proceed, and seems to be asking the therapist to take charge and tell her what to talk about. These attitudes, coupled with her history of mostly unsuccessful therapy, might not be considered strong positive indicators for a successful analytically oriented treatment, and it is easy to imagine that the therapist may, at this point, have felt disinclined to recommend beginning an intensive therapy.

Therapist: Where would you like to start?
Patient: I really have a problem with that. I don't have a place to start. I don't know where to start. I was hoping you were not going to ask me that. (*laugh*)
T: That's an interesting place to start. Why is that?
P: I don't know; because I don't know where I'm going; I'm just very unfocused about all of this, so I need guidance and help. I really don't know.
T: Hmm. It looks like you have a lot of feelings about that. Are you feeling something in particular about that?
P: I don't know. I don't know. I mean I don't know what it is I'm feeling. I want you (*laugh*) I want you to say "talk about this" or "let's do this" or something like that. (*pause*) And this is important for you to know, also: I have a history of brief attempts at therapy of one

kind or another or another, all of which to me have been disappointments. Not that I knew what I was doing then either. I was unfocused then and I am now. I don't have an experience with doing this sort of thing that tells me, well, this is the way it works.

T: Mm.

P: And I just don't, I just don't.

T: Well, tell me about the disappointments.

P: Maybe I wasn't committed; maybe it was me more than anything. I just felt like we're not getting anywhere. I already knew all of this so what's the big deal about this? I just didn't get it.

T: Hmm.

P: The experience I have was starting back when my marriage was failing. We went to marriage counseling. That was terrible, just terrible . . .

The patient goes on to describe in some detail her disappointing experience with marriage counseling, and her subsequent treatment with a psychiatrist. Although the antidepressant medication he prescribed helped with the symptoms of inability to eat, weight loss, and sleeplessness, she did not find the therapy useful. She then began group therapy, where she was able to form good bonds with some of the women in the group, but she did not think it was very valuable in terms of personal growth. The therapist subtly acquires more information about the extent of Ms. M's actual helplessness and inability to proceed by asking about her previous disappointments in therapy, and Ms. M responds by speaking quite freely.

P: So anyhow, the point of all of this is why I don't know (*laugh*) where to begin or what to talk about.

T: You know, when you've had that many disappointments and then to think about exactly how, in a positive way, how this is going to go. . . .

P: That's right.

T: You've had those disappointments but yet you're hopeful.

P: Absolutely. Absolutely.

The therapist goes on to ask her thoughts about her depressive episode during that period.

P: I never imagined much of a mood swing at all, and then this hit me. I just felt like a real roller coaster with my emotions. And that they were absolutely out of control. I don't think this really happened, but it felt like a constant battle to me just to keep from breaking down and crying at any minute. I suppose I didn't lose control of my emotions at inappropriate times.

T: Mm.

P: So for thirty years I was at a perfect balance and then all of a sudden, boom, this terrible thing happened that I had no control whatsoever.

T: Triggered by the abortion?

P: Triggered by the abortion.

T: Sounds like you don't think it was just about that.

P: Well, I guess I don't think it's just about that. . . . At the same time, through this whole period and even after I had the medication for a few months, I felt very special. In some ways, probably for the first and only time in my life, I felt really special. I felt like I could walk into a room, and eyes would turn. I was noticed when I would walk into a room, or just down the street or whatever. It's funny, it's funny to try to talk about. Well, it's just a feeling. I felt very special.

T: Do you think, do you think you were just letting it in?

P: That's possible.

T: Or is your idea that there was a difference in how other people responded to you?

P: Well, I think that there's a little, uh, truth in both.

T: Mm.

P: I do believe that I put out vibrations or signals or something that were different, that did sort of electrically charge things. On the other hand, I think that one of my real problems—I'll say *problems* just because I can't think of a better word but something that I'd like to change—is it's very easy for me to get to feeling invisible. Not feeling unattractive. I'm not talking ugly or I'm not talking about feeling ugly or anything like that, just unnoticeable.

T: Huh.

P: And at my best I feel attractive in an electrically charged way.

T: Right.

At this point, the therapist may be wondering about the severity of Ms. M's pathology. Ms. M describes mood swings, which might be cyclothymic or perhaps even manic depressive in nature, and describes as well what could be interpreted as ideas of reference and apparently strong dependency needs. The therapist's reservations about whether Ms. M would benefit from psychotherapy could well be heightened at this point, and she may wonder whether medication might be more useful. However, the therapist's estimation of Ms. M's disturbance level will become more favorable, as will as her estimation of Ms. M's capacity to use therapy, as a consequence of the patient's response to an interpretation about the meaning of a symptom, her crying spells.

P: When I moved here, I got pretty much back to business, I would say. I think I'm the same with people as before this whole this period happened. Yeah.

T: Yeah.

P: What happens now, as though I still have a very connected feeling with lives of other people, people who I know or people I don't know. So I fight back tears frequently over crazy things. Over anything. Over hearing stories, or reading stories, or watching TV. Just anything will bring tears to my eyes now.

T: What sorts of stories will trigger your feelings?

P: It just seems like anything that has anything to do with emotions. Someone else's emotional challenge or that sort of thing. Just almost anything. The Olympics. I cry at every event at the Olympics, for instance.

T: Uh-huh. The achievement. Yeah.

P: I mean, I'm just giving you an example of the really silly things.

T: The achievement of it.

P: That's right.

T: Yeah.

P: That's right.

T: The hard work and the achievement and the effort. Mm-hmm.

P: Yeah.

T: I was remembering how you were crying Monday (*during the initial session*) at the thought of wanting to share happy events and I was wondering if it was happy events, or well, achievements would fit into that.

P: Uh-huh.

T: Accomplishments, getting what you want.

P: Truthfully, I think that may be right. I think, now that you mention that, I think that may be why. Right. That may be more of a pull on my emotions. More so than difficulty overcoming; or falling into the trench (*laugh*) kind of things. You know, it's the pulling out of the trench that seems so emotionally charged to me. I think that's right.

T: That's very interesting.

P: It's interesting to me, too. (*pause*) I don't know why. I don't know what the meaning of that is. (*pause*) Well, one thing I think that connects: I think what these therapists I've had in my past have done that's annoying to me is they've said, "Well, it's been very difficult." Or they've tried to make me feel (*pause*) I don't know. I know I feel annoyed when someone says, "You've had to do something very difficult." I don't know why that's so annoying to me when therapists say that. First of all, it seems sort of condescending to me. And it seems untrue. I mean, it seems like this is in their book of how to be a psychologist, that says be empathetic and here's a way to say "Well this is a very difficult thing." (*laugh*)

T: Yeah.

P: It's annoying to me because I think that my view of myself is one who, though I've lived through hard times, so what? A lot of people (*laugh*) have lived through hard times, you know. If it's hard you work harder. (*pause*) I mean there's nothing more to be said than that. That's not where the focus needs to be (*laugh*) for me. I don't know where the focus does need to be but . . .

T: Well, that leaves the achievements, the positive.

P: I think that's right. I think that's right. Maybe this doesn't feel exactly right, but I appreciate the positive, the accomplishment, once it's done, and feel proud and happy about it.

   The patient begins the next hour (*the third session*) by taking up the therapist's interpretation about why she wept watching the Olympics, or hearing or reading other stories about achievement.

P: This morning I started thinking about what you men- tioned last week, which was maybe that the things that caused me to be emotional are examples of people feel- ing pride or joy or that sort of thing. More so than the other side. So since Thursday I've sort of paid attention to each time I felt that, and what was causing it. And it's true. That's accurate. That every time that I felt that well- ing up of tears and so forth was an occasion where people were feeling particularly joyful about something. When I cried here the first time I met with you it was because I was trying to explain to you how I longed for sharing those moments about my own children with other people. And that's what I've been thinking about since Thursday. I mean I haven't gotten anywhere about that, those particu- larly joyous feelings. I mean more specifically sharing the specialness, maybe. That's what makes my children so spe- cial to me. And I wished that they were equally special to someone else so that I could have that bond with them.
T: Mm.
P: And I suspect all of this has something or another to do with my fear of finishing life without ever getting to the point where I'm secure with my own sense of specialness for myself.

This interaction during the first two treatment sessions enhances our evaluation and understanding. Ms. M had ini- tially asked for a fee that was lower than that determined by the sliding scale used by the clinic at which she was being seen, thereby jeopardizing her chances of being accepted for treatment. She then invited the therapist to pathologize her by announcing how ineffective her previous treatments had been, and by emphasizing the severity of her symptoms, especially her frequent crying spells. In other words, she masochistically invited the therapist to either reject her for treatment, to see her as extremely troubled, or to condescend to her with useless sympathy. Instead of arriving at a diagnosis of cyclothymia or other mood disorder, the therapist attempted to understand if any consistent meaning was represented in Ms. M's crying.

The therapist tried the interpretation that Ms. M's crying spells expressed a wish to share happy events, such as achievements. This interpretation of the meaning of her crying spells clearly interested the patient. It engaged her in the therapy process, and seemed to have an organizing effect on her. From the standpoint of evaluating Ms. M for treatment, the therapist was able to observe how effectively the patient was able to work with a trial interpretation, carrying her thoughts about it into the next hour. Ms. M's positive response was probably also related to the therapist's refusal to be drawn into a sadomasochistic interaction. Ms. M quickly begins to appear less troubled, and agrees with the therapist that she wishes to focus on accomplishing something of which she can feel proud. This interaction also provides some evidence of the narcissistic conflicts that are part of Ms. M's depression, that is, the sense she will never achieve being special. This early interaction between therapist and patient can be viewed from the framework of interactions structures. Repeatedly during the treatment, the therapist feels compelled to rescue Ms. M from her masochistic feeling of not being worthwhile or special and her related depression.

It is through the intervention process itself that we can reach a more complete understanding of the nature and meaning of the patient's symptoms and what intervention strategies might be most effective. The process of evaluation is continuous with the task of introducing the patient to therapy, which should be done in a manner that facilitates the development of a therapeutic process. Introducing the patient to therapy provides continuing opportunities to evaluate what kind of relationship may develop with the therapist, and what anxieties and resistances may obstruct the development of a therapeutic process.

"Is This the Right Treatment for Me?"

There is now a wide range of mental health interventions available to patients. Some patients will have encountered media reports about the presumed superiority of one type of therapy over another for particular problems. Professional organizations have promulgated often controversial guidelines about what ought to constitute the standard of treatment for patients who meet criteria for *DSM* diagnoses. The use of medication for treating depression and anxiety, as well as many other psychological problems, has increased enormously. In fact, physicians in general practice routinely prescribe antidepressant medication to patients who complain of dysphoric affect. It is hardly a surprise that as a consequence, many individuals are often uncertain about what treatment might be best for them. Analytically oriented therapists must often respond to confusion, questions, and worries about their method of treatment, and its status and effectiveness relative to other treatment possibilities.

In the following segment taken from the first session of a treatment, the patient's question about what kind of therapy he should have is quite effectively linked by the therapist to an understanding of the nature of the patient's problems.

Patient: I had a good friend of mine who said that she had read a book about cognitive behavioral therapy. Basically describing a different type of therapy. She went through it, and she said it just made a huge difference. It really helped her reflect on where her thought processes are and kind of nip her thoughts at the bud when she started thinking negatively and so forth.

Therapist: Mm-hmm.

P: Of course you're familiar with it. So, I was interested in that and contacted the center where she said she took eight courses. They said they had nothing available at the moment.

T: Mm-hmm. (*The interview continues for another 30 minutes, during which the patient describes feelings of harsh self-criticalness and depression that have plagued him since childhood.*)

P: What do you think so far? I mean, from a doctor's standpoint. Let me ask you this: Do you think that an extended, intense therapy is going to help me?

T: Yeah. I think you're motivated to do it now. I think you have a pretty clear sense of the problem . . . but it's like the tip of the iceberg. You know the problem, but you don't know really what keeps you motivated to treat yourself in this way.

P: Yeah. Yeah. So understanding the past as it applies to where I am at, and then in extended therapy sessions, we'd be exploring the past but dealing with what would be coming up in my life in the present, as well. And then I can change it, hopefully?

T: Yeah, that's the idea. If you can understand why you are so persistent in being critical of yourself, putting yourself down, what keeps that going. If you understand that, you'll have much more freedom to see, Well, gee, are there other options? Are there other ways to treat yourself that make sense? But for now, somehow, this way seems to make a kind of sense for you, so that's what you do.

P: Initially I thought, maybe I'll take some cognitive behavioral therapy sessions. I mean do you think this therapy will be something for me? Coming two times a week? Or do you think it's something that I can overcome by doing cognitive-behavioral therapy? I think cognitive-behavioral therapy, it's more like a present thing. You're not necessarily addressing things that occurred in the past. I mean what do you, what do you . . . What angle do you like to take as a doctor?

T: Well, the kind of therapy I offer includes a cognitive point of view. It includes understanding why you think the way you think and if there aren't other options. But it goes beyond that in a way that I think is important for you. You've told me this way of thinking has lasted a very long time. It's very knit into your personality.

P: Mm-hmm. Yeah, totally.

T: Those things don't change with just a few seminars, you see. They're too woven in and there has to be a very strong motivation for maintaining them. I think you've already seen that through your previous attempts [at change].

P: That's a fear of mine, though. How you described that—the knit—that's a great way of describing it. I've never heard it put that way. The way I think is sort of knit into my personality. It makes sense, but I'm afraid what I know of my identity . . . do I hate it so much? It's like I love parts of it. But I don't really know what I love and I can't stand parts of it, but I don't want to lose that. And that's what I fear, that if I go into some type of intense-type therapy that . . .

T: . . . that therapy would it take away?

P: Oh, no. That's a ridiculous worry.

T: No, I don't think that would be a ridiculous worry.

P: No, but it's not really a worry, in all honesty. I know that life is a process and a journey and it can't do anything but help me. Initially, when you were saying that, I was like, wow, I don't really want to change, I don't want to end it. It will unravel and I will just spiral down.

T: That's a good way of putting the worry.

P: But that won't happen, though, because it's going to be a positive thing doing therapy. It's not like I'll have a doctor who's just going to allow me to spiral down while I'm dealing with this shit.

T: You see, the perspective of the therapy I offer is that if you can understand this, then it's up to you, if you feel you want to change. It's not something that is imposed upon you. If you can understand something about yourself, then you have greater freedom to do what you want.

P: So do you think this is something that I should do? As a doctor?

T: I think, yes, you should be in therapy. I think you need an extended therapy because, from what I am understanding about your life, this has been going on for a long time, this tendency to criticize and blame yourself and worry that you are too hurtful to people.

P: Totally. It is a huge issue.

T: This is a great time in your life to do it and take care of this. So, I would absolutely recommend that you proceed in therapy.

It becomes clear that the appeal of a brief course of cognitive therapy lies in the fact that the patient perceives it as less threatening. An intensive analytic therapy holds for the patient the possibility of being changed in ways he does not wish, or even precipitating a downward spiral. The patient is, in essence, asking if analytic therapy is safe for him. This underscores the fact that a patient's request for a particular, although often only vaguely understood, type of treatment (or therapist) frequently represents a wish to have, or to avoid, a particular kind of relationship or kind of experience. The therapist's recommendation for treatment is direct and forthright, and tied to her understanding of the nature of the patient's problem. The therapist explains that psychoanalytic therapy, in addition to many other matters, does interest itself in patients' thinking. In fact, a study of the Berkeley project (Ablon and Jones 1998) demonstrates that psychodynamic therapists focus on irrational thinking, self-punitive ideas, and pathogenic beliefs as much as do cognitive therapists, but also concern themselves with interpersonal experience and developmental history to a much greater extent. The patient in fact did begin treatment on a twice-weekly basis.

In the next illustration, taken from an early session, the patient is troubled by her family's criticism of her therapy; they are urging her to seek medication and cognitive-behavioral therapy. Although the patient is pleased with the course of her therapy so far, these criticisms have stimulated doubt and caused her to question her judgment.

Patient: My father and my sister think (*laughs nervously*) I'm in the wrong kind of therapy.
Therapist: Because?
P: They think that since Alice [patient's sister] had treatment—I think she was in cognitive therapy and had some

medication, Prozac, to go along with that. And she's telling my father about that versus psychotherapy . . .

T: Is she still on Prozac?

P: Yes she is, but she has that and therapy.

T: Mm-hmm.

P: And (*laughs*) I see with her that she's fine as long
as she's on the medication, but when that needs to be
upped, when they need to increase the dosage, she re-
sumes kind of being depressed again.

T: Mm-hmm.

P: And that's a little bit frightening to me. She was telling my father that you could do a therapy that works a
lot more quickly than psychotherapy. When they were
talking with me, they seemed really perturbed (*laughs*)
that I had chosen this path.

T: Because he sees you as losing ground, or what?

P: My father wants me to be okay and as quickly as I can,
to get over what's bothering me.

T: How are you?

P: Well, (*laughs*) I'm feeling better.

T: Well, do you feel that we're on the wrong beam?

P: I don't. I feel pretty happy with this. I don't think that
it's easy, but I feel happy with where this is going.

T: But something about your sister wants you to be like
her. Or she's worried about how you're doing. What is
your understanding of this, and her recommendation?

P: She and my father had been talking about how, for example, how I have a tendency to handle crushes, which
we've talked about here.

T: Yeah.

P: Intensive crushes, and they were worried about that. She
(*laughs*) isn't a doctor, but because we're sisters and because we have had some of the same kinds of problems

and thought processes, she thinks that it's partly chemi-
cal, according to her. (*Patient discusses her sister's views for
some time.*)

T: I wouldn't recommend Prozac for you, right now. I
mean, I don't see all of you, but I don't have a sense
that, here's a woman that Prozac would be really helpful for at the moment. If you feel that I'm missing a
kind of bleak depression that you don't talk about in
here, then we need to talk about what keeps you from
telling me.

P: Oh, I've been completely forthright.

T: I assumed so.

P: But I don't feel that I'm really in need of medication.
They might have (*laughs*) a different opinion, but I know
how I feel and think and what goes on in my mind, and
I don't feel like I'm that severe. Every now and then I
come to see what I'm doing with my sister, which I don't
think is necessarily all that good. I don't know about her
therapy; that's her business.

The patient goes on to note that her sister claimed
psychotherapy was too slow, since it was concerned with
why someone was doing something rather than focusing on
helping patients stop doing what they are doing. She wonders if medication or cognitive therapy might work more
quickly.

P: It might not work as quickly. I personally don't know if
it does or not. And I don't feel like I'm qualified to
make that judgment. But uh . . .

T: I think they're quite different. It's apples and oranges.
I think Prozac can be quite helpful, when needed. And
it can be helpful to keep somebody feeling in the groove
when otherwise they'd feel quite despairing and quite
overwhelmed by intrusive thoughts.

P: Well, let me ask you, now, how about cognitive therapy because that's what she was comparing, I think.

T: You know, like any therapy, it partly depends on whose hands it's in. And it partly depends on what suits you.

P: Mm-hmm. Well, from what I understand, psychotherapy has come a long way from the Freudian model. They were talking to me as if it were still very much in that model.

T: What do you mean? Do you know what in particular?

P: My father was telling me that psychotherapy is almost like a luxury. It can go on for years and years.

T: What's wrong with luxury?

P: (*laughs*) I guess over, over the long term, it could be expensive.

T: Mm-hmm. Depends on what it yields.

The patient, who had been relying on her father to pay the costs of her therapy, then goes on to consider the possibility of paying for the therapy on her own. The therapist systematically and patiently explores the meanings and resistances underlying the patient's thoughts about the desirability of other forms of treatment. The therapist subtly assists the patient in taking an independent view of herself in the face of her family's pressure that she have the same treatment as her sister. Although the therapist remains open to the possibility of medication, both therapist and patient agree that it is not indicated. In response to the patient's questions about the usefulness of cognitive therapy, the therapist points out that in psychological interventions, the practitioner is perhaps more important than the treatment model, something often overlooked in the era of manualized treatments.

What in this evaluation phase appears to be external pressure from the patient's family is an early form of an interaction structure. In the interaction pattern that develops, the patient herself insistently pressures the therapist to fix her quickly under the threat of termination, despite reporting that she is feeling better. In response, the therapist continually felt coerced and beset by worry that the therapy was in jeopardy.

Educating Patients about Therapy

Many patients have only vague and often erroneous notions about what to expect from a therapist, and about what they ought to do in therapy. It is often helpful to educate the patient a bit about therapy: "Our goal is to get to know your mind, and how it works, by your listening to yourself, and by our listening to you together." Instructing the patient about free association is often a very useful way of informing the patient about how to proceed. At the same time, close attention to the patient's responses provide a way of assessing how well the patient might be able to use psychoanalytic therapy. The following illustration, taken from the third session of a therapy, is a clear, straightforward introduction to free association. The first two sessions were consultations during which the therapist evaluated the patient, who was an obsessional, overly intellectualized law student, and made a recommendation for treatment.

Therapist: I don't know how you've worked in psychotherapy before. In the work I do I put a lot of emphasis on free association.
Patient: Mm-hmm.
T: I regard that as a very productive way for you to proceed. By free association I mean allowing your thoughts

to come to mind on their own and trying to give voice to them.

P: Mm-hmm.

T: So that your spontaneous thoughts, images, memories, whatever, lead us rather than your conscious, directed . . .

P: Mm-hmm.

T: . . . effortful thinking leading us. There may well be times when there's simply something you want to tell me, and so you just go ahead and do that. That's what you've come with, but in general, particularly for those of us who are overly intellectual . . .

P: (*laughs*)

T: . . . and I include the two of us in that. Most people with a good deal of education put so much emphasis on rationality and the use of reason . . .

P: Mm-hmm.

T: . . . free association is a kind of antidote to rationalism, and helps us avoid becoming limited by your own attempts to overpower your problems by reason.

P: Mm-hmm.

T: It's an unnatural thing to do, to give voice to thoughts that are occurring to you on your own. Particularly to someone you don't know well. I don't expect you to be particularly good at it right away. I take it as part of my job to help you, help you learn how to do it, help you relax a little, and render yourself up to it . . .

P: Mm-hmm.

T: . . . a bit more as we go along. But I want to indicate now that it is a kind of guideline and an answer to the question, how do I start? or what should I talk about?

The therapist offers a brief explanation about free association, and why it is useful. He has obviously already observed the patient's inclination to rely on intellectually oriented defenses, and shapes his description of free association in such a way that he begins to address this important aspect of the patient's character.

Several therapy sessions later, the patient complains about his difficulty in letting his ideas come spontaneously to mind, and speaking his ideas freely.

P: I am interested in finding out more about the part of me that's blocking my speaking, or voicing the thoughts that come up in here . . . and that's resisting these other things in my life. And I really don't know how to do that, 'cause like I said last time, it's like . . . I don't know, it's just a catch-22. It seems like that sometimes. I was wondering if you could talk to me just a little bit about that or help me get some idea about what to do about it all or, or what it'll be like to deal with it.

T: Okay. I think that it's something that you'll learn about as we continue to do this. The way you put the question was "I want to learn more about whatever it is in me that blocks certain things and that resists various other things." It is that thing which devotes itself to maintaining things as they are and as they have been for a long time. In your case it is bound up in your depressiveness. In psychotherapy the resistance is what? Since psychotherapy is all about helping you get off the dime, then resistance here tends to be mobilized, uh, becomes more palpable and stands as a specific obstacle against speaking your thoughts as they occur to you spontaneously. So as you try to speak thoughts as they occur to you spontaneously, it is everything within you that says, "I don't want to do this, it's too hard, I'm tired, what's the point?, I don't believe in a unitary self anyway . . ."

P: (*laughs*)

T: It's that feeling of futility, weariness ... "No, I don't want to do this. ... What's the point?"

P: What does one do about that?

T: Try ... an act of faith.

P: Hah, (*laughing*) that's precisely what I don't have.

T: Yeah, but here it's just a kind of approximate act of faith. If you don't begin to see some promise in this, in at least the foreshadowing of some real benefit, within at least a few months then ... You know, it's not like signing up for some belief whose validity won't be established until the next life.

P: (*laughing*) Right.

The difficulties the patient experiences are not uncommon, particularly in the beginning phase of treatment. In fact, the difficulties patients experience can provide an opportunity to gauge how well they might be able to use a psychoanalytic approach to therapy. The therapist attempts to turn this patient's strength of intellect to understanding his difficulties in free association and explaining the nature of his resistances. He also appeals to the patient's motivation for change. In the following illustration, taken from a subsequent hour, the nature of the patient's anxieties about therapy, which are represented in his difficulty talking freely, begin to emerge. The example also demonstrates the therapist's ability to listen empathically to the patient's struggles, as well as demonstrating the constructive use of the patient's silence.

P: (*lengthy silence*)

T: You stopped talking abruptly.

P: Uhm . . . I think I want to know more about the rights of, the legal rights of, psychotherapeutic and psychiatric patients in general. That's a large part of it for me. It'll require a little bit of research. (*pause, sigh*)

T: You mean about things like involuntary admissions and electroshock and things of that sort?

P: Yes. It was very frightening for me to say that because . . . I mean there's a reason I go to a psychologist rather than a psychiatrist. It's because I'm a little bit afraid of the old medical institution, the psychiatric institution. Uhm. Well, for instance, a friend of mine in Alabama, her psychiatrist prescribed antipsychotic medication for her, and a mutual friend of ours said to her, "Well, you know Elaine, you seem really depressed and all but those are some pretty heavy drugs you're on. You should ask for a second opinion or something." She told her psychiatrist that and her psychiatrist told her that if you do that we might have to put you in the hospital. And that seems to me more akin to social control than to healing or treatment. (*silence*) Uhm . . . I am wondering what you're thinking.

T: Well, you said that you thought that you wanted to learn more about these things. I wasn't clear whether you were asking me or whether you planned to do some research on it. I think it's a good idea. Not because I see it as an issue in your case, but because you're worried about it. I regard these worries of yours like any other sorts of things that might occur to you as you sit here. They are things that we want to explore and understand for their meaning. And, in addition, you may want to explore them in a different sort of way outside. To me, it is important and valuable that you've given voice to these thoughts because they weren't just born a minute or two ago. They've been here every time we've met but this is the first time I get

to know about them. It helps me to understand you better. And what's at stake for you as we talk.
P: Freedom.

The therapist hears and accepts the patient's anxieties
about being controlled by the therapist and loss of independence. Through his empathic listening, and through allowing the silences to continue, the therapist creates an
atmosphere in which the patient can reveal the frightening fantasies that underlie his resistance to treatment.
His acknowledgment of powerful worries about losing his
autonomy helps clarify why he relies so strongly on
his intellectual defenses. The analysis of these resistances
and the uncovering of these fantasies actually mark the
initiation of a therapeutic process. This patient's deep
anxieties about being controlled foreshadow a gripping interaction structure. In this interaction pattern, the patient
repeatedly attempted to control the therapist and render
him ineffective by disavowing his own obvious hostility,
and remaining obtuse in the face of the therapist's interpretations. The patient's refusal to use the therapist's
ideas sometimes provoked an angry countertransference.

The orientation described in this chapter underscores
the limitations of static, pretreatment diagnoses in understanding and treating patients and the advantages of assessment by means of the ongoing treatment process. Interactions in the beginning phase of treatment can yield a
knowledge and understanding of the patient that are
helpful to the therapist in assessing the patient's capacity
for self-reflection and ability to work with interpretations.
Thoughtful attention to the nature of the treatment process that evolves with the patient is essential in forming a
diagnostic and psychological understanding of the patient.
The next chapters discuss how particular therapeutic inter-

ventions foster the integration of mental representations of self and other, and the capacity to represent and reflect on experience, within the framework of interaction structures. Chapter 3 addresses how the use of questions, clarifications, identifying themes in the patient's conduct, and memory and reconstructions can contribute to this end.

3

Creating Opportunities for Self-Reflection

Patients often approach therapy with the expectation that the therapist will relatively easily comprehend why they feel as they do, and then deliver transformative explanations. They consciously or unconsciously hope that the therapist will provide knowledge, resolve conflicts and dilemmas, and advise them about how to conduct their life. Most patients must learn that self-understanding, as opposed to received wisdom, will be the means by which they are able to change and sustain their change. The foremost goal of analytic therapies is to help patients understand how they think, how they feel, the nature of their relations to others—in short, to understand their mind and how it works. Much of what the patient does in therapy will be in the form of learning to perceive, express, and reflect on experience. The patient's self-observation is a necessary precondition for a change process to occur. Some basic techniques for developing these capacities in the patient include questions, clarifications, confrontation, identifying themes in the patient's experience or conduct, using memories or reconstructions of the past, and linking perceptions or feelings with past experience.

These intervention strategies are considered within the context of the model of therapeutic action introduced and illustrated in Chapter 1—interaction structures. Interaction structures refer to the repetitive ways in which patient and therapist interact. These patterns of interaction, which are usually slow to change, reflect the psychologies of both patient and therapist. Although these observable, repetitive interactions are not the same as what is unconscious, they do represent some aspect of the unconscious mental life of patient and therapist that has come alive in the interaction. In this respect, they provide a way to bring disowned feeling states and related mental representations into awareness and allow their modification through integration with conscious and more differentiated mental processes. Particular therapist actions, such as questions, clarification, and confrontation, are best viewed within an interactive sequence occurring over time. The meaning of the intervention for the patient is derived from an intersubjective field, created by therapist and patient, in which the therapist's actions take place. Although the therapist may have a particular intent in intervening in a certain way, its effect depends on the patient's subjective experience at that moment.

Questions

There has been considerable discussion about the uses of questions in analytic therapies. The difficulty in discussing questions as a technique is that as a rhetorical form or grammatical construction, questions can be put to many uses, and potentially have many different connotations to patients. Questions can in themselves be interpretations. A common use of questions is, of course, to discover more about the patient's difficulties and to clarify the nature of problems. Questions may also serve as a means of inviting the patient's curiosity, or to point the patient toward a domain of inquiry that the therapist thinks might be productive. However, there have been concerns among some psychoanalytic clinicians about the role of questions. Questions may, for example, implicitly require the patient to submit to the therapist's interests or agenda. They may also mask the introduction of ideas, or even criticisms, and contain suggestions.

Questions, like all therapist actions, can be thought about in terms of interaction structures. For example, if a patient is passive and does not easily reveal much about himself, the therapist may feel prodded to ask questions. Over time, the therapist may find himself reflexively accepting the role the patient is forcing on him, falling into a pattern of taking over the therapy sessions and guiding the patient with a series of questions. This would constitute an interaction structure, a way in which therapist and patient relate to one another that likely has important meanings. The questions may gratify the patient's need to evoke interest and concern, or represent a way to avoid thinking about himself. For the therapist, the routine of questioning might express a need to be seen as an authority, or mask impatience or criticism of the patient's passivity. The meanings of such an interaction structure, for which questions are verbal "markers," should be explicitly recognized and understood.

It is impossible to know what patients' experience will be of a question posed by the therapist. Their reactions must be considered within the subjective and intersubjective experiences of a particular moment in treatment. Questions may allow one patient to experience the therapist as involved and responsive, but lead another to experience the therapist as intrusive and controlling. In general, the role of questions as a technique in psychotherapy is best understood in the interactive field created by therapist and patient.

There are a few generally agreed-upon guidelines
about the kinds of questions therapists should *not* ask.
Therapists should refrain from asking questions out of self-
interest. They should not, for example, ask a patient the
least traffic congested route to a destination, or to repeat
the name of a good hotel. A somewhat more complex
example is refraining from asking a foreign-born patient
about cultural practices out of a sense of personal interest
or curiosity. Such questions can be easily rationalized as a
means of furthering our understanding of the patient. The
point here is that therapists can experience the urge to
question for a variety of reasons, and should try to be aware
of their motives. Less experienced therapists sometimes ask
questions out of a sense of not knowing what to do. Anxiety or difficulty tolerating silence can also be motives for
asking patients questions. It is important for patients to
have some uninterrupted silence for thoughtful reflection.

Another guiding principle might be to ask questions
not necessarily for the purpose of obtaining an answer, or
to evoke a particular reaction, but rather to stimulate further thought. It is often useful to anticipate what the question will precipitate in the experience of the patient, and
what the patient will think the therapist is trying to evoke.
The patient's experience of a question can often be sur-
mised from the nature of the interaction patterns dominant at that particular point in the treatment.

One long-standing reservation about the use of questions among some psychoanalytic clinicians is the possibility that questions may hamper the free-association process,
requiring the patient to rely upon more rational, reality-
oriented forms of cognition. However, it cannot be assumed that a question forecloses or opens the possibilities
for exploration. Everything depends on the experience of
the question for the patient in the context of an ongoing

interaction with the therapist. Similarly, it cannot be assumed that questions represent a demand on the patient to accommodate to the therapist's interests. Contemporary two-person or intersubjective approaches remind us that the therapist's agenda cannot avoid emerging just because the therapist is silent or avoids questions; the therapist's interests and priorities are continually communicated both directly and indirectly. Exploring the meaning of the therapist's question to the patient, as with any other aspect of the therapist's activity or presence, may lead to new understandings or awareness.

One good use of questions is to provide a model for self-reflection and to help patients develop a sense of subjectivity. In the following illustration the therapist's questions are directed at the patient's wish to avoid thinking about herself.

Patient: (silence) Hmm. A lot of times when I try to think about myself it is a real effort.
Therapist: Mm-hmm.
P: I mean, I start thinking about other things. (*pause*) I don't remember what I was thinking about it.
T: Well, what do you imagine happening? If you were really to think about yourself?
P: I think it would be hard (*pause*) and painful. But when I see the difficulties of it as a challenge, the pain of it is short term. But still, really painful.
T: Mm-hmm. Perhaps that helps explain why you feel so slow, and why you may not like to do it so much.
P: (pause) Yeah.

The intent of the therapist's questions is to bring into focus an aspect of the patient's defenses and the purpose they serve of avoiding painful affect. The therapist also ties this to the meaning of the slow, effortful quality of her thought.

The next illustration demonstrates the use of questions to clarify the nature of the patient's problems. The therapist inquires about a patient's complaint concerning difficulty in leaving her house, which has the effect of bringing into the open additional facets of the patient's difficulties.

Therapist: Have you had any ideas about what might be contributing to this problem?
Patient: Not leaving the house?
T: Mm-hmm.
P: Well, I'm essentially shy. And I guess I figured if I don't leave the house, I won't have to take chances and I won't get hurt.
T: Hurt in what ways?
P: Oh, rejected or (*pause*) ignored. Or any bad experiences.
T: Have there been bad experiences in the past?
P: Oh, not bad, but not rewarding. (*long pause*) I do make myself go—when the people that I work with are going to be there, I make myself go. But I have to make myself go.
T: And what's it like when you get there?
P: It's all right.
T: You enjoy yourself?
P: Eventually. It takes time.

The patient's response to the therapist's questions quickly make it clear that her presenting complaint, fear of leaving the house, involves the nature of her relations with others and her fear of feeling rejected and hurt. The therapist's questions in another session are aimed at determining the reasons for the patient's abrupt decision to end her vacation early and bringing into the discourse her troubled self-image and related difficulties.

T: You mentioned like the, going off on a vacation and then turning around and coming right back.

P: Yes, I went to a resort. And I was planning to stay and enjoy the weather and enjoy the beautiful place up there. One of my co-workers has a motel up there, and I dropped by to see him, and he wasn't there at the time and these places were very expensive. So they pointed out some other places where I could stay, and I went and I looked at them and (*pause*) I didn't want to stay there. And I wanted my own mattress and I wanted my own house. I turned around and came all the way back.

T: Did you think it was something more than just being displeased with the accommodations?

P: (*Pause*) Well, part of me is cheap. I have I never realized how fast time is going by. But I did realize about five years ago that I'd have to hurry and try to get some money together for my old age. And so ever since then I've been trying to live on half my income. So part of it was the fact that it was an expense. But no, no that wasn't the whole thing. It's just that I didn't see anything. It used to be that I used to enjoy lying on the beach and sunning myself. And since I've put weight on, I (*laugh*) didn't want to lie on the beach, and I just couldn't see anything that I wanted to do, so I just turned around and came home.

T: Mm-hmm. You say that this change—you began noting about five years ago?

P: Mm-hmm.

T: What, what was going on back then?

P: Well, um, weight for one thing has been going on for about eight years.

Questions can be effectively used to encourage the patient to consider long-held assumptions about themselves, to begin to reconsider certain ideas or thinking in new ways about their self-image.

In the next example, the therapist's questions help the patient voice her sense of futility and lack of agency in determining her life.

Patient: So like even now when I'm making choices—or making decisions, rather, and I—I just don't make them. I just put them off until the last minute and then I kind of go with how I feel at the last minute.

Therapist: Uh-huh.

P: I don't look at all the options and like research all the choices. I do that, you know, on my own time, but I just never make that last final step of actually choosing.

T: What do you notice internally—during that time, I mean—do you have a sense of what may stop you, what may block you?

P: Well, I guess a few things. In one sense I kind of think, well, whatever happens with that, well, no matter what I decide, something's going to happen anyway.

T: Something meaning what?

P: Kind of like destiny sort of a thing. I know that there's a situation somewhere that I'm supposed to be in, and no matter what happens between now and then, I'll be there (*laugh*). Sometimes it's kind of like that . . .

T: Really? You don't feel like you have a choice not to be there?

P: Some I do, but there's always that little thought lurking in the back of my mind that no matter what I choose, I'm not sure that it will affect my future. I mean I can be in a different situation, but I'll still go through whatever is meant for me to go through.

The therapist's questions prompt the patient to put into words a perhaps inchoate felling that she is fated to have little control over her life, while at the same time providing an opportunity to reflect on this assumption.

In general, questions should not distract the patient from his or her train of thought, and should not be random, too frequent, or hasty. Repeated and unnecessary questions can disrupt a therapy session. Such questions can express countertransference feelings, a need to control patients, or uncertainty about how to proceed.

In the following illustration, the patient is clearly reluctant to talk about the death of a close cousin. The therapist, instead of noting this reluctance and the patient's wish to stay away from painful feelings, asks repeated questions about the details of the funeral. The therapist has a sense that the patient has not completely mourned the loss of this relationship, and seems to hope to encourage this process by pressing the patient to recall the event. The patient complies with the therapist's wishes but responds in a way that suggests the questioning is not helpful.

Therapist: Tell me again about how you heard about his death.
Patient: Oh, I don't even remember. I suppose they called. Dad's brother probably called the boy's father. And then he told me about it, I guess, I don't, I don't remember.
T: Did you go to the funeral?
P: Mm-hmm.

T: Where was the funeral?

P: It was . . . well there may have been two. Seems like there was one, I think there was one at the Methodist Church and then one at the church at home. He and I had sung at some of our older relatives' funerals together on a few occasions.

T: The two of you together . . .

P: Mm-hmm.

T: . . . would have been there?

P: We both sang in the church choir. Did specials for the church, duets and . . .

T: Well, as you say, it's more than losing a cousin. It's losing a companion, like a brother. Someone that you were teamed up with. A comrade.

P: Yeah, and he was a junior and I was a junior. And we were both the oldest sons of the only two boys in our dads' families.

T: What was it like at the funeral services then? Did you, did you wind up seeing, did they have an open casket at all?

P: Well, I think so. Can't remember very many funerals I've been to where they didn't.

T: Did you touch him, or?

The strategy of pressing the patient for the details surrounding a possibly traumatic event derives from some questionable ideas about the treatment of traumatic syndromes. Its aim is to evoke whatever feelings of grief, terror, or pain the patient felt during the event, with the mistaken assumption that the reexperience of these emotions is in and of itself curative. In this example the repeated, intrusive questioning blocks rather than promotes exploration. It also demonstrates how questions can demand a submission to the therapist, rather than promote responsibility for participation. The therapist takes control, and in this is a subtle derogation of the patient's need for defense against overwhelming emotion.

Clarification

Clarification is a therapist action that involves restating or rephrasing the patient's statements or ideas, or re-presenting an affective tone, in a more clearly recognizable form in order to render more evident the meaning of what the patient has said. Clarification involves a sharpening, and often a subtle extension, of the patient's intended meaning. The purpose is to bring into focus and heighten awareness of some aspect of experience. A rephrasing of the patient's comment can provide another vantage point from which the patient may begin to consider what he or she is thinking and feeling. A good clarification or reflection has the effect of turning patients' attention to their mental processes. It also helps foster a greater sense of subjectivity in emphasizing that the patient is author of his or her thoughts and feelings. Clarifications, like all therapist actions, can be considered from the standpoint of interaction structures. If the therapist finds himself routinely clarifying a patient's frequently vague, confusing, or incoherent statements, this may signify his participation in a repetitive pattern that has important meanings.

In the following illustration, the therapist captures and provides greater clarity about the conflict the patient experiences between obeying the rules and feeling rebellious. This comment helps the patient achieve a clear view of her internal states and how she is affected by them.

Patient: I feel like if I was ever just really going off to some extreme, like being really depressed, or just like being in a bad mood to the point where I was being antisocial or something, well, I just kind of behave automatically, according to the rules, and I wouldn't have to think about anything.

Therapist: Uh-huh.

P: Sometimes I think they're kind of silly, because they are usually times when I'm feeling self-confident, and then I'll do things like kind of rebel against them.

T: Rebel against the rules?

P: Yeah, like, I don't know, like I'll walk outside the crosswalk. (*laugh*) I mean the grid that's actually painted on the street. I'll walk on the edge of the grid or I'll walk in the pavement (*laugh*) or I'll jaywalk (*laugh*) or something.

T: So, you have two different states. One is you stick by the rules—your own internal ones or external ones. And this other state, or other mood you might have of rebelling against them—your own choices or others.

P: Yeah.

Through this kind of clarification, the therapist represents the patient to herself as an intentional being who can be understood in terms of mental states. It also lays the groundwork for further understanding of the link between the patient's depressed moods and a sense of submission, and the association of her feeling self-confident with being defiant. The recognition of these mood states, and knowing that feeling good means breaking the rules while feeling depressed is linked with a sense of submission will, through similar repeated interactions over time, help the patient understand and gain greater control of her depressive feelings.

This next illustration represents a reflection of a different kind in which the therapist underscores and emphasizes a changing awareness in the patient. The therapist helps the patient capture the stance she struggled to maintain in a violently angry confrontation with her husband. The patient has some awareness that she responded differently and more effectively to her husband than in the past. The therapist's articulation and clarification of this new stance helps the patient reflect on the fact that, beyond being angry and frightened, she also knew what she wanted and that she does not fully appreciate her own agency in achieving it.

Patient: I can't really describe how he is abusive; it's not a describable kind of abuse. (*laugh*)

Therapist: Hmm.

P: You know. But he was . . . I don't think I threw anything that time. But I just said, "Fuck you," and I left. But this time you see, I stuck. I didn't just, say, throw the boots at him and say good-bye. This time I said about probably about thirty-five times, uh, "Don't ever throw anything at me ever again or I'll kill you. I'll go after you with anything. Don't ever get mad at me and treat me like this . . . don't touch me."

T: You told him exactly what this was. Yeah.

P: I said it again and again and again and again and again. And yeah I told him exactly, not just . . . get out of here, or I'm leaving, but, you know . . .

T: Hmm.

P: So there's something, I'm not exactly clear (*laugh*) what's different about the whole thing. I think there is something different. Because it wasn't just a one shot, and then leave.

T: Right. Well, you told him he was responsible for the interaction, . . .

P: Yeah.

T: . . . and that you weren't going to engage in it anymore, . . .

P: Right.

T: . . . rather than "we have to separate." Which might imply that your temper was too hot, too, . . .

P: Yeah, right, right, right. Right.

T: . . . that you were not protecting him as much as you have in the past.

The therapist captures and extends the emotional tone that is implied but not fully expressed in order to help the patient experience her emotional state more clearly, and to be able to direct her attention toward this aspect of her experience.

In the next illustration, another patient attempts to understand his motives for forgetting to come to the previous session. The therapist helps to clarify how the patient's state of mind relative to his sexual feelings contribute to his forgetting and mental blocking. The intervention helps foster in the patient a greater appreciation of how the strength of his conflicts influences his mental functioning.

Patient: I was thinking about why I missed last time and what sort of reading I would put on that. Because it was really . . . it was just like completely blanked out. And I looked at my watch to see how much time I had before I had to do this other thing, and then I realized, Oh my God, you know. So it was, yeah, it was definitely a mental block, or slippage, or something like that. And one thing that came to mind is that I was going to, like, ask on Friday, like more about what it means to face something, what it means to face feelings, face . . .

Therapist: Conflicts?

P: Conflicts, tensions, yeah. Um . . . and then maybe, part of it is that I didn't want to know the answer (*short laugh*). Maybe, I don't know. And the other part is, that I was going to see [girlfriend], and just like you said, we ended up spending the night together (*sighs*). I guess that's really another tension or conflict, uh, yeah, that's my read on it. It's still a tension or conflict because . . .

T: Before you go on, let me just restate this as a small version of what you said and to underline it. That your sexual conflicts have the power to . . .

P: Fuck me up.

T: . . . to produce a kind of shutdown of mental functioning.

P: Yeah.

T: I forget the word you used for it. It was a real mental . . .

P: Slippage or block.

T: Block. Yeah, to produce a real mental block.

P: Mm-hmm.

T: I think it helps both of us understand better, or have a deeper appreciation for how strong these conflicts are.

Confrontations

Confrontations are interventions in which the therapist directs the patient's attention to a behavior or thought that is problematic in some way. Confrontations are especially useful if the patient's behavior is dangerous or destructive, and when the therapist's failure to comment might be construed as acceptance or a sanction of the action. Confrontations often show there is more meaning to the problematic action than initially assumed by the patient. The following illustration is from the treatment of a very obsessional young man who has a strong tendency to discuss his problems in an abstract and intellectualized manner. His preoccupation with psychosomatic complaints and his defensively dismissive style has brought the treatment to a virtual standstill. The therapist confronts the patient's lack of genuine interest in his own mental life and the way in which this limits the patient's ability to reflect usefully on his own thinking.

Patient: What's going to get chopped off next? What's going to break down next?

Therapist: You need to confront that thought as a psychological matter.

P: What . . . Castration . . . or what?

T: Well, that wasn't what I was thinking. That's what came to your mind. Yeah, that's a start.

P: (*laughs*) What do you mean "confront it"? I mean . . .

T: Just what you did. That is, to take up the question— What does it mean that I have this fantasy about myself?

P: In what terms, though? I'm kind of . . .

T: Since you're not a knight and since no one is hacking pieces of you off, and since, in fact, all of your pieces are still here and since they actually work, then you could raise it as a psychological question: "Why, given all those things, do I have this fantasy about myself?"

P: Because I feel powerless, I feel like I've . . .

T: That's, that's too quick.

P: Well, that's why I'm asking. What's the intermediary term, or the, ah, term beyond that?

T: The first thing that came to mind was castration.

P: Right, 'cause as I was saying . . .

T: Let's, let's see what else comes to mind.

P: I'm saying this to a shrink and um, what else. Ah . . .

T: The first thing to be noticed is that you're not really interested in the matter. That's the first thing.

P: Well, interested? I'm just frustrated.

T: No, no no. That's also too quick. It tells us something about the attitude you have toward your body, that this exaggerated and bloody fantasy that you have about it is really not of interest to you. You don't say, you don't think, "Now that is odd—why do I think about myself in that way?" "It's castration, it's this, I'll tell him that because he's a shrink. It's because I feel powerless." That's really a failure to take seriously the question. It doesn't really interest you much.

The therapist forcefully confronts the patient with his superficial, ironic accommodation to what is expected in therapy, emphasizing that in this way the patient avoids thinking about himself. The therapist also confronts him with his fundamental lack of interest in his feelings and fantasies, an attitude that, until it is brought into the patient's awareness and understood, will prevent the possibility of change.

The next illustration is taken from the same treatment. The patient has criticized himself for arriving late, and then too quickly and facilely claims this must have been an act of aggression. The therapist confronts the patient not only about his coming late for therapy sessions, but even more importantly about the patient's attitude about his lateness.

T: No, I don't think that's an accurate way of construing the problem with reference to being late for our meeting.

P: Mm-hmm.

T: You weren't being too aggressive. In fact you were, um, apologetic and mortified, as I said.

P: Mm-hmm.

T: And you had been aware that you were making yourself late as it was happening. But, if I understand it correctly, you never said to yourself, and you never said to me, "You're not going to like this and I don't care."

P: (*laugh*)

T: And when you're not here you didn't say, um, "I'm late. I knew that you wouldn't like this and what I was doing was more important to me." Which would have been aggressive.

P: (*laugh*)

T: But that's not what happened.

P: Mm-hmm.

The therapist confronts the patient's stereotyped and placating attitude about his lateness, and the patient's assumption that this was an aggressive act. In this way, the therapist opens up the possibility for exploring the action and understanding it differently.

Identifying Themes

A common intervention is the identification of a recurrent theme in the patient's experience or conduct that may be related in some way to the patient's difficulties. Our research (Spence et al. 1993) has demonstrated that identifying themes fosters greater free association in the patient, and that sometimes this effect extends into the next two or three treatment sessions. In the following illustration, the therapist identifies a recurrent oedipal theme in a patient who repeatedly finds herself in romantic triangles. These triangles involved competition with another woman and prevented her from having intimate relationships with men.

Therapist: But there's just that striking similarity. In your relationship with John, where you couldn't really get as close as you might have . . . because there was a wife in the background. And in another relationship you couldn't get that close because there's a female friend in the background. And, of course, with your father, there's your mother in the background.

In the following illustration, another patient is describing an experience that has been repeated many times in her life: she does work, and then allows a man to take credit for it. She has recently repeated this painful experience at a new job. The therapist is able to show her that this is a repetitive pattern, noting that she has conducted herself in this way with her father, her boyfriends, and her husband. The therapist's aim is to demonstrate to the patient that she is actively participating in creating this experience, and that for some reason, yet to be understood, she has a powerful inclination to create this kind of relationship. This is also a first step in recognizing a repetitive interaction structure that may already exist in subtle form in the treatment relationship. By recognizing this conduct pattern, the patient may then go on to understand more about her motives and intentions toward important men in her life.

Patient: I had this terrible experience at the law firm. And then (*sigh*) just, you know just trying to, basically I think trying to make a living more than anything else. And then I got into interesting work. But still no personal reward in it; I mean all it ever was, was finding something very helpful (*laugh*) to our client and then giving it to the attorney. Then the attorney could go and stand before the judge and say, "La da da da." (*laugh*)

Therapist: And look great, huh?

P: And the prosecuting attorney could go "Oh no." And there I was, still at home, you know.

T: Just like you used to do with your father and Dave . . .

P: Yeah, that's exactly what it is. Mm-hmm.

T: . . . and all your boyfriends.

P: It's the same thing.

In the next illustration from another treatment, the therapist identifies, in the patient's description of her response to adversity, a characteristic reaction—redoubling her efforts. The comment prompts the patient to reflect on this inclination in herself. She apparently does not yet have much understanding of this response, but the therapist has underscored this aspect of her behavior and both therapist and patient note this as something to be thought about further.

Patient: I thought about this before because, I just noticed that in relationships (*pause*) they seem to go a lot better. There's something that, you know, we have to overcome. Something.

Therapist: Mm-hmm.

P: Sometimes I do a lot better in a class where I'm doing really bad, but some time during the semester, I have to like make up for all the lost time. (*long pause*)

T: That kind of really gets you into high gear then. Overcoming that kind of adversity. Either in school or with somebody.

Remembering, Reconstructions, and Therapeutic Action

A discussion about how to foster patient self-reflection must inevitably turn to memory, and the act of remembering. The role of memory in psychotherapy, and indeed the very nature of memory itself, has been rethought in recent decades. A brief survey of the various ways in which memory has been understood, and of current ideas and controversies about how we remember, will be helpful in orienting the contemporary clinician to new ideas about the role of memory in the change process.

How much do psychotherapists need to make links with the past, and why? Memory and recollection of childhood experience and early personal history have had an important place in psychoanalytic therapies. Experienced psychotherapists know that some patients can remember little about the past, or have gaps in their memories. Others seem uninterested in their past, or unable to connect past with present. And other patients refer frequently to the past and use it to help understand themselves. The phenomenon of forgetting, and the role in therapeutic action played by remembering early experience, was central and clearly defined in early psychoanalytic theory. In contemporary theories of therapeutic action the conceptualization of their role has become more complex.

In his early work, Freud signaled the importance of memories in his assertion that hysterics suffer mainly from reminiscences (Breuer and Freud 1893). Symptoms and inhibitions were considered to represent past, usually traumatic, experiences; they were understood as substitutes for forgotten feelings and experiences. In a sense, patients' symptoms were considered a form of memory in which they preserved the past. It was important to recall certain expe-

riences and the emotions associated with them that had
been forgotten or repressed. One of the therapist's functions
was to help the patient remember, to reconstruct these experiences. As gaps in hysteric patients' memories were filled
in, it was thought that symptoms would be alleviated. This
view of the role of memory in therapeutic action was tied
to the topographical model, which emphasized bringing
unconscious desires and conflicts into awareness by overcoming repression. As the structural model and ego psychological approaches were developed, hysteria no longer served as
a prototype of etiology and repression was understood to be
only one of several important defensive processes (Kris
1956). Nevertheless, as we shall see, this early model still
exerts a significant influence, particularly in the recent debate about childhood sexual abuse and the role of recover-
ing memories of childhood trauma in psychotherapy.

The link between remembering and therapeutic action
has become less straightforward with more complex contemporary conceptualizations about the nature of memory.
What is remembered may not necessarily be historically,
photographically accurate. Much of current research suggests that memory, especially memory from childhood, is
more than simple recollection of the past. This is due to
the intermingling of fantasy, desire, and perception, fil-
tered by the effects of children's level of cognitive development. Research on memory suggests that all memories
are a mixture of an historically accurate reproduction of
the past and reconstruction. The memory of an event is
influenced by its personal significance, the emotional experience associated with the event, the amount of time
that elapses between the experience of the event and remembering it, the reasons why the person is remembering the event, and to whom the person is remembering
(Morton 1997).

Memory is an interaction between past and present; present feelings and interests supply the incentive for viewing the past from a particular standpoint or with particular emphasis (Kris 1956). Why, for instance, are some experiences remembered and others forgotten? Memory is, to a certain extent, a reflection of current interests and conflicts, shifting and changing correspondingly. It has even been argued that the historically true past is for the most part inaccessible. Spence (1982), for example, holds that all interpretations regarding the past are in actuality constructions, and that historical truth is a less important aspect of therapeutic action that is usually assumed. He narrows the distinction between "narrative truth," or constructions that are appealing and persuasive, and historical truth. Although this position may appear extreme, it is actually not so different from some of Freud's later views:

> It may indeed be questioned whether we have any memories at all *from* our childhood: memories *relating* to our childhood may be all that we possess. Our childhood memories show us our earliest years not as they were but as they appeared at the later periods when memories were aroused. In these periods of arousal the childhood memories did not, as people are accustomed to say, *emerge*; they were *formed* at the time. And a number of motives, with no concern for historical accuracy, had a part in forming them, as well as in the selection of the memories themselves. [Freud 1937, p. 322]

Appreciation of the complex connections between memory, fantasy, and reality has led to different approaches to the use of memory and reconstructions of past events in psychotherapy, as well as to a different view of its role in therapeutic action. Memory is now not necessarily seen as a reproduction of an historical event, but rather as "psychic reality"; the subjective significance rather than objective reality of an event is crucial in determining the impact of an event. Early childhood conflicts and their consequences and developmental influences are often more important than actual historical facts (Blum 1980).

Reconstruction is now often undertaken in the spirit of reexamination of the facts, for example, the nature of the family situation or parental behavior that might be denied or distorted. The following example illustrates an attempt at this kind of reconstruction. The therapist is helping the patient reconstruct the period of his life preceding his mother's death. Although the patient was about 10 years old at the time of her death, he has only vague and unclear memories of that period of his childhood. His difficulty in recollecting this period is likely associated with what may have been intensely painful feelings that, even as an adult, he prefers not to experience.

Patient: I mean, I guess I did stuff with my mom. I think she drove me places, sometimes. (*pause*) I can't remember specifically things that I did with my mother in the summers.
Therapist: What I mean is that if you were spending your time at home . . .
P: Mm-hmm.
T: . . . reading, watching TV, listening to records, who was in the house with you?
P: Nobody.
T: So your mother wasn't there?
P: No, I mean, well, I don't really remember when she was alive is what I'm saying.

T: Hmm. I see.

P: I don't know if it was the same way when she was alive as it was afterwards, which is the period I'm recalling.

T: I see. I thought we were talking about the years when you were 10 and 11 when you were playing basketball; you're wondering whether . . .

P: Mm-hmm.

T: . . . you just did it because that was what boys did. And that perhaps it kept you from doing what you would have done naturally. And so then we'd've been on the question of what you might have done naturally.

P: Mm-hmm.

T: And you were saying that during the summers—around 10 and 11 you were staying home . . .

P: Mm-hmm.

T: . . . not doing much.

P: Mm-hmm. Mm-hmm.

T: She was alive then.

P: Yeah. At first. I mean, she got sick pretty soon after we moved into that new place and I got moved. Schools got moved. And actually there was when we first moved there, when I was in the fourth grade. So, when I was what? Ten, 10 to 11. Around in there. (*pause*) Nine or 10. It's like when I was around 10. I was still going to the old school. Until the end of the year. And I ended up going to the new school. (*pause*) And the school where I was really happy.

In the next illustration, Ms. M (see Chapter 2) recalls in detail her experience of her brother's death during her childhood. These memories help her to acknowledge the profound sense of loss she felt at the time, a loss she continues to feel as an adult. During the course of this patient's treatment, she becomes aware of the relationship between her chronic sense of guilt and depression and the loss of her brother.

Patient: I thought [my mother] felt that I, or I thought that I had been responsible somehow for [my brother's] death and she knew that. So she hated me. That's what she felt, I guess. I want to go back—I really felt sorry for her. I felt sad for her. It never occurred to me to feel sorry for me and I needed to feel sorry for my own loss. But it seems like I, for reasons I don't know, never got around to that. I guess I didn't get around to feeling sorry for myself, for my own loss, in part because it wasn't recognized by anyone else. Not only was it not recognized but it was sort of treated like, "Well, she doesn't understand anyway." So I probably didn't feel like I had a right to feel the loss. And partly I probably didn't feel the loss because I was busy feeling (laugh) guilty about being responsible for the loss.
Therapist: Hmm. Oh, yeah . . . makes a lot of sense.
P: But I do think it's real important for me to remind myself. I'm not sure why it's important, but it feels important to remind myself that it was also my loss.
T: It was a big loss for you.
P: It was a big loss for me.
T: That you feel all the time.
P: Mm-hmm. I do feel it all the time. So, this confuses it even all the more to me. In any event, for years I looked at it as her loss. I felt sorry for her, for having such a loss. I felt like I should just stay out of the way. There was a difference up to the time that [my brother] died.

The question of the extent to which memory and reconstructions are, and should be, historically accurate is a subject much discussed. Most clinicians acknowledge the problems stemming from the inherently composite nature of memory. However, narrative accounts of the past must at least approach the truth in order to contribute to psychological knowledge about the self. Not any account of the past will do. Reconstruction is often a gradual process that involves memory as well as the reconstruction of reality events. Reconstruction often requires inferring substitutes for missing memory and gaps in history. New meanings may be given to past experiences. Freud (1937) emphasized that "we do not pretend that an individual construction is anything more than a conjecture which awaits examination, confirmation or rejection" (p. 265). While noting that reconstruction of the past is less emphasized in modern technique, Blum (1980) points out that reconstruction aids in restoring a sense of continuity and cohesion in the patient. It can provide the patient with an important sense of integration, as well as offer explanations of the repetition of problematic conduct in life and in the transference. Reconstruction can also foster an appreciation of the connection between fantasy, memory, and reality in the patient (Arlow 1969).

Memories of Childhood Trauma

This discussion must now join a related set of ideas and controversies, that of repressed memories and the false-memory syndrome. The scientific debate regarding memories of childhood sexual abuse dates back to Freud's seduction hypothesis, in which he stated that repression of early childhood seduction was implicated in the etiology of adult hysteria. He later revised this hypothesis, and pursued a

direction that was decisive for the development of psychoanalysis, arguing that many memories of childhood seduction were in fact fantasies representing childhood sexual interests. However, there remained an important place for
traumatic events in the etiology of psychopathology (Freud
1937). Current research suggests that childhood sexual
abuse is likely more common than previously realized, and
that some individuals may in fact have no recollection of
the event.

The recent debate concerning recovered memories
has been intense and often vituperative (see Loftus 1993,
Sandler and Fonagy 1997). Recovered memories are repressed memories of traumatic events, particularly sexual
seduction in childhood, that surface after years of complete
amnesia for the presumed events. In this debate, memory
and its role in therapy is viewed as it was by Freud in his
early theorizing about hysteria. The memory of childhood
sexual abuse is thought to be repressed. It is further believed that the recovery of these memories, and the accompanying emotional catharsis and putative explanation for
current life difficulties that these memories offer, is therapeutic. Since such recovered memories usually, though
not always, arise in therapy, controversy emerged around
the possibility that therapists might incorrectly suggest to
patients that they had been sexually abused as children
and had repressed the event, even when there was little
indication that such abuse might have occurred (false
memories). Many patients and some therapists hunger for
dramatic, conclusive revelations in psychotherapy, and an
overemphasis on the recovery of memories of traumatic
events may be an expression of this desire. It is important
to distinguish between an event and the trauma. It is the
meaning of events for the child, either at the time or
later, that should be the focus in therapy.

Some patients are traumatized by an atmosphere in the family that does not always make clear the limits of permissible behavior, thereby creating an ambiguity about whether the child's fantasies could be realized. When there are elements of uncontained impulsiveness and sexuality in the family, in the child's mind fantasy may not be reliably distinguished from actual events. A chaotic family context may foster a sense of unreality through denial and concrete thinking or even a lack of thought (Fonagy and Target 1997). Consequently what may be fantasy may nevertheless point to a psychological truth for the child. If therapists focus only on what may have actually happened, we may not appreciate the very real trauma that was suffered because of the child's inability to make the distinction between what actually happened and fantasy, itself a result of an atmosphere in a family that did not foster adequate reality testing.

Ms. R, a 30-year-old divorced woman, came to me for analysis complaining of depression and problems with sexual responsiveness. During a previous treatment she realized, with the help of her therapist's insistent confrontation of her defensive denial, that she had been sexually molested during high school by an athletics coach. The patient now wondered whether she had been sexually abused during childhood, and whether the molestation by the coach simply repeated earlier sexual abuse. She had married one of her high school teachers, which she also saw as evidence of a pattern of romantic and sexual involvement with older male authority figures.

She began analysis with real trepidation, fearing that analysis would try to prove that she had in fact not been sexually abused, and that this idea was only a fantasy.

And she feared that even if I agreed she had been abused, I would believe that what happened was her own fault. Both the patient's parents were severe alcoholics. The household was characterized by a sexually charged atmosphere in which the parents and neighbors swapped sexual partners, and an adolescent sister would strip tease for her high school classmates. Ms. W reported dissociative experiences, particularly when hearing music of the kind her father played on the piano while he was drinking. During a three-year analysis she had vague memories of sitting on an uncle's lap. We nevertheless deliberately restrained ourselves from prematurely reconstructing an experience of traumatic sexual abuse, and the patient developed a greater capacity to tolerate her uncertainty. It was never conclusively established whether Ms. W had been a victim of childhood sexual abuse. What was remembered and reconstructed with conviction was traumatic forms of parental neglect, sadism, and physical abuse. An important focus of the therapy was Ms. W's pervasive difficulty in knowing. For example, she had real difficulty knowing that her father was a severe alcoholic, though he died of an alcohol-related illness. The focus on mental processes, that is, on her defenses and her related difficulty in conceptualizing her experience, was far more therapeutic than establishing with certainty that she had been the victim of sexual abuse.

Dysfunctional and abusive family contexts can create in individuals reared in such environments a strong sense of not knowing what actually occurred. The patient's press to know what really happened may contribute to the therapist's countertransference wish to reconstruct traumatic experience. The repeated effort during therapy to establish what may have actually happened can constitute an interaction structure, a process of reciprocal influence, in which the therapist responds to the patient's inability to know with a sense of conviction about what actually did happen. In short, therapists should be alert to the possibility that historical reconstructions represent some aspect of the present therapist–patient interaction displaced into a version of the patient's past.

In fact, traumatic experience is usually not forgotten. Most individuals who were traumatized as children recall the trauma directly and are sometimes emotionally preoccupied with the event. Memories of childhood abuse that have been more or less continuously available prior to any therapeutic encounter are likely to be true at least in part (Brenneis 1997). Nevertheless, some who have experienced childhood trauma do not recall the event (Viederman 1995, Williams 1994). Those who were very young at the time of the abuse and those who were molested by someone they knew are more likely to have no recollection of the event (Williams 1987). It is much more difficult to ascertain the accuracy of memories of abuse reported for the first time in treatment. It is certainly possible that memories of this type, presumed to be historically accurate, are in fact distorted through a fantasied and defensive reconstruction.

It is unlikely that the recall of traumatic events, guided by a cathartic intent and without emotional preparation or interpretation, is helpful. The understandable hope is that conscious awareness of a victimization will automatically lead to a settled score with the victimizer and a resumption of normal life. What this point of view underestimates is the developmental and characterological consequences of trauma of all kinds, when it has in fact occurred, and the challenges such formative experiences pose to bringing about change in mental representations of self and other in psychotherapy.

Contemporary Approaches to the Use of the Past

What, then, is the role of remembering and reconstructing the past in therapeutic action? As we have seen, it is not easy to be clear about what is meant by the "past." In psychotherapy, there is no such thing as pure history, a rendering of facts about the past. The past is not simply the facts about the patient's life or developmental milestones, nor is it the way in which the patient represents his or her personal history. Personal meaning is always attached to history. The past is an amalgam of facts about the patient's life, the way the patient was treated in early life, the child's reaction to this, the parents' response to the child's reaction, and patient's fantasy about all of this (Joseph 1996). All this must be considered the patient's history, the patient's psychic reality. The emphasis, then, should not be so much on discovering new facts about the past, but on the meaning of this psychic reality.

There are a number of difficulties in relying on history to explain the patient's current experience. First, this kind of attention to history can become an intellectual exercise. Second, it is a common defense to implicitly blame history or parents for problems. Third, it can be defensively convenient to resort to historical or reconstructive interpretations out of the therapist's needs, for example, to avoid the patient's criticism in the present. All too often, when there is some difficulty in the treatment, the therapist retreats to history to attempt to explain it. It is more useful to identify representations of the patient's history in the present and how, for the patient, they are plausible representations. Therapists should remain alert to the possibility that some aspect of the transference-countertransference in the present is displaced onto, or represented by, a reference to history, or by a memory of an event or emotion that is related to current feeling or experience (transferring the present to the past).

The following example illustrates what may be the most common difficulty. The therapist and patient are drawn into an abstract, intellectual discussion of the patient's history. The therapist makes an unproductive attempt to link the meaning of a patient's chronic, nagging psychosomatic complaints to his mother's mortal illness when he was a child.

Therapist: Remembering more may also take some of the pressure off of your body.

Patient: Hmm. You mean just the actual act of remembering things?

T: If you can remember more about your childhood, which includes your mother, then there may be less of an unconscious pressure on you to enact her ailments.

P: Hmm. Hmm. (*pause*)

T: The idea being you don't have a choice, you're going to remember one way or another. (*long pause*) Remember it in your writing, your poetry, . . .

P: Mm-hmm.

T: . . . in your aches and pains. In your living out of your relationships with other people. But most destructively, at least in the last few months, has maybe been the living out of it through somatic pain. The remembering of it through your body.

P: Mm-hmm.

The main question centers on how the patient uses the past in the present. Contemporary approaches emphasize the limitations of starting from the past and trying to explain the present and current problems with what one believes one knows from the past. The focus is more usefully on how the patient defends against reexperiencing the pain felt in the past, how the past has been translated, how the patient helped cause the past, and now uses and perpetuates it (Joseph 1996). All of this can be known more directly by observing how patients deal with the past rather than making inferences from the facts of their history.

Interaction structures (see Chapter 1) can be thought of as a new version of history relived in the context of psychotherapy. Through these repetitive interactions, some part of the patient's psychic history is lived out, or repeated, without being understood. Although many therapists are inclined to focus on patients' autobiographical memories, interaction structures, which are observable behavioral and emotional components of the transference-countertransference, reveal another reality, the psychic reality, of the patient's past and present experience.

Contemporary research in cognitive psychology and memory makes a distinction between explicit and implicit or procedural memory. *Explicit memory* can be reproduced as narratives of autobiographical events. *Implicit memory* is nonconscious knowledge of how to do things, including how to relate to people, and the quality of relationship experiences. In other words, two forms of organization of personal memories can be posited: the selection and reconstruction of explicit memories, and another that cannot be articulated but is constantly expressed through the shapes it lends to relationships, personality, and ways of speaking and thinking (Target 1998). The notion of implicit memory fits well with psychoanalytic ideas about internal mental representations of self and other, assumptions about how we will relate to others, and how others will relate to us. The experiences, fantasied and real, that lay the groundwork for these mental representations cannot, of course, all be remembered explicitly, since some of this experience was itself originally outside of conscious awareness.

Interaction structures are likely to be shaped by the patient's implicit, procedural memory, along with the therapist's countertransference. The procedural memory enacted in interaction structures will show part of patients' history, especially their psychic experience with caregivers in childhood. Some clinical theorists hold that memories that are expressed implicitly in the transference, and memories relating to the transference, are better evidence of the patient's self-object representations than what might be inferred from historical events. While this is undoubtedly true, neither explicit nor procedural memories can provide a historically accurate account of past events. Memory, explicit or implicit, can convey only what was experienced and understood, or misunderstood, by the child at that time, that is, the child's psychic reality. Moreover, this point of view seriously underestimates patients' need to retreat from transference feelings in the here and now to memories or reconstructions of the past; that is, it underestimates the *defensive use of memory*.

In contemporary approaches to the use of memories and reconstructions, there has been more emphasis on patterns than on exact events. A greater appreciation of the alive and active mix of past and present in any given moment in therapy has led to a refocus on the here and now of transference, that is, an emphasis on linking memory and reconstruction to the transference-countertransference (Wetzler 1985). The following illustration is from the case

of Mrs. C (see Chapter 1). The analyst connects the
patient's experience of not knowing or understanding
matters in therapy with a reconstruction of how she must
have felt knowing things of a sexual nature when she was
a child. The example captures how memories and reconstructions can be considered as part of the effort to identify and gain insight into repetitive interaction structures.

Therapist: Now, I remember one thing about that Sunday
    afternoon, that I thought of and you didn't bring up
    in connection with it. It came up in another way. There
    was another time, when you were taking a nap, when
    you were a little girl. And you were supposed to be
    sleeping, but you weren't. And you saw something. You
    saw the rabbits and the dogs. And you were troubled
    by it, but you couldn't tell anybody. You couldn't talk
    to your mother about it, because that would mean let-
    ting her know that you weren't sleeping. That you
    weren't taking your nap. You'd seen something you
    couldn't own up to. But you had to, in effect, play stu-
    pid about. Play dumb about it. Muddle up. And the
    very thing you're just describing, this incident today,
    but you've been doing it increasingly, I think, since,
    since Sunday afternoon. You didn't want to really go
    into that, or tell me about it much.

    The patient's forgetting and not knowing, and the
therapist's countertransference of exasperation over the
need to provide the patient with a lengthy explanation,
represents an interaction structure. The therapist ties the
patient's "playing dumb" in the treatment to her feeling
that there were matters she ought not to know as a child.
The here and now of the patient's transference (not wanting to tell the analyst much about an event) is linked to

the reconstruction of an event in early childhood in which she thinks she saw something, presumably sexual in nature, that she felt she should not have. This reconstruction allows the patient to observe how she inhibits her capacity to know and perceive, and provides an explanation anchored in the patient's personal history for the need to inhibit herself. The useful integration of the past can best be achieved if the therapist's starting point is interaction patterns that can be experienced and observed in the present.

Along with self-knowledge, insight, and greater capacity for self-reflection, patient change occurs as a result of a shift in emphasis between different mental models of interpersonal relationships. Remembering may illuminate these mental representations of self and other, bring them into explicit awareness, and help in their exploration. But the recovery of memory will not likely in and of itself lead to change, or sustain change (Fonagy and Target 1997). Therapeutic action, or the impetus for patient change, lies in the discussion, reflection, and elaboration of mental representations as these become manifest in the transference-countertransference. The aspects of mental representations that are most observable, and hence accessible, to both therapist and patient are repetitive interaction patterns, in which mental representations are lived out and emotionally experienced.

4

Bringing Defenses and Unconscious Mental Content into Awareness

An important aim of psychoanalytic therapy is to bring into patients' awareness how they avoid knowing about themselves. Many patients have limited capacity for self-reflection. The difficulty in self-reflection and self-observation is often associated with a narrow range of mental activity—of thoughts, feelings, and fantasy. There is much that cannot be allowed into awareness, and there is a reliance on defensive strategies of various kinds that permit only a constricted range of experience. This chapter considers those therapist actions that are intended to draw the patient's attention to the manner in which feelings, ideas, and wishes are warded off. Particular emphasis is placed on bringing into greater mindfulness those aspects of subjective experience the patient regards as wrong, unacceptable, inappropriate, or dangerous, with the aim of increasing the patient's self-knowledge and self-acceptance.

An essential component of bringing unconscious mental life into awareness is the activity that has come to be known as "defense analysis." Threatening information and other mental content can be kept out of conscious awareness by an abundantly varied set of defensive processes, which are themselves typically outside of patients' awareness. A central goal of psychoanalytic therapy is to bring these defensive maneuvers into patients' awareness. The therapist observes, along with the patient, how and when these protective measures are active. The objective is to promote self-observation in patients, as well as greater understanding of how they avoid knowing about themselves and avoid experiencing repudiated feelings and ideas. Observing such processes repeatedly over time, and gaining an appreciation for the reasons the patient relies on them, ultimately allows greater adaptive control over formerly automatic protective measures. A diminished reliance on defensive processes enhances the capacity for self-reflection and self-knowledge. It also allows the more effective representation of experience in words and in thought, and the greater integration of undifferentiated or disorganized self-object representations. Therapists often wonder just how and when defensive processes and unconscious mental content should be pointed out and interpreted. A premise of this discussion is that the therapist's awareness of interaction structures can inform what aspects of defense and unconscious mental activity might be most usefully interpreted at a given moment in the ongoing interaction.

Defense refers to an intrapsychic process; resistance refers to the interaction with the therapist, and is expressed in the transference. It could be said that resistance is the interpersonal manifestation of defense (Gill 1982). In recent years, the term *defense* itself has, among some psychoanalytically oriented therapists, come to assume a negative connotation, as has the term *resistance.* They have argued that terms such as *defense* and *resistance* have embedded in them implied criticism of the patient. The patient is being "defensive," unwilling or unable to look at himself honestly; or being "resistant," oppositional, recalcitrant, or even combative. Schafer (1976, 1983) has pointed out that such terms as *defense* and *resistance* refer to the patient not behaving in a way that is expected, collaborative, or otherwise desirable. He argues that these terms have pejorative connotations and incline therapists to an undesirable adversarial view of the therapy relationship. He encourages an orientation toward defense and resistance that does not connote blame or criticism of the patient. Protective mental processes are of great importance to patients, who rely on them for very good reason. He urges therapists to assume an attitude toward these mental activities that helps establish an atmosphere of safety in which they can be observed, considered, and understood.

The interaction structure construct is consistent with a nonadversarial stance toward the patient since it encourages a broad, interactive conception of defense and resistance. Within a repetitive interaction framework, defense and resistance are not simply self-protective or oppositional, but are in part shaped by, or even constitute reactions to, the therapist's countertransferences and counterresistances. The patient's resistance to improvement and health may stem, for example, from a guilty and masochistic intolerance of gratification as well as a sadistic wish to defeat the therapist's evident need to heal. At the same time, the therapist's intolerance of his own aggression may not allow him to see and interpret the hate and destructiveness in the patient's negative therapeutic reaction.

How to Observe and Identify Defensive Processes

Defense analysis has assumed a prominent place in contemporary American psychoanalytic thinking and clinical practice. This emphasis derived from Freud's later structural theory, and his view of the importance of the ego in assessing danger and safety. He observed that the greatest analytic gains are achieved through the analysis of defenses and related resistances. Anna Freud's (1946) cataloging of various defense processes, such as denial, constriction of the ego, and identification with the aggressor, fostered a shift in focus in analytic treatments from interpreting unconscious mental content to attending to defensive processes. In subsequent decades defenses became too narrowly conceptualized as special, discrete mechanisms of the mind, specifically and almost exclusively devoted to purposes of defense. Brenner (1982) later provided a corrective to this tendency to view defenses as specific mechanisms by broadening notions of defense to include whatever psychological processes result in a diminution of unpleasurable affects, including pain, anxiety, and depression. His conceptualization of defense is a functional one: "It is the function served by what one does that determines whether it is properly called a defense" (p. 79). In other words, defense is an aspect of mental functioning that is definable only in terms of its consequence: the reduction of anxiety and depressive affect associated with a wish or desire (i.e., drive derivative) or with remorse or shame (i.e., superego functioning). In his view, there are no special ego functions used only for defense; any psychological process, such as an attitude, perception, or alteration of attention or awareness, can be used for the purpose of self-protection. Modes of defense are part of normal functioning, and as richly diverse as mental life itself. Identifying and bringing into awareness defensive processes overlaps what has been called character analysis (Reich 1933), that is, bringing into awareness the psychic function of those routine and automatic patterns of comportment, self-expression, and cognitive style that are seen as the individual's personality.

Attention to defenses is not limited to ego psychological approaches derived from drive/structural theory. Object relations theorists, particularly the neo-Kleinians, are centrally oriented to the analysis of defense. They place special emphasis on splitting, denial, repression, projection, introjection, idealization, and identification used defensively. Schafer (1997) notes that Kleinian analysis of defense takes up both defense and the motivation for defense, such as pain and danger situations. Defensive operations are viewed both as expressions of unconscious phantasies and as mechanisms. In other words, they are understood as both content (specific phantasies) and form (e.g., projection). Projective identification is seen as a mechanism (form) that also has an unconscious phantasy of expulsion of parts of the self (content).

A conventional technical guideline is that defenses and resistances must be confronted. This guideline tends to align with the view of defenses as being in opposition to the treatment, an adversarial conception of resisting, rather than something the patient is doing for very good reasons. It is quite true that patients frequently behave in ways that can be readily described as insincere, superficial, contentious, or defiant. These actions include coming late for therapy sessions, missing sessions, arranging their schedules to create conflicts with sessions, or in other ways disrupting the continuity of treatment. To this list can be added the failure to pay, overt dishonesty, withholding associations, and dismissively rejecting the therapist's comments or observations. Less obviously oppositional defenses might include silence or the disinclination to talk, avoiding certain topics, not listening to the import of their own words, being rigidly unemotional, or remaining unaware of self-destructive or otherwise maladaptive actions. The conventional view holds that the therapist must help the patient become aware of his or her defenses or resistance, particularly because these are usually ego syntonic, that is, they are not a source of conflict or emotional distress and hence do not invite the patient's attention and curiosity. Patients take them for granted without awareness of their purpose and meaning. Confrontation is considered as an important initial step in the analysis and modification of resistance and defensive processes. As Greenson (1967) states, "Our task is to get the patient to understand *that* he is resisting, *why* he is resisting, *what* he is resisting, and *how* he is resisting" (p. 104).

In contemporary thinking there is a greater sensitivity to the fact that confrontations, or even simple observations about patients' defenses by the therapist, can be experienced by patients as a criticism. Patients can feel accused of their defenses, hurt, misunderstood, unfairly treated, or confused, and they may become submissive, enraged, or frightened. This can, in turn, engender further resistances in the treatment. The terms *defense* and *resistance* tend to direct attention to what patients are against, or what they are not doing or should be doing. Modern defense analysis emphasizes what patients are doing, rather than what they are not doing. "What is this person doing? What is this person aiming at? What are they for? Why is he or she doing it? How are these actions wish-fulfilling?" (Schafer 1976, p. 257). In this view, the emphasis should largely be on what resisting is *for* rather than simply what it is *against*. The importance of understanding the protective function of defense and resistance was implied in earlier approaches, but is now more thoroughly emphasized in contemporary approaches. Overtly oppositional forms of conduct are most usefully viewed as expressions of the patient's need to maintain, or avoid, particular states of mind, and as indications of significant unconscious conflict that must be understood.

There is, as well, another side to patients feeling accused of their defenses or resistances, what Racker (1968) has termed *counterresistance*. In his view, a good deal of the resistance to uncovering the resistances stems not from the patient but rather from the therapist. Therapists often fear that they will bring up the topic of resisting tactlessly, irritably, or coercively, or that simply pointing out defenses is too aggressive. Therapists' interventions are inhibited by concerns about their own need for control or dominance, and their denial of the patient's aggression and wish to triumph over the therapist expressed in the resistance. Counterresistance can also take other forms. For example, a therapist may see and understand something about the patient that seems important but does not point it out to the patient. Racker notes that counterresistances usually coincide with resistances in the patient that concern the same situation. It is as though there were a tacit understanding, a "conspiracy of silence," between therapist and patient to keep quiet about certain topics.

Interaction structures usually involve the patient's most central and characteristic defenses, as well as the therapist's countertransference responses to them. Therapists can experience gripping countertransferences in response to patients' resistances and defenses. Among competent therapists, ineffective clinical work usually occurs in the context of such countertransferences to patients' resistances. Therapists' awareness that they are involved in a pattern of repetitive interaction provides a stable point of reference in what can be a sea of turbulent emotion. The patient is resistant, obstructive, defiant, or attacking. In response, the therapist may feel helpless, frustrated, or angry. In a reactive effort to move beyond a difficult stalemate, perhaps to save the treatment, the therapist may make poorly thought out, desperate, or even punitive interventions. The therapist has then become involved in a collusive transference–countertransference enactment with the patient in the form of an unconscious, repetitive interaction.

The case of Mr. S (see Chapter 1) describes a particularly devastating form of resisting that undermined the analyst's wish to empathize. Mr. S's suspicion, tendentious argument for argument's sake, and derisive reactions to the analyst's attempts to understand had the effect of stifling the analyst's hopefulness, interest in the patient, and objectivity in estimating the extent to which the analysis was in fact going forward. It is helpful if the therapist considers that he or she might be caught up in a repetitive interaction. This can help protect the therapist's investment in the treatment, and orient the therapist toward a greater neutrality. The recent greater awareness of the intersubjectivity of the clinical encounter has given rise to questions about the extent to which it is possible, or even desirable, for therapists to maintain a neutral stance. The effort to maintain a neutral stance does help safeguard the therapist from unconscious involvement in confusing and emotion-laden repetitive interactions that can lead to ill-advised and unproductive interventions.

It has long been accepted that defensive processes should be addressed before the underlying content, which is often outside of awareness or unconscious, is addressed. This is often described as "beginning with the surface," or taking as a starting point what can be directly observed by the patient before taking up feelings or fantasies that the patient is defending against. Technique in modern defense analysis (e.g., Gray 1994) tends to emphasize working with defensive processes almost to the exclusion of other approaches—for example, interpretation of unconscious conflicts, dream interpretation, or historical reconstruction— at least at the beginning of treatments. Defensive processes are more directly observable, and the interpretation of unconscious fantasy and conflict may involve too much speculation and guesswork on the part of the therapist. Disagreements about the validity of differing interpretations or formulations of the same case material are commonplace in clinical work, and constitute important grounds for criticism of the scientific basis of the psychoanalytic clinical method. It is particularly in the activity of formulating patients' unconscious dynamics that analytic therapists encounter the problem of validation, since plausible alternative interpretations of the same clinical material are often possible. Nevertheless, not all psychoanalytic clinicians agree that bringing into awareness defenses that can be directly observed by both the therapist and the patient should necessarily precede the interpretation of unconscious mental content. The neo-Kleinians, who have emphasized the defensive aspects of unconscious phantasy, hold that direct interpretation of content that is remote from consciousness, if accurately formulated and directed at an aspect of the transference, can be accepted and used by the patient.

How to Interpret Resistances

Resistances often coalesce or are expressed around what has been termed the "frame" of the therapy situation, that is, issues of time, the scheduling of appointments, and lateness. In the following illustration, taken from a sequence of sessions, the therapist points out, and gradually begins to interpret, the meaning of the patient's difficulty in scheduling sessions. The therapist is tactful in confronting the patient's resistance, is careful to note that the difficulties are not deliberate or conscious, and refrains from prematurely interpreting the meaning of the patient's behavior.

Patient: I'm really not consciously aware of forgetting about the scheduling conflicts as being an avoidance of anything, if that's what you're getting at.
Therapist: If you were consciously aware of it, you couldn't do it.
P: Right.
T: So my question is, it's not clear to me what is being avoided. I assume that particularly since both of the forgotten events concern K [patient's girlfriend].
P: Mm-hmm.
T: So I'm not ready to jump to a conclusion about what's involved. But the last time we met you were unusually late and then the next thing that happens is that you discover that you can't keep the next appointment. And then the next thing that happens after that is you discover you can't keep the one after that either. It's so unusual and I think it would move our work along if we could learn something about it. I take it to be, since you forget about these events, something that happened unconsciously, not for conscious reasons.

The following week, this patient forgets his session. In the subsequent session, the therapist takes up the difficulties with remembering the appointment times. The patient himself gives meaning to his behavior as a way of undermining his recent greater involvement and progress in treatment, though this understanding remains intellectualized.

P: I'm sorry about last time. It was my understanding that my acupuncture appointment would be for an hour. And

I took my watch off; I had to take my watch off for the treatment, so there wasn't any way of keeping track of time. And as I was walking out I realized it was ten past four. And I was there without my car.

T: Hmm.

P: Um, now I'm sure it's resistance, too. I mean (*laugh*), you know, I mean it's a pretty obvious explanation as well.

T: Well, I imagine it is and let me tell you why. The first is that it comes right on the heels of those . . .

P: Right.

T: . . . two other mistakes you made about appointment times.

P: Right.

T: So it seems like it is part of a series. And (*pause*) if I ask myself, as I have, why if this is resistance, as you put it, why is it intensified now? That is, if it is part of a series.

P: Mm-hmm.

T: When I ask myself that, what occurs to me is, among other things, that the last time you were here we did some work. (*pause*)

P: Meaning, we got somewhere.

T: You told me new things from your past.

P: Mm-hmm.

T: You were rather involved in talking about it. And it seemed to me that it had been an important meeting.

P: Mm-hmm.

T: But at any event, I start off with all that so as to not simply put you on the spot.

P: Thanks.

T: That it's work we do together, and try to understand if it is resistance, if that is what's happening.

P: Well, that would fit in with the idea that I, or that some

part of me sort of sabotages myself when I succeed at
something.

T: Mm-hmm.

P: I mean it would fit in with the theory.

T: Mm-hmm.

P: I'm inclined to believe that theory just because (*laugh*)
my experience seems to bear it out.

The next illustration, from a different psychotherapy
case, is taken from a session after the patient abruptly
announced her intention to terminate. The patient was
made anxious by the therapist's upcoming vacation; she
has difficulty mentally representing her feelings, and instead has a powerful impulse to act. The therapist is able
to link the patient's sudden wish to end her treatment to
his impending absence, and to wanting to leave first, before the therapist left her. In the following session, the patient has difficulty speaking, and falls silent.

Therapist: You had a thought.

Patient: Just that I'm scared into silence.

T: Scared?

P: I don't know ... I don't want to put my foot in my
mouth.

T: What are you worried you might say?

P: I don't know, just what I've been thinking.

T: (*one minute pause*) Seems like you're reluctant to say
something.

P: I was thinking ... that ... I'm not sure ... I mean it
feels like it could be time to make the move, but I'm not
sure where that feeling is coming from. I wish leaving
wasn't such a big thing in my life. I don't know how to
make it not be, though. I mean it doesn't solve things
to ... try to leave first. And I wasn't really thinking about

leaving first when I told you that Monday would be my last day.

T: I think that's why you did decide on Monday being the last session. Because you didn't want to think about this stuff, you didn't want to think about me leaving, you didn't want to think about any of this.

P: Yeah.

T: And you didn't want to have the feelings that go with it.

P: I don't know, like I've got a lot of feelings lately and I don't know what to do with them, so you know, I feel like they're just sort of there regardless of what I decide.

The therapist interprets the patient's sudden wish to terminate as not wanting to think about and experience feelings connected to an anticipated disruption in their relationship. As a result of this interpretive work, and the patient's greater understanding of her feelings toward the therapist, the patient was able to continue in treatment.

Silence is a common form of resistance, and often means the patient is unconsciously, or consciously, unwilling to communicate his or her thoughts and feelings. In some instances, the patient may be aware of this unwillingness, or may simply have the feeling that there is nothing on his mind. The therapist's task of understanding the silence and conveying its meaning to the patient is captured in the following illustration.

(lengthy silence)

Patient: And (*pause*) I don't know, I don't know. I just got back to thinking, I know that it's not true, but I feel as if saying things directly, mainly, well. I guess almost any-

thing. I don't like to be very direct in almost any way.
(*two-minute silence*)

Therapist: And I think that's part of the reason that you're
so often silent, and quiet, and don't say anything. Because you're trying to get control of the words before
you say them, in case something comes out that you
don't have control over, and will have terrible consequences.

How to Interpret Defenses

Resistances have an interactive quality; they are interpersonal manifestations of defenses. Defenses are characterized
by the avoidance of certain thoughts, feelings, or experiences, and have the appearance of being less overtly directed at the therapist. The following illustrations do not
attempt to capture specific defense mechanisms. Instead,
they reflect Brenner's (1982) broad definition of defense
as any psychological process that results in the diminish-
ment of unpleasurable affects, such as pain, anxiety, and
depression. Identifying and interpreting defensive processes involve close attention to alterations in the patient's
affect, flow of associations, or shift in topic. The therapist
may explicitly verbalize how the patient's active and productive efforts at exploring or understanding a difficulty
came to an abrupt end. The therapist might then raise a
question about why the patient's efforts stopped at that
particular moment, or at moments in which the patient
shifted the topic or became frustrated, guilty, or despairing, or began to externalize the problem or blame the
therapist for not being more helpful. Defensive processes
can often be traced to the inhibiting effects of critical,
self-punitive, even attacking attitudes toward feelings or

wishes coming into awareness that the patient feels are inappropriate, wrong, dangerous, or in some way bad.

In the following example, the patient, a young writer whose mother died when he was a child, had been talking for some time in an intellectualized manner about psychoanalysis and mothering. The patient is aware that his interest in writing about his experience in therapy has little to do with solving his problems, though this does not seem to particularly concern him. Instead, he is frustrated at his inability to make use of his therapy in his creative efforts. However, he seems largely unaware that this attitude toward his experience in therapy serves as a bastion of defense against what must be feelings of painful loss and child-like vulnerability.

Patient: You know, it's weird. When I think about all the effort it would take to actually construct something out of it, my first thought is, well, what can I write about it? (*laughs*) Immediately, it's like I'm deciding whether it's going to be worth the effort. It's like, not, well, will I become a more integrated, mature, you know, well-adjusted human being. It's, well, what can I write about it? Will it make an interesting work of art or piece of writing? Um . . . and to that I sort of have to emphatically say "no." It's like that's what everybody and his brother's been writing about for the last twenty years.

Therapist: To me that thought means something different. "Can I write about it?" to me means "Will I be able to get a hold of it intellectually quick enough so that it won't hurt me?"

P: Huh. Huh. (*sighs*) Hurt me how? If I'm afraid of something, I really don't understand what I'm afraid of or why. Unless it's of feeling like a child and feeling vulnerable and small and bereft or something.

T: Well, that would be bad enough if you really felt it.
P: (*silence*)

The therapist points out to the patient how the immediate wish to write about something of personal relevance that emerges in the treatment can be a way of distancing himself from very painful feelings. He interprets the patient's attitude toward his treatment, and the wish to use his intellect to transform his experience in therapy, as a defensive avoidance motivated by the fear of being hurt.

The next illustration is taken from the middle phase of Mrs. C's analysis (see Chapter 1). The analyst interprets the patient's "muddling up her thoughts," and not thinking about his observations, as a way of remaining stupid, or not knowing something about herself. This interpretation of a defensive process occurs in the context of a repetitive interaction. The analyst makes it clear that this way of not knowing is repetitive; it requires the analyst to provide a detailed description and explanation of what the patient is doing, which is accompanied by countertransference feelings of exasperation, frustration, and being stymied.

Therapist: The point I'm trying to get at, it's as though all week, what you have been doing—for, I think, a very particular reason—is muddling up your thoughts. All last week . . . everything I said you sort of heard it, and then dropped it. And you even commented on how you hadn't dealt with the things I had said. . . . But I think you're keeping yourself from trying to put them together. You're finding it necessary to be stupid, to stay in this state, to not know.

This interpretation of the patient's defense of "being stupid" in the context of a repetitive interaction allows the patient to admit to consciousness a memory of another, related repetitive interaction she had with her father during her adolescence. It also becomes clear that what the patient wishes to not know or remain stupid about is her sexual interests, and her wish to provoke and arouse men. Indeed, her remaining stupid and ignoring the analyst's observations, and the analyst's response to this, enacts in the transference-countertransference the need to provoke, arouse, and exasperate.

P: I used to try to come to the dinner table in my slip. (*laugh*) And it made perfect sense to me then, because I would take off my clothes when I came home, you know, just to be more comfortable. And I'd be studying, and I could have put on a house coat, but I wouldn't. And knowing my father's reaction, I can't even believe I would go down, try to come to dinner in my slip.

T: How old were you?

P: Well, I must have been in high school..

T: (*interrupting*) You can't believe it, huh?

P: Um-hmm.

T: Well, that's the point. See, that's exactly the kind of trick you're playing. You have to be stupid about it, you have to not know it. But now you just remember doing something that's unbelievable.

These last examples have shown how the interpretation of a resistance or defense can lead to some warded-off mental content or affect, a thought, desire, or fantasy. In a sense, the distinction between defense and underlying mental content is an artificial separation. In fact, defensive processes and fantasy or unconscious content are often one in the same. The neo-Kleinians in particular emphasize the defensive function of unconscious fantasy. Let us say that during treatment a patient becomes aware of a rescue fantasy. This fantasy might have the form of the patient helping a friend or loved one in difficulty, or perhaps saving a friend from a risky or dangerous situation. For example, while driving in heavy traffic on the way to his therapy hour, a patient becomes aware that he is fantasizing that a colleague's car has broken down in a dangerous stretch of freeway where his car could easily be struck from behind by oncoming traffic. The patient, through his quick thinking and decisive action, extricates his colleague from this precarious situation, and the colleague is appropriately grateful. This fantasy (and others similar in content), which was itself initially warded off or outside of conscious awareness, may in fact serve to defend against awareness of anxiously competitive, angry, or sexual feelings. The content of the warded-off fantasy itself represents a defensive process.

The following segment illustrates how a previously warded-off fantasy serves an important defensive function. The patient is a young woman in long-term psychotherapy who became quite severely depressed at the death of her grandmother. The patient has just received a batch of her grandmother's old letters, and does not wish to read them for fear they may somehow spoil her idealization of her grandmother. The idealized fantasy aspects of the patient's image of her grandmother constitute an important defense against her own self-representation as a weak, defective, and destructive person, and provides the patient with a mental representation of strength, safety, and refuge.

Patient: To me, my grandma is a saint. I realize that she probably had her negative side. I know she did. But there were so many other negative aspects of my child-hood that I'd like to hang on to her as one of, you know, the one-hundred-percent positive ones. And she was entitled to her share of mistakes.

Therapist: But it sounds actually like an important thing to try and understand more about why it shakes you up so much to think of learning anything more about her that doesn't fit the role that she had in your life.

P: I think one part of it is that I feel like I'm the product of two so extremely miserable and destructive parents. But in Grandmother, I had a positive role model. Yeah, I can say she was strong. Not that she was extremely successful financially or career-wise. She had a good little tailor business; nothing that made her rich, but it provided for her. A security. And she was successful as a human being; she was liked and she was a good person. And she was sober. And she wasn't addicted in any way except to pastries. So I can feel like I have some strong good genes, too, you know.

T: It sounds like you're saying one reason that it shakes you up is because if you see anything negative in her, it taints you.

P: Yeah, it does. It does.

T: How does that work?

P: Because I tried to convince myself that despite the destiny of my parents, I'm strong. And the reason I'm strong is because I've been with her and she was a healthy person. And that's where I have gained my strength.

T: It sounds as if you don't believe that the strength that you've attained is now yours.

P: No.

T: That it requires maintaining an image of her, as if she is still making you strong. Not that you've separated from her and from all of them, really, and developed your strength within the context of your relationships. But now it doesn't sound like you feel like it's really yours or that you're apart from her.

P: I think it's hard for me to trust in my own strength.

T: Mm-hmm.

P: It's so hard for me to be optimistic about my own qualities and my life in general. If there's something that I have been able to trust in life, it's the goodness of my grandmother. And if I can't even trust that, how can I trust my own capacity? I mean, if that's even not true.

T: Well, I guess the question is how true does it have to be in order for it to be true? You know that it was true for you.

P: Yeah.

T: But it sounds again like the idea of getting any information about her that doesn't fit could negate the truth that you feel. And it sounds like you feel in some ways like you need to really walk around with blinders on. You don't want to open these letters.

P: Mm-hmm.

T: But then the cat was out . . .

P: Mm-hmm.

T: . . . of the bag. And it sounds like it's thrown you.

P: Yeah, well, I had anxiety for the remainder of that night and I have thought about it afterward. But I've decided that I'm not going to feel bad about it because it didn't have anything to do with my relationship with Grandmother. But I realized that, yeah, it does upset me and I realized that, no I'm not really ready to look at that.

T: Mm-hmm. Mm-hmm.

P: I'm not. It gives me anxiety. I need Grandma to be perfect for me another couple of years. (*pause*)

T: It's interesting that you know this about yourself. That you know some other truth might exist about her but it doesn't shake your feeling that you just don't want to see what they are. You need to keep her alive in exactly one way in your mind.

P: Mm-hmm.

T: In order, in order for what?

P: Yeah, well. For me to feel safe!

T: Ah.

P: I don't feel safe otherwise. Like I said, she's the only person that I ever have been able to trust and rely on and she still is. My husband is close but he's never going to measure up to the way . . . how safe I can feel with my grandmother. And as long as I don't feel more safe inside, this is what I still hang onto in many ways. We all need things to hang onto. And I don't see what benefits there would be in choosing, you know. Well maybe I do. Maybe . . .

T: Like what were you just thinking?

P: Well, I was thinking. I was trying to see the benefits of me letting go of this ideal picture of my grandmother and start trying to see different sides of her and I guess that would be . . . something I'd have to go through in order to really, you know, gain, personal strength. I mean, my strength.

The patient is able to be aware of the purpose of the defensive idealization of the grandmother. The therapist's tactful, systematic effort to engage the patient in a dialogue about this defense is noteworthy. The interpretation of a defense is not usually a single pithy, succinct utterance. More often, it takes the form of gradually clarifying the nature of the defensive process, understanding the patient's purposes for maintaining it, and the implications for the patient of no longer needing to rely on such protective maneuvers.

How to Interpret Unconscious or Warded-Off Mental Content

Interpretation of unconscious or warded-off mental content can be mutative by fostering the recovery of threatening ideas and feelings, and is linked to the possibility of new action, including new ways of thinking, being, and behaving. Most often, warded-off mental contents are aspects of self and object representations. Bringing them into clear awareness helps to reorganize and integrate such repudiated unconscious mental representations with more differentiated and complex mental content and thought processes. The recognition, experience, and identification of previously isolated or conflicted mental representations permit a more integrated self-concept and a less discordant set of self-object representations. Unconscious mental content must, by definition, be inferred from an understanding of the patient's psychology, and more immediately, from the patient's language, emotion, attitude, or other directly observable behavior.

In formulating unconscious mental content, the question arises as to how the clinician can arrive at a sense of confidence about the validity or correctness of the interpretation. The question of the validity of psychoanalytic formulations, especially of unconscious dynamics (or motivational forces) or other mental content, is an issue that goes to the heart of the debate about the scientific status of psychoanalytically oriented approaches to treatment. Moreover, there is the possibility that particularly premature interpretations of unconscious content may provoke greater defensiveness in the patient, that is, lead to intellectualization or outright rejection of the interpretation. It is also possible that the patient will comply with the therapist's interpretation even if it is incorrect or only partially true. This is one of the reasons why some theorists (e.g., Gray 1994) advocate restricting the attribution of meaning to aspects of the patient's character, behavior, or affect that are readily observable to both therapist and patient. Some contemporary clinical theorists argue that the therapist does not have a privileged position in regard to knowing more objectively or accurately the nature of the patient's unconscious mental life. There is an "irreducible subjectivity" (Renik 1993) in the perceptions of the therapist as well as in those of the patient. In this view, it is the prerogative of the patient to draw inferences and make conclusions about those ideas and feelings that may lie outside of awareness.

In the following illustration from a brief therapy, the therapist points out the patient's self representations of being either dependent and weak or wishing to be taken care of. If the patient allowed herself to experience dependent longings, she would be a weakling like her brother and mother. Bringing this mental representation (contemptibly weak self being cared for by a strong other) into awareness allows to be tested against reality, and to be integrated with other, more positive and adaptive self-perceptions. This in turn may allow the patient to fear her dependency less, and allow herself to be cared for when it is appropriate and necessary. Note that the therapist is also able to link this warded-off self-other representation to the interaction in the transference.

Therapist: What was it like to have a mother who didn't take care of herself?
Patient: I hated it, I really did. I remember that, I remem-

ber that. Maybe that's one reason I got to be as I am. She always said, "Oh, you just took after your father; I wish you'd taken after me." She always said my brother took after her and I always consider my—it's terrible—I always consider my brother a weakling because he let others take care of him, too. He did the least he could do and he even married a wife that just took over, you know.

T: To let others take care of you makes you feel weak, because of what you saw with your mother.

P: Maybe, I never thought of it, or connected the two, but that's true. And we always had this, "I was like my father, he was like her," and there was a line right down the middle. Uh huh. And my father always made everything work.

T: You see, now you are in a position where you kind of want to have people take care of you.

P: I wouldn't mind.

T: You are in a rough spot. There is a part of you which says I can't do that, I'd be weak; and then you see your mother and you say if she'd only been stronger then, I wouldn't have these feelings now.

P: That is absolutely right. I look down on people who do that.

T: You're being real good and logical; and talking. And I think you are finding it very hard to let me take care of you in some ways.

P: Do you really? Because I hope not, I want to be helped. I know I do. I have the desire, but I guess I don't know how to let loose, to let you, because I never have, I guess.

The patient accepts the interpretation and acknowledges its validity. The interpretation does not touch on mental content that is deeply unconscious, since the patient appears to have ready access to the conflict concerning her fear of being dependent and weak and her longing to be taken care of. In focusing the patient's attention on these aspects of her self-other representations, and emphasizing their role in her conflict, the therapist creates the possibility these ideas can be reexamined, and modified relative to her current adult reality and integrated with other more differentiated and nuanced representations of the self. The patient is surprised by the realization of what this might mean in terms of her relations with the therapist and seems to understand the possibility for change afforded by experiencing these conflicts in a new relationship.

In the next illustration, the therapist is able to show the patient that he has an unconscious punishment fantasy that has been actualized and intensified by a surgery that brought him close to death. The mental representation that is elaborated is of a person who is guilty for not having done everything he should, of a criminal who deserves retribution, but has so far managed to barely escape his just punishment.

Patient: Since the operation—I got to keep going back to that. I am obsessed with that operation, 'cause I still don't understand it. I just cannot accept it, that I had the damned thing. Somewhere along the way they stopped my heart and put me on a machine, and then jolted me back in again at the end of the operation. You know, all of these things are just unreal to me.

Therapist: What is it you can't accept about it?

P: Well, (*sigh*) this wasn't supposed to happen to me. I did all the right things. (*pause*) You know what I mean? And

yet (*pause*) it was in a sense the retribution I've been
expecting all of my life. "They're going to get me." By
God, it really got me.

T: You described the operation in the context of three or
four things that had happened in your life . . .

P: Yeah.

T: . . . that were dreadful experiences. Where you felt afterward sort of like "Wow, I'm all here." This experience
brings those back, and it brings some of those feelings
back of—what, amazement that you survived? Or almost
a discomfort that you survived. Sort of, "Oh, I wasn't
supposed to."

P: Right, yeah. Because I really was a fraud and I didn't
really do all the things I was supposed to do.

T: Yeah, those are the fantasies connected with it. You had
deserved the disaster, that was the myth.

P: Yeah.

T: And in fact it didn't happen, so you felt almost guilty
about surviving.

P: (*pause*) Yes. In a way, I never thought about that, but
in a way there was a certain guilt about surviving. I really should have died. Everything pointed to the fact
that I . . . I should have died. I think I told you, something happened during the operation when I could
have ended up (*pause*) as a vegetable. And I beat that
one. And I keep beating the rap. Sometimes I feel like
a criminal who hasn't been caught yet.

One of the patient's self representations is of a person who did everything right, and who doesn't deserve
those life events that he experiences as punishments. Another is that he is a guilty criminal who has remained one
step ahead of calamitous retribution. In bringing these

good and bad mental representations more sharply into the patient's consciousness, the therapist creates the possibility for their integration, which would lead to a more differentiated sense of self. As a consequence the patient would then also give a different, more adaptive (less punitive) meaning to difficult or traumatic life experiences.

In the opinion of many theorists and practitioners of brief therapy, brief treatments should have a focused, concrete, problem-solving orientation. The following illustration, taken from a twelve-session therapy, demonstrates that repudiated, warded-off mental contents can be interpreted in a useful way in a very brief therapy. The therapist interprets the patient's wish to be close to her father, and the related unconscious fantasy or belief that her competitive wishes and feelings of oedipal rivalry were powerful enough to have killed her mother. The patient confirms the therapist's interpretations, providing additional corroborating material, thereby allowing the therapist to address the various levels of a central conflict in a relatively rapid sequence of interventions.

Therapist: So Mom says, even from the grave, that you can't have your father. He's really for another woman; then, at that point, you'll step back and say well that's the way it should be.

Patient: (*laughs*) (*pause*) I guess so. (*laughs*) (*lengthy pause*) I don't know, is that sort of a common thing for girls to feel that way? About their fathers?

T: It seems like it's something that makes you feel uneasy. You know, in various ways you're saying that the edge she had over you, which you would have liked, was a marriage to this terrific guy, your father. And that allowed

her to not work, that gave her life a direction, and gave
her a guy she could rely on.

P: Yeah, yeah.

T: When we ended last week's session you were saying
that your father's objection to traveling with you is that
people might mistake you for his wife or lover, and
that seemed troublesome to him. It seemed like it might
be, in some ways, kind of exciting for you.

P: (*pause*) Yeah, I guess so (*pause*). I think part of it, too,
is that it would be nice to travel with someone who I get
along well with. Most of the traveling that I've done has
been alone, and it gets kind of lonely. And we have a lot
of similar interests. After once traveling with someone
who I didn't know very well, I resolved never (*chuckles*),
ever to do that again, you know.

T: You know, I think probably someone else in your situation might even have some thoughts in her head like,
this would be more fun if mom weren't around.

P: Hmm. Yeah, but I still feel kind of guilty about it.

T: Exactly. I think it's even hard to let yourself think those
thoughts.

P: Yeah.

T: 'Cause it makes you feel like you're a very hurtful kind
of person to even think that.

P: Yeah, it does. (*silence*)

T: And I think also that where you may be getting yourself into some trouble, is that thinking that having
thoughts like that could actually hurt her.

P: (*silence*) I don't know (*pause*) I don't know if she . . .
thought about that . . . or not. She knew that I wanted
to do more things.

T: Well, I suspect what makes it so troublesome for you is
that when you were growing up that you may have

thought, "Gee, wouldn't things be more exciting, or more fun, or more adventurous if Mom weren't around?" But finally, when she's not around, because she dies, it makes you feel like you're somehow responsible. That just because you had those wishes, that somehow you magically killed her off. As if thoughts and wishes had the power to do that.

P: I know they don't (*pause*) but I guess that I still kind of feel that. (*silence*) um (*20-second pause*) I don't know how to . . . change (*patient becomes tearful*).

T: Change what?

P: To change how I felt or feel.

This exchange, in which the patient verifies the therapist's interpretations concerning her irrational guilt about her mother's death, ends with a common question or demand: "How can I change the way I feel?" After acknowledging threatening, previously warded-off mental contents, patients often long to be free of such feelings, to dispose of them; they may even struggle to re-repress them. This patient continued to feel guilty and responsible for her mother's death despite the knowledge this was based on her feelings of rivalry and magical, omnipotent thought. Indeed, some patients maintain painful ideas and feelings in the face of all evidence and common sense. It can safely be assumed that the patient has a good reason for doing so; that is to say, the maintenance of such troubling self-object representations must serve an important psychic function. It would have been useful to encourage this patient to explore further why, despite her new insight and awareness, she continues to feel responsible for her mother's death, and what it would be like if she did not.

In the next illustration from a longer-term psycho-therapy of an academic, the therapist is able to interpret the patient's painful psychosomatic symptoms as a way to destroy his interest and excitement in his work. The therapist does not assume a privileged position as the one who knows what is going on in the patient's mind. Instead, he introduces his interpretations with a collaborative attitude, inviting an exchange, and encouraging the patient to modify or verify how he understands the patient's experience. This strategy will likely increase the accuracy of the therapist's formulation, as well as help the patient to accept the interpretation.

Therapist: At the point you experienced this excruciating pain in your wrist . . .
Patient: Uh huh . . .
T: How long had you been writing?
P: Fifteen, twenty minutes.
T: Fifteen, twenty minutes. Well, let me tell you my idea and you tell me if I've got it wrong.
P: Okay. Okay.
T: I imagine that you were enjoying yourself and that you were excited about the ideas you had.
P: Uh huh. Yeah, to a certain extent. I was very uncertain about how I was going to teach the course, or how it was going to fly, and a lot of trepidation about that. But certainly I was interested in the texts and the ideas involved. (*pause*) So getting the pain in the wrist is sort of a reaction against my getting excited about my work or something?
T: Well, until that important detail surfaces . . . that is, that you were very interested, even excited about what you were doing, which it hadn't up until my bringing it up
. . .

P: Uh huh . . .

T: The picture looked rather different.

P: Uh huh.

T: The picture was of a man, of a burdened academic who was wandering around campus, near to screaming in his loathing and disgust for his university, his department, and his place in it. And there was not even a hint in that discussion that this was a man who was very interested and excited about the prospect of teaching.

P: (*sighs*) Well, I think that we like to do things that we are successful doing and that we don't like to do things that we are not good at or that we don't feel capable of doing. And I guess the way I'm relating to it now is that it just seems like an impossible task. It just seems like there's no way that it's going to work for the students. I mean, I could sit down and read those essays and have a great time. But trying to teach them how to write is another thing. You know, it just sort of occurs to me today that I just don't like teaching composition. I don't want to have to teach these people how to write. (*laughs*)

T: But these aren't the thoughts that cause you trouble. This is a well-worn groove. The thoughts that bother you and that create all kinds of problems are thoughts of excitement and interest.

P: (*sighs*) Yeah, that's what I don't get. I mean, I am on some level interested and excited about what I'm doing. I'm much more interested in my writing now that I've thought a little bit more about how it relates to my life and thought some more about its relation to modern consciousness. Yeah . . . it's hard for me to say that I'm excited about teaching.

T: But you did.

P: I did. Yeah, I did.

T: And I think you can even remember that feeling before your wrist hurt, in that ten or fifteen minutes.

The therapist is able to capture the patient's fleeting awareness of his excitement about his work, and to interpret his largely unconscious need to destroy this gratification by means of his psychosomatic pain. The patient's desires, and his conflicts, find expression in opposing or contradictory self and object representations that are affectively imbued. The therapist helps the patient begin to integrate a self representation of a man who can work creatively and effectively and enjoy it with the more dominant mental representation of a suffering, inadequate, alienated person. Bringing this unconscious self representation into greater awareness will foster a less discordant and more complex, differentiated, and integrated self-object representation.

In the next illustration, taken from the middle phase of Mrs. C's analysis, the analyst interprets the largely unconscious feelings of resentment the patient has toward her new baby as linked to her own feeling of having been left out when her younger brother was born.

Therapist: But the way you've been feeling makes a great deal of sense as a way that you must have been feeling around the time when [your brother] came, when your mother was pregnant with him, when you felt shut out from what your mother and father were doing. When you felt left out, when all the attention went to [brother]. When your father turned to him, when your mother was preoccupied with him. When you must have felt very, very left out. When you hit your mother, it's clear that you were really attacking the baby. It's hard to understand it any other way. You were saying that you didn't want that baby to be there, as curious as you might have been. That baby interfered with you, made you feel left out. And your anger at it would be quite understandable, and your feeling left out and unloved. I guess what puzzles me is that *I say* this after all the things you've said, and you don't.

Patient: (pause) Well, that puzzled me, too. Because yesterday, or whenever the other time was when you said it, pretty much the same way, all I could concentrate on was the way things are now, and how people are being to me now. How could I feel this way when they're being this way to me now? And also, I think the other thing that keeps troubling me is the thought that it's my baby now and how can I feel threatened by it in the way I did with my brother? How can I lose the whole context of how things are now?

(two-minute silence)

I don't know, first I was thinking well, there have been other babies born after [brother] that I've been closely connected with. But in a way that's not really true. This is really the first baby that has meant much to me. Because I mean, [cousin's] first one did, in a way, because it was exciting. Still, it was her baby and she was part of another family, in a way. It didn't really affect me. And so this is really the first one, and I suppose that might be why.

A few sessions later, the analyst continues this line of interpretation. It is quite common for therapists to interpret the same or related aspects of a patient's conflicts or mental contents repeatedly in the course of several, or even many, sessions. The interpretation, its verification, and exploration of its sequelae take the form of an ongoing dialogue between patient and therapist.

T: You see, I think there's absolutely no question, at least there is none in my mind now, but that you have strong feelings about [the new daughter] that you are not letting yourself become aware of. One of the things, for example, that struck me was when you said now that you couldn't call her by her name for a long time. I was very struck by how casually you mentioned her name to me when you first came in this week. It must have meant something that you told me her name the way you did. Not by telling me her name but by casually referring to her. And so exaggeratedly casual.

P: Yeah, I was aware of it, too.

T: And that means you're hiding something, I'm sure. From yourself.

P: (*silence*) I, I'm remembering just (breathes deeply) the first few weeks at home when I just sort of mechanically took care of her. And I, if anything, felt maybe resentful. But certainly I wasn't enjoying her, and I didn't feel any great warm feeling toward her. And I felt very guilty about it because everybody always says how wonderful it is to have a baby, and suggesting that immediately there is this strong warm feeling. And I just didn't have it. And I'm enjoying her more now, and I don't know whether it's because I've repressed whatever the real feelings are, or if it's something else. It's almost like I've gone through a thing of convincing myself a girl can be just as nice as having a boy. I think I've done that, to an extent.

T: But the need to convince yourself implies the opposite feeling.

The analyst offers a relatively deep interpretation, that is, an interpretation of feelings or motives that are relatively remote from consciousness. He also links, by way of a reconstruction of the past, her current feelings about her new baby to feelings she had as a child when her brother was born. The analyst continues to interpret the patient's defenses, that is, that she is hiding something from herself, and to explore the patient's feeling that she would have preferred to have a boy. This is ultimately linked to the feeling she had when her brother was born that her parents, particularly her father, greatly preferred her brother. This illustration demonstrates how, with the collaboration of the patient, interpretations of unconscious motives can be confirmed and validated through an ongoing dialogue with the patient. Note that these interpretations occur in the context of an interaction structure. The analyst once again feels frustrated and is drawn into providing lengthy explanations. Mrs. C's defenses require the analyst to know because she herself feels too threatened to know ("playing stupid"; see Chapter 1). The patient pressures the analyst, and most likely others in her life, to represent disavowed aspects of the self.

Observing defensive mental processes, identifying them, and showing the patient how he or she relies on them is a central activity for many psychoanalytic therapists. Equally important is the formulation, interpretation, and the verification or modification of interpretations about the patient's unconscious or warded-off desires, fantasy life, and self-object representations. Most often protective measures and warded-off feelings must be recognized and interpreted many times over before patients slowly feel it is safe to know about themselves. This is what is meant by "working through." They can then begin to make observations about themselves and attain insights with less assistance from the therapist. Bringing defenses and unconscious mental content into awareness is a central component of therapeutic action. These processes enhance patients' capacity for self-reflection, their ability to effectively represent experience, and the integration of undifferentiated or disorganized self-object representations.

The extent to which therapists rely on these strategies may differ depending on their theoretical orientation. Those who have been strongly influenced by self psychology, for example, may place greater emphasis on empathic mirroring and the containment of anxiety and other overwhelming affect. Some therapists may elect to foster identifications with themselves, particularly with narcissistic patients. Newer ideas about the use of the therapist's emotional experience and countertransference to understand and interpret the patient's projective identifications have also been influential among contemporary psychoanalytic clinicians. However, the interpretation of defensive processes and underlying mental contents is compatible with any of these several emphases, and indeed can be viewed as an important component of many. The next chapter takes up a topic that is central to the clinical work of virtually all analytic therapists: the use and interpretation of patient transferences to promote patient change. More conventional views of transference and countertransference are recast in terms of interaction structures, the two-person patterns of interaction that actualize the unconscious forces at play between therapist and patient.

5

Interaction Structures in the Transference-Countertransference

This chapter summarizes the evolution of the concepts of transference and countertransference and places them within the framework of interaction structures, the patterns of interaction that occur over and over again between patient and therapist. These slow-to-change two-person patterns actualize unconscious forces at play between patient and therapist. They represent not only how the patient's conflicts are represented in the transference, but also the therapist's reaction to these conflicts.

Transference was initially conceptualized as the patient's distorted perception of the real nature of the therapist. These distortions were thought to be caused by the patient's wishes, mental representations, emotional reactions, fantasies, or experiences from the past. Later, transference began to be understood as a plausible construction of something real or actual about the therapist, or about the nature of the interaction, that reflects a repetition of the patient's conflicts. Most recently, there has been a tendency to view transferences as co-constructions of patient and therapist, that is, as interactive phenomena in which both participate. As we shall see, these more contemporary views of the transference and countertransference fit within the framework of repetitive interaction structures, the two-person patterns of interaction that bring to life mental representations and related affective states in the interaction between patient and therapist. But first, an overview of the evolution of the key concepts of transference and countertransference.

Transference and Therapeutic Action

Freud (1912) held that transference was a form of repetition in which the patient acted unconsciously in place of a capacity to remember. The feelings and reactions that emerge in relation to the therapist were thought to be representative of the patient's conflicts, primarily over wishes and desires. He emphasized transference as a distortion of the perception of a more-or-less neutral and objective therapist. It was important to demonstrate to the patient that these feelings and reactions did not fit the person of the therapist, and that they must stem from previously held fantasy or experience. Distortions through transferences were a way of protecting against certain wishes and desires from being uncovered and brought into contact with rational thought and reality.

> The unconscious impulses do not want to be remembered in the way the treatment desires them to be, but endeavor to reproduce themselves in accordance with the timelessness of the unconscious and its capacity for hallucination. Just as happens in dreams, the patient regards the products of the awakening of his unconscious impulses as contemporaneous and real; he seeks to put his passions into action without taking any account of the real situation. The doctor tries to compel him to fit these emotional impulses into the nexus of the treatment and his life-history, to submit them

to intellectual consideration and to understand them in the light of their psychical value. This struggle between the doctor and the patient, between intellect and instinctual life, between understanding and seeking to act, is played out almost exclusively in the phenomena of transference. It is on that field the victory must be won—the victory whose expression is the permanent cure of the neurosis. [Freud 1912, p. 108]

Transference was, then, a repetition stemming primarily from a resistance to the awareness of fantasy or wish, to recalling certain experiences (fantasized and real) from the past. Therapeutic gain was thought to result primarily from the conscious experience of these mental contents—wishes, conflicts, and memories. Therapeutically useful transference was considered to occur only in hysterical, obsessional, and anxiety neuroses, what Freud termed the transference neuroses.

Later conceptualizations of transference placed greater emphasis on the role of the therapist's person in the nature of the patient's transferences. The therapist was now considered to be a participant-observer in the patient's conflictual patterns, not only the recipient or target of the patient's emotional attitudes carried over from the past. This change was accompanied by a number of distinctions that were beginning to be made about transference. The term *transference of defense*, for example, was introduced. It referred to the patient's character style, habitual modes of conduct or relating, or other forms of adaptation that served to avoid or ward off transference reactions. It became generally accepted that particularly these forms of transference were ever present and observable from the beginning of treatment. Gill (1954, 1982) made the distinction between the facilitating transference, which is the unobjectionable positive transference, and the transference resistance. He argued that defining transference as distorting a realistic relationship fails to recognize the conscious, unobjectionable positive transference, or what some have termed the "therapeutic alliance."

The therapeutic alliance has become a popular construct and is useful to consider in relation to the views of the transference. The alliance construct has more than one definition, but can be broadly defined as the extent to which patient and therapist are working collaboratively and have formed a trusting bond. More specifically, the therapeutic alliance construct is an attempt to make a distinction between transference and the realistic relationship, for example, the extent of agreement about the tasks and goals of treatment. It has been argued (Gill 1982) that the various alliance concepts fail to distinguish between present and past determinants of the patient's attitudes. Alliance concepts emphasize the present and cognitive determinants; realistically appropriate behavior on the therapist's part is taken for granted. Moreover, such concepts tend to de-emphasize any examination of the actual situation, and imply that the therapeutic alliance can and should be fostered in a variety of ways. In Gill's view the unobjectionable positive transference that Freud argued was the necessary context for cooperation in the analytic work (certainly one broad definition of the therapeutic alliance) is not something that has to be fostered by special means. The therapist does not have to act in a special way in order to create an alliance. The progressive clarification, interpretation, and understanding of transference reactions in and of itself helps build a collaborative working alliance.

In later views, transference was seen largely as the result of patients' efforts to realize their current desires and wishes. Recalling childhood or infantile wishes and experience became less central. Therapeutic gain was still considered primarily the result of reexperiencing these wishes through transference reactions to the therapist, coupled with the realization that they are determined by something preexisting within the patient. Greater emphasis was given to the experience of something new as it was engendered in the interaction with the therapist, to whom the wishes are now directed. The therapist's ability to refrain from fulfilling or reacting to the patient's transference expectations contributed to therapeutic change, since it fostered recognition of the fantasied aspects of the relationship with the therapist. The therapist is not simply a new object, different from the patient's frustrating and disappointing objects in the past, who provides a new and better interpersonal experience. The therapist's neutral, nonreactive, yet compassionately concerned stance provides the backdrop for analyzing transferences. It allows the comparison of the patient's attitudes with other possible ways of experiencing the actual situation, and how these are related. The patient, for example, has the opportunity to consider whether the therapist was actually being provocative or condemning, or whether the therapist's comments could be seen in another light. Patient and therapist together examine this new experience, and the new experience is further formed through a continuing understanding of the interaction between them.

The view of transference as in part the plausible interpretation of some aspect of the therapist or the interaction has also been influenced by object relations theory, which reconceptualized the role of wish, desire, and conflict in mental life. Wish and defense are seen as components of internalized self and object representations. These determine mental structure and unconscious mental life. Intrapsychic conflict constitutes two or more opposing or incompatible sets of internal mental representations of the self and other ruled by powerful emotional dispositions. In treatment, the patient scans the therapist, consciously and unconsciously, for those characteristics that can be construed to support a view of the therapist that is similar to a representation the patient needs to encounter in reality. The patient in this way transfers the intrapsychic aspects of the self onto the interpersonal field. Although the patient's representations of frustration and disappointment are most often experienced as caused by others, including the therapist, these are also representations of aspects of the self. The relationship is not simply a repetition of the patient's internal conflicts now externalized; it is also a response to the person of the therapist and the therapist's countertransferences.

In contemporary approaches to analytic therapy, interpretation of the here-and-now transference is usually considered more effective than historical transference interpretations, i.e., those linking the transference to early developmental or formative experiences. Along with a greater understanding of the complex nature of memory has come a realization that the link between remembering and therapeutic action is not straightforward. Much of what is remembered, especially of early childhood experience, can be unreliable because of the combined influence of fantasy, desire, and perception, as well as children's level of cognitive development. Remembrance in therapy can represent an interaction between past and present, since present needs can select and color specific memories of the past. It is often appealing for therapists to resort to historical or reconstructive interpretations in an effort to extricate themselves from a difficult transference–countertransference impasse (see Chapter 3 for an extended discussion of contemporary approaches to the use of the past in psychoanalytic therapy). The useful integration of the past is often best achieved if the therapist's starting point is the repetitive interaction patterns that can be experienced and observed in the present transference-countertransference state. This offers greater emotional immediacy, and hence therapeutic usefulness. In a sense, repetitive interactions are distillations of the history of the patient's mental representations, actualized with the therapist.

Countertransference and the Uses and Abuses of Subjectivity

Conceptions of therapeutic process and the therapist's mental and emotional life during treatment have evolved from a view of the therapist as a more-or-less objective observer, to that of participant-observer, and more recently to a therapist who is an affectively immersed participant-observer in an evocative intimacy that necessarily touches on aspects of the motives, fantasy life, and experience of the therapist. Countertransference was originally seen as the therapist's conflicted emotions, enactments, and other reactions to the patient's transference that stem from unresolved conflicts in the therapist. Such therapist reactions were thought to occur largely as responses to particularly intense or disturbed transferences and behavior, occasionally in conjunction with particular circumstances in the therapist's life. Later, countertransference was extended to include all that is infantile in the emotional relationship of the therapist with his or her patient. Most recently, countertransference has been used to refer to all of the feelings and reactions that arise in the therapist as psychological responses to the patient.

Concern about therapists' countertransference, in addition to the prevailing theory about the nature of therapeutic change, contributed to the establishment of the principles of therapist neutrality, abstinence, and anonymity in psychoanalytic treatments. These three principles probably also contributed to the stereotype of the analyst as a "blank screen." Psychoanalytic neutrality implies refraining from overt judgment and from deliberate suggestions, at least in more usual circumstances, about how patients should conduct themselves. A neutral therapist would not, for example, tell a patient that the relationship she is in is not a very good one, and that she should consider getting out of it. Neutrality also connotes giving equal attention to all the patient's thoughts, feelings, and associations, and maintaining a respectful equidistance in relation to the various aspects of the patient's conflicts, that is, not becoming an advocate for one wish over another. In addition, neutrality implies refraining from gratifying certain wishes of the patient, for example, for inappropriate intimacy.

Abstinence refers to avoiding the unconscious, or even deliberate, exploitation of the patient and the treatment situation for more purely personal motives. These include less obvious motives such as loneliness or voyeurism as well as the more blatant use of patients sexually or financially. The therapist ought not, for example, eat lunch and exchange gossip with the patient during the session, that is, relate to the patient like a companion. In a published personal account of a treatment, a patient described how his therapist talked about personal matters, including his deceased wife and former patients. At one point, the therapist told the patient where he should spend his vacation, insisting he should stay at a particular hotel, and even phoning during the treatment hour to make reservations

for the patient and his wife (Gopnik 1998). In this example, the therapist uses the patient for personal gratification, even living through the patient vicariously.

Anonymity refers to exerting care about what the
therapist discloses to the patient about his or her personal
experience and inner life. Inappropriate therapist self-
disclosure can be troublesome for patients. For example,
in response to a young woman patient's inquiry about
whether the therapist liked her and thought she was a good
person, the therapist replied that she reminded him of his
daughter toward whom he felt affection. The patient subsequently felt burdened and obliged to behave like an
affectionate daughter.

Neutrality, abstinence, and anonymity are closely
linked to a theory about therapeutic action. Many psychoanalytic clinicians continue to find it useful to minimize the
realistic interpersonal aspects of the therapist–patient relationship and identify them, as much as possible, as components or companions of transference. Neutrality should
not be confused with inactivity. Neutrality is sometimes
construed to mean the therapist should remain silent and
unperturbed in the face of pressing patient anxieties and
conflicts. A therapist may be quite active, but still neutral
in response to a patient's conflict about whether or not to
undertake a particular course of action. The therapist's
activity would focus on an exploration of the wishes, fantasies, inhibitions, and the like that are expressed in this
conflict. Nevertheless, as relational theorists have pointed
out, even when a diligent effort is made to maintain neutrality, it is impossible for the therapist not to communicate something about his views. What is most important is
what the patient makes of whatever the therapist says or
doesn't say. Even silence will have a meaning for the patient. Whatever the therapist does or does not do plays a

role in determining the patient's experience of the actual situation, and hence the transference. No matter the extent to which therapists may limit the range and intensity of their behavior, or allow themselves free and spontaneous expression, there is a structure of interaction between patients and therapists that reactivates past experience and fantasy life in the present. Nevertheless, neutrality allows the therapist greater freedom to observe the effects of his or her interventions, personal characteristics, and behavior and the effects of the therapeutic situation on the patient's experience of the relationship.

As we have seen, in the last decades there has been greater emphasis on the mind and subjective experience of the therapist and a correspondingly more nuanced view of the nature of countertransference. One contemporary view of countertransference is that it is "formed by the projected object (or self) responses unconsciously elicited by the patient's interpersonal pressure and by the pre-existing aspects of the analyst's subjectivity" (Gabbard 1997, p. 21). The therapist is seen as immersed in a relationship that necessarily evokes his or her own motives, wishes, fantasies, and resistances. This view has led some clinical theorists to assert that therapists do not have a privileged position in terms of either the perception of objective reality in the treatment situation or the interpretation of meaning. Therapists therefore ought to take into account the relativism of their own psychic reality (McLaughlin 1981). What both therapist and patient perceive to be true in the therapeutic situation is influenced by mutual and ever-present transference processes. Indeed, this book develops a view of therapeutic action as occurring to a great extent in transference–countertransference interactions (see Chapter 1).

The therapist's personal motives, anxieties, and other feelings, both conscious and unconscious, are routinely aroused by the patient. The extent to which this constitutes a necessary and inevitable, and even useful, element in the therapeutic process, and the extent to which this may lead to countertherapeutic defensive measures in the therapist, is an issue that is currently under debate. The most radical position is the therapists' subjectivity is irreducible, that is, everything therapists do or do not do in therapy is based on their personal psychology. This view argues that therapists cannot eliminate, or even diminish, their subjectivity, and that the widely accepted principle of avoiding countertransference enactment should be discarded. Therapists become more effective and comfortable not because they reduce the extent to which they act out of personal motivation, but because they become less defensive about it and more confident about being able to explore their patients' reactions to expressions of their own personalities. Acting, in this sense, does not refer only to physical movement or motor behavior; enactment can also be expressed in attitudes, feelings, and intentions.

According to the view that argues for the supremacy of the therapist's subjectivity, it should not be assumed that acting in a way that satisfies personal motivation will necessarily be detrimental to the therapeutic process. A commitment to abstinence and efforts to maintain an objective stance provide no real protection against exploitation of the treatment situation by the therapist. Therapists' use of the clinical setting for personal gain is in fact more easily rationalized, and effective self-analysis impeded, if they minimize the personal involvement and subjectivity of their participation in clinical work. It is argued that unconscious personal motivations expressed in action by therapists are not only unavoidable, but also essential to an effective therapeutic process. Entering spontaneously and genuinely into such actions provide a crucial series of gratifications and frustrations to the analysand that form the basis for a successful analytic process. Continuous examination of them as they occur, and the retrospective understanding continuously reached and refined, is what we usually refer to as the analysis of transference. We can emphatically agree with Boesky (1990) when he observes, "If the analyst does not get emotionally involved sooner or later in a manner that he had not intended, the analysis will not proceed to a successful conclusion. [Renik 1993, p. 564]

Certainly, countertransference and subjectivity are inevitable. They may affect the therapist's perceptions, choice of focus, depth of inquiry, and tolerance of intensity around specific affects. But this does not mean that since therapist acting out of more personal motives cannot be avoided, anything the therapist does will ultimately be therapeutic. Moreover, recognition of the therapist's subjectivity does not mean that the validation of one's understanding of the patient is unrealistic and unachievable. The therapist's subjectivity provides different information or knowledge. Meaning in therapy is best arrived at mutually through discussion between therapist and patient. It is also likely that under more usual circumstances, therapists will be less subjective than the patients, that is, they are *relatively* more objective. Therapists must, for instance, sometimes help patients distinguish fantasy from reality. Indeed, patients expect that their therapists are relatively more objective as a function of their role. They often implicitly rely on therapists to help them understand their incomprehensible feelings and behavior, and to caution them against making potentially disastrous life decisions.

How can truth and meaning be established in the therapy situation where the subjectivities of patient and therapist are central? During his analysis, Mr. S (see Chapter 1) would sometimes fail to appear for a session. He would then declare at the next session that psychoanalysis would surely explain that his behavior meant that he was angry. But he was not at all sure about that. He asserted his absence had no meaning at all. I would attempt to interpret meaning directly: "Perhaps you didn't come because you felt I humiliated you during our last meeting. Maybe this is your way of getting even." Mr. S rebuffed such interpretations with scornful attacks: "There is no evidence of that; it could mean anything." At this point, Mr. S had been in analysis with me for some years. I understood him, and the state of the transference-countertransference, and knew a great deal about his difficult early experience. I was quite convinced of the accuracy, or validity, of my interpretation of his absence, at least as far as it went. In this example, if the patient's subjectivity and claim to knowledge were privileged, then both Mr. S and I would be in the position of not being able to know anything with a sense of conviction about this recurrent conduct pattern. In essence, neither I nor the patient would be allowed to think about the contents of his mind and to know and understand something about him. In this instance, I believe I was relatively more objective about the patient's psychic reality, and this certainty allowed me to continue to function analytically.

The idea of a real, external, shared world that therapist and patient can be more-or-less objective about is indispensable for patients to know their thoughts and feelings as their own, as well as for therapists' capacity to know their thoughts as their own. In short, self-reflection cannot occur without the presumption of an objective reality (Cavell 1998). And it was through reflection on this repetitive interaction that Mr. S was gradually able to know, with a sense of conviction, the meaning of our enactment.

The radical subjectivist perspective has implications that are clinically and theoretically problematic. Still, this point of view is helpful in cautioning therapists against an authoritarian stance regarding knowledge and meaning in the treatment situation. There is an inclination for therapists to assume, or allow patients to place them in the position of being the "one who knows" what is in the patient's mind, and what is really going on. Analytic therapies place real emotional demands on the therapist. Therapists often feel an inner pressure to know what is going on with the patient as a defense against doubt and uncertainty about how to intervene effectively. A source of objectivity in the therapy situation is the effort to maintain a certain attitude toward one's own subjectivity and countertransference—making ourselves (that is, our countertransferences and subjectivity) the subject of continuous observation and analysis. This is why therapists' personal analyses have traditionally been considered a sine qua non for carrying out analytic treatments. It is primarily through a personal analysis that therapists acquire the necessary habit of self-reflection and the proper stance toward their own subjectivity.

Analytic treatments require of therapists a certain self-discipline and ongoing awareness about maintaining the therapeutic role in order to create an environment of safety for both participants. Neutrality and caution about self-disclosure is useful not necessarily to facilitate the transference (as it has sometimes been assumed in the past) but to facilitate a safe setting that allows often emotionally charged interactions to be explored and understood. Self-revelation tends to intensify analysts' personal engagement and, possibly, their countertransference. Therapists' ability to observe is diminished, and boundary violations and abuse of the patient can occur. The danger increases not in relation to particular information that the patient has about the analyst (decreased anonymity), but as a function of the analyst's own deepening, countertransference-ruled involvement with the patient. Therapists can, of course, discover they are using a patient for their own needs and attempt to understand and gain control over this aspect of their countertransference. The danger is in the extent to which this is enacted with the patient.

The following description of an interaction structure illustrates the difficulty.

The patient had been repeatedly telling her therapist her irrational anxieties about applying to graduate school. In exasperation the therapist finally suggested that she meet with Ms. W, who was already a student at the university to which the patient hoped to gain admission. The patient complied and arranged a meeting with Ms. W. In a later session, once again in response to the patient's persistent anxiety about graduate training, the therapist asked to see a copy of the patient's application. The therapist, without the patient's knowledge, showed the application to Ms. W. In the following session, the therapist referred in passing to Ms. W's impression of the patient's application. The patient was shocked by this breach of confidentiality, noting she had not given the therapist permission to show the application to others. The therapist then replied that Ms. W was his girlfriend. The patient understandably felt angry and used by the therapist and his girlfriend. This interaction repeated her experience of her father's poor boundaries and her mother's intrusiveness.

These kinds of boundary violations are not uncommon, and can be troublesome, confusing, and painful to patients. Any extratherapeutic relationship, in the broadest sense, will remain problematic and charged because the patient's transference to the therapist as a parental or authority figure will remain uninterpreted and unresolved. The conscious, deliberate effort to maintain neutrality, abstinence, and anonymity in the work with the patient helps to maintain a safe environment for both patient and therapist.

Interaction Structures in the Transference-Countertransference

The interaction structure construct is a way of formulating many contemporary ideas concerning the transference, the countertransference, the therapist's subjectivity, and the nature of therapeutic action. These slow-to-change patterns of interaction reflect the psychic structure of both individuals, as they become manifest in their perceptions, fantasies, and experiences of the therapeutic situation. Racker (1968), who was the first to conceptualize therapeutic process as "bi-personal processes," stressed the analogies and correspondences between transference and countertransference. He attempted to specify the manner in which the therapist's countertransference shapes the patient's transference. The therapist's relation to the patient is an ongoing emotional experience. This does not mean that patient and therapist are necessarily co-equal creators of the patient's transference experience. The therapist's desires, frustrations, and anxieties are real, though under ordinary circumstances, not as intense or dominant as the patient's. In most circumstances, the patient's transferences are typically the more powerful. The countertransference, however minimal, necessarily fluctuates with shifts in the transference. In the end, Racker argued, the therapeutic outcome depends to a large extent on the therapist's capacity to maintain a positive countertransference over and above the countertransference neurosis.

How is it that the therapist countertransference affects the therapeutic process? The countertransference can heighten or help resolve the patient's conflicts. Moreover, since it determines the therapist's attitude toward the patient, "it also determines the destiny of the transference; for the analyst is the object of the transference and the analyst's attitude represents the object's attitude, which in its turn influences the transference. The countertransference is thus decisive for the transference and its working-through, and is also decisive for the whole treatment" (Racker 1968, p. 18). From this point of view, countertransference cannot be entirely separated from technique. Indeed, therapists' various internal attitudes toward patients influence, among other things, their focus, capacity for empathy, and how aggressive or confrontational they might be. The therapeutic process, then, necessarily involves therapists' attitudes toward themselves.

The transference–countertransference constellation is expressed in repetitive patterns of interaction. Considering the clinical situation in terms of the interaction structure construct can alert therapists to the presence of such repetitive patterns of demeanor and action. Subsequent self-reflection on their countertransference involvement in these interactions, and on their subjective experience while these are occurring, can help inform therapists about the nature of the patient's projected self representations. Thoughtful consideration of such interactions will also foster an understanding of the conscious and unconscious responses elicited by the patient's transference and interpersonal pressure on the therapist's own mental representations and subjectivity. For example, a male therapist reduces his fee to allow a young woman to begin therapy. Some months later, the patient finds new employment, and the therapist expends considerable effort to accommodate her new work schedule so that she can continue in treatment. The patient nevertheless suddenly declares her intention to terminate, thereby demonstrating in action that she is innocent of any interest in the therapist and, more unconsciously, in her father and men in general. The therapist feels rejected and hurt that his efforts on the patient's behalf count for so little. In this way he identifies himself with the patient's mental representation of her father, with whom she had not spoken in a number of years. This kind of interaction had in fact been repeated in a number of smaller, less obvious ways during the therapy. If the therapist does not become aware of this identification, he will continue to react out of the role ("role responsive") in which he is placed by the patient's oedipal guilt feelings and related sadomasochism. Awareness of interaction patterns can help form the basis for interventions, particularly transference interpretations, which are often made in response to transference pressure.

How to Interpret the Transference

An important aspect of psychoanalytic therapy is identifying, understanding, and interpreting the patient's transference reactions. A question that frequently arises concerns timing: When should transferences be interpreted? Transference interpretations are not useful until the patient's emotional reactions, or avoidance of them, become palpable. Transference interpretations are often made in the context of a countertransference reaction. This is why questions about the timing of transference interpretations so often arise; the therapist is aware of a certain countertransference response well before the patient is remotely aware of his or her transferences. Gill (1982) makes a useful distinction between (1) interpreting resistance to the awareness of the transference and (2) interpreting resistance to the resolution of the transference. The assumption is that transference is ever present, and bringing these reactions into conscious awareness is central to therapeutic change. It is not uncommon that patients seem unaware of their transference reactions, that is, they ward off, defend against, or resist knowledge of their feelings toward the therapist. Alternatively, while they may have some awareness of such feelings, they are kept secret, and any fantasies about the therapist are withheld. In the following illustration, the patient denies that she has any feelings about the therapist or about the time constraints of the therapy. This constitutes an important resistance to the awareness of any transference reactions, which the therapist identifies and attempts to interpret. The therapist has been feeling a sense of frustration, and feeling that the relationship with the patient seemed somehow barren and lacking in real emotional involvement. This is the subjective, countertransference context in which the therapist interprets the patient's resistance to the awareness of the transference.

Therapist: Over time, whenever I ask you questions about your feelings, for instance, about, oh, any number of things that come up between us, you know your response has always been that it strikes you as odd that I should be asking these questions. And that it would be stupid for you to get too attached to somebody that you know you're going to be leaving.

Patient: But I would be leaving, you know, if there was a time limit set up by the [research] project or not.

T: Sure, but I wondered if it was different.

P: I don't know.

T: It might be different if you felt that the time and the way things ended really came from you and the two of us as opposed to from anything external to this relationship.

P: I don't know. I hadn't thought about that at all. (*pause*) I don't know. (*pause*) But I don't think so because I've thought, two years like we were talking about was plenty of time, to see how I felt. I mean, I thought that was a long time and ah (*pause*) I have no problem with it. And I think I would feel the same way as far as how I would relate to you even if it was timeless because of the character of the relationship. It's not the time limits, you know, that anybody would set up, whether it was us or them. It's the character of the relationship that is so unequal. I don't see the situation as a relationship with my therapist. I see this as a time for me to be selfish, a relationship between me and the different aspects of myself. A place where I come and I try to figure things out and I can be emotional. A place where I also can try to intellectualize things and where I can get some intellectual response from you. I just see it as a place where I develop a relationship with myself, you know, and not through you, on an emotional level but with the help of your educational background and your intellect. That's how I feel.

T: Well, that's very clearly how it feels like. You really don't view it as an emotional relationship.

P: No.

T: You don't want emotions to enter into it. I wonder why you feel that way.

P: Because I don't know you, I don't know anything about you. How could I possibly know if I like you or not as a person. I like you as a therapist, I think you're great. But how could I like you as a person when I don't know the first thing about you? I couldn't develop any emotional connection to anybody I didn't know as a person.

T: How are you able to control your feelings that way, to keep them away?

P: No, I don't have to control them. They just don't come. Like I said before, if I don't have a situation where you give, and you get, feedback and there's an equality in terms of giving and taking, then you can't get to know each other, and you can't start caring for somebody on an emotional, personal level.

T: Yet clearly you do have strong feelings about the things that I ask you or that I tell you. Like when I asked you about being late.

The therapist brings out the patient's wish to avoid a more personal relationship. The patient feels that this is justified in view of her experience of the inequality of the relationship, and the therapist goes on to point out that this is just where some of her most important feelings lie.

It is often most useful to begin interpreting the resistance to the awareness of the transference from whatever the patient is responding to in the therapy setting

or interaction. This can be accomplished by articulat-
ing what appears to be a disguised expression of the
patient's transference that has not been made explicit.
In the following illustration, the therapist links the la-tent
mean-ing of the patient's self-criticism and thoughts about
suicide to his transference reactions to the therapist's
criticism.

Therapist: You mentioned once, very explicitly and then
   again just now by implication, that maybe you are very
   inconsiderate.
Patient: Mm-hmm.
T: And when you mentioned it earlier you said maybe you
   should jump off the bridge.
P: Mm-hmm.
T: I said last week that I was angry about the lack of con-
   sideration that you had shown.
P: Mm-hmm.
T: And it makes me wonder today about what your reaction to my having said that has been.
P: Mm-hmm.
T: One seems to be that it makes you feel, that maybe
   you're just a bad, just an irredeemably bad person who
   ought to do himself in, totally.
P: Mm-hmm. Mm-hmm.
T: The other reaction, and you may have more than one,
   (*pause*) may be that you're in the hands here of a luna-
   tic who doesn't know what he's doing and he's telling
   you to do things in the wrong way. And I'm in the image of the new clerk or typist or whatever she is at work,
   who doesn't listen and doesn't get it. And gives you bad
   advice. But that if you just keep cool around her or me
   you'll be all right. Probably.
P: Hmm.

The therapist is referring here to an encounter that the patient had with a new secretary at work concerning his paycheck. The patient was angry because he felt she did not listen to him and gave him off-hand, bad advice. However, he resolved not to show his annoyance so there wouldn't be more trouble. The therapist treats this description as a displacement of the transference. It is one mental representation the patient has of the therapist; the patient sees the therapist in these same terms as he describes the secretary. The therapist has first interpreted the patient's self representation as a worthless person. He then articulates the patient's related representation of the therapist as an inattentive, unreliable, even crazy object who gives bad advice that can lead to trouble, and around whom it is best to "keep cool" to be safe.

Patients can know about their feelings toward the therapist, but be unaware that these feelings have their source, at least in part, in transference reactions. An interpretation that an attitude is indeed transference is an interpretation aimed at the resolution of the transference. In the following illustration, the therapist points out that the feelings the patient is experiencing are transference reactions.

Patient: So it was really interesting that I have all these rules I live by, and statements coming from other people. Yet I depend on myself to interpret all the rules. I never bother to ask for help, or understanding from the point of view of the person who set the rule at any given time.

Therapist: How are you thinking about it—in terms of the sessions and things like that? What sort of things were you thinking about?

P: Hmm. Because I'm doing ... if I even could ask you questions, I mean.

T: If you could?

P: Uh-huh. Not in terms of whether or not it's allowed. But also in terms of like whether or not you can even answer them.

T: What did you think?

P: I think I'm the only one who can answer my questions. I mean, ultimately, I guess. It's almost like asking the questions would be kind of a waste of time. Sometimes, too, I know when I get in conversations with other people, I somehow touch upon questions that I'm asking myself, although I don't directly come out and say it. I think I really weigh whatever they say too heavily. I really get carried away with their answer ...

T: Mm-hmm.

P: ... and forget about the focus of mine, my own answer.

T: So do you think that plays out in here? Where you may want help, but you won't ask for it, or you kind of expect it from me, or something from me, but ...

P: Yeah.

T: ... maybe are reluctant to let it happen.

P: Yeah.

T: In what way? How do you think it plays out?

Interpretations referring to the here and now of the interaction are intended to promote the resolution of transference reactions. Another category of interpretations aimed at resolving the patient's transference reactions are genetic or historical transference interpretations, which link the patient's current transference reactions to the therapist to past experience. For example, "You believe I am critical of your interest in sex; that is very similar to what you believed your mother's attitude to be." In this way patients may be helped to reflect on how their perception of the therapist is influenced by their personal past. Genetic interpretations can also involve attempts at reconstructions of the past. In the continuation of the previous example from the same hour, the therapist and patient together attempt a reconstruction of past experience that is linked to her transference reaction.

P: Not really being able to ask questions almost feels like when I was living with my stepmother. It means smarter or stupid. I mean being smart like acting up or I think "you're being dumb," that I didn't have any common sense. But I should be able to figure myself out.

T: You might have felt really hurt by those things because you might have just been asking the questions because you didn't know and you wanted to be helped.

P: Yeah.

T: Maybe some of that is happening now. Because one of the first things you said, you kind of were wondering if you could ask me questions. And it sounds like you're kind of afraid to ask me questions, for some of the same reasons.

P: Yeah. (*cries quietly for a minute, blows nose*) I mean I can't ask questions, or feel like I can't ask questions. I mean, my employer and my friends, I feel like I'm bugging them. (*two-minute silence*) Can I ask questions?

T: What would stop you from asking questions?

P: I don't know.

T: You know I can't promise that I would answer every one of them. But I'm kind of curious as why you think you couldn't.

P: Mm. (*pause*) Because they seem like—I'm not sure that they lead to anything.

T: Yeah, but that's a different point, whether or not they lead anywhere is, you know, open to see, but something stops you . . .

P: Mm-hmm.

T: . . . from even getting to the point of feeling like you can ask me a question. I mean independent of whether I answer it or whether or not it leads somewhere. I think it provokes some feelings inside you, that old feeling you said. (*pause*) Feelings of being what—being smart or being called stupid, or feeling like you're bugging somebody.

P: Mm-hmm. (*pause*) Also, I don't know. I've got to use your common sense to answer questions. I'm not using my common sense. (*silence*) I feel like I'm trying to get everyone else to live my life if I can't answer my own questions. (*silence*) Sometimes I think I do all kinds of dumb things, so I can find answers without having to ask anyone.

T: So it may be less painful perhaps, to do those things rather than put yourself in the position of asking people questions.

P: Yeah.

T: Well, it sounds like you're struggling with some of that in here. You have given me lots of information or lots of cues that you really want to ask me some questions but are hesitant to.

P: It still doesn't feel right. It seems like I am not supposed to ask questions.

T: Well, what's interesting about that is, I've never said anything to that effect. I don't remember any rule like that being talked about, yet it feels that way to you. Like you were saying before, it's one of these rules that you've come up with about how you and I relate; one of the rules you've come up with is, you don't ask questions.

P: Yeah.

T: But it sounds like the same thing is happening in here that happens outside of here. Like you're saying with your friends and with your boss and maybe with your stepmother.

A frequent topic in discussions of technique is whether, or to what extent, therapists should answer direct questions posed by the patient. Of course, much depends on the context in which the question is asked. Note, however, that in not responding directly to the patient's question, "Can I ask questions?" the therapist allows more of the patient's feelings about this to emerge, and is able to link what is occurring in the transference with early experiences as well as the patient's current relations outside of the treatment. The next illustration, taken from the same treatment, illustrates an interpretation aimed at the resolution of a transference reaction. The therapist demonstrates that the feelings behind the patient's unexpected and abrupt declaration that she is terminating the treatment is indeed a transference reaction provoked by his upcoming vacation.

P: Um, Monday's going to be my last day.
T: Oh really?
P: Yeah. I accepted a job offer. And, you know, I think it will just be better to stop Monday. I think it'll be better for me to stop on a Monday, than on a Friday. You know . . .
T: Stop?
P: Coming into therapy.
T: That's kind of interesting. That's the day that my holiday begins.
P: Oh, yeah. (*pause*) And you're going Friday, right?
T: Mm-hmm.
P: Yeah. Yeah. I'll be in town until September second, first or second.

T: Why did you think that would be such a good idea? It's almost like, leaving me before I leave you.

P: (*pause*) Yeah. That's true. Hunh.

Later during that same hour, as the patient talks more about her sudden impulse to end the treatment, additional important transference reactions emerge more sharply into the patient's awareness.

P: There are still some things that I want to talk about, but not *now*. (*laughs*)

T: Well, I think you said that last time, too. You were talking about all these things. And in a sense you're worried about what I'm going to see. And if I see something, what am I going to do with it? And I think you're *worried* that I might have some reaction to all the stuff you're talking about, that you're putting out on the table.

P: Mmm. Like being bored.

T: Yeah. You're worried that I'm going to not be interested in you.

P: Yeah. Yeah, I think that's really hard for me too right now. Because things are just sort of like . . . okay for once. I mean, (*laugh*) there's nothing major going on. It's just sort of like (*pause*) I still feel like nothing's happening. It's just, there's (*laugh*) no crisis going on.

T: Well, I don't think that's a small point in how you feel about being here. I think you're saying that it's more uncomfortable to be here unless there's a crisis.

P: Yeah.

T: And that you're worried that unless you're in a crisis, I'll be bored.

P: (*pause*) Yeah. That's why I'm thinking, it's easier to go.

T: So part of your motivation for leaving may in fact be an attempt to, what? *Do* something so I won't get bored or something.

P: Yeah.

T: (*pause*) Rather than, say, staying here, when there's no crisis.

P: Yeah.

The therapist is able to bring into awareness some of the patient's transference reactions to the actual situation (the therapist's impending vacation) as well as some of the patient's transference wishes (that the therapist be interested in her) and fears (that he will be bored, or worse). The therapist's interpretations contributed toward resolving the transference, at least insofar as the patient was able to continue in treatment.

In contemporary technique, experienced therapists are careful not to overemphasize memories of the past in the interpretation of transference. What is remembered is influenced by fantasy, desire, perception, and level of cognitive development at the time of the event (see Chapter 3). There is a complex connection between memory, fantasy, and reality, and therapists can focus too much on the events of the past rather than on how the patient construes these events. Reconstruction of past experience lacks the immediacy and certainty that accompany reexperiencing them in the transference. When some aspect of the transference has been brought into awareness, priority should go to further work within the treatment situation instead of attempting to relate the patient's reactions too quickly to historical or contemporary extratransference connections. Most often, efforts are more usefully directed at promoting the resolution of the transference within the

therapy situation. This is accomplished especially by using
features of the interaction as a point of departure for the
exploration of the patient's transference attitudes. The
resolution of transference does not come about by recovery of the patient's history, or by cognitively connecting
past experience to what the patient is experiencing now
in relation to the therapist. It occurs largely in the ex-
plication and understanding of the transference reaction, and the accompanying increased capacity for self-
reflection and self-knowledge.

The following illustration is from a sixteen–session
brief therapy. The therapist seems anxious in the face of
the patient's sense of abandonment about the impending
termination. In what appears to be an attempt by the therapist to avoid his own guilt about ending the treatment, the
therapist moves too quickly to the patient's memories of
past events rather than progressively elucidating (as in the
example above) the manner in which the interaction is
being experienced by the patient.

Therapist: You have a very vivid picture of how I must be
   feeling. I think your concern is that I might be feeling
   some worry and some regret . . .
Patient: Mm-hmm.
T: . . . and some feelings of almost helplessness that we've
   got to stop, and I can't quite give you what you need.
P: Yeah.
T: Yeah. I said earlier that I thought that a lot of these feelings that you're having now are a reversal. They are feelings that you would have at any point in the therapy. In
   stopping . . .
P: Mm-hmm.

T: . . . it's because of the feelings you had when it was time to leave your parents, or when they left you.

P: Mm.

T: You picture me as having the same feelings, I think.

P: Maybe so.

T: And part of your question about whether we can go on is really, not that you don't think you can make it. I actually think you're quite confident.

P: But are you going to desert me, too?

T: Well, what I'm saying is that the feelings that I'm in your spot.

P: Mm-hmm.

T: Feeling "Gosh, I wish I could do a little bit more." See that's what you felt with your parents, when in fact you couldn't.

P: Yeah.

T: I mean in fact the real reason for us to stop now is we're done! We've done our job.

P: Yeah.

T: We set ourselves a task, we're finished.

P: I think we have. I really think what you've just said is very important. (*pause*) That somehow—and I suppose if this went on for another three years, it would be even worse—my feelings become intertwined with what I want your feelings to be. You know, what I anticipate they will be.

T: As part of how the work proceeds.

P: Right. And I want you to feel as strongly as I feel, or you *are* me. You know, and you are going to feel what I feel.

T: Well, that's what your parents said to you.

P: True.

T: How could you feel anything but what I want you to feel?

P: Right.

T: And it was very painful for you.
P: Yeah.

The therapist is anxious and controlling in moving away from the here and now of the therapy relationship to past experience, thereby interfering with the patient's expressing fully and in his own words his feelings toward the therapist. As we have seen, contemporary psychoanalytic theorists do not regard transference as simply and primarily a distortion of the present by the past. The present, as well as the past, is represented in the transference. Transference attitudes are often based on what the patient sees as plausible responses to the interaction with the therapist and the overall therapy situation (in this last illustration, the impending termination), and to the therapist's countertransference. The resolution of the transference is not accomplished by the recovery of the patient's history, the presumed origins of the transference, but by the elucidation and understanding of what is transferred in the context of the patient–therapist interaction.

Understanding Countertransference through Interaction Patterns

As we have seen, definitions of countertransference have evolved over time. Contemporary views emphasize that the therapist is immersed in an intimate relationship that necessarily evokes the therapist's own wishes, fantasies, and resistances. Countertransference is those responses unconsciously elicited by the patient's transferences together with already existing aspects of the analyst's subjectivity, which may then be projected onto the patient or the treatment situation. Racker's (1968) creative theorizing has helped to specify the processes that promote countertransference in the therapist. He noted that the intention and effort to understand sympathetically creates a predisposition to identify with the patient. As a result, every transference situation provokes a countertransference that arises out of the therapist's identification with the patient's (internal) objects or mental representations. This view of countertransference fits well with the idea of interaction structures, two-person patterns of interaction that reflect the psychological structure of both patient and therapist in a transference–countertransference involvement. It is these transference situations and the therapist's response to them, and in particular his or her understanding and interpretations of them, that are of decisive importance. In Racker's view of therapeutic action, these are the moments when the cycle of patients projecting their inner world, evoking certain responses from others, and then reintrojecting and reinforcing a maladaptive representation of the world can be interrupted and observed or perpetuated. In a progressive therapeutic process, therapists will be emotionally engaged and experience their countertransference, often with real intensity, but should be able to maintain a kind of split in their consciousness that allows the use of these reactions to further understand the patient.

Let us return for a moment to the case of Mr. S presented in Chapter 1. During the early phase in his analysis, Mr. S closed himself off to my every interpretation and effort to help and to understand. He derided my comments, and reproached me for the uselessness of the treatment, claiming in an angry, defeated way that there was no hope for change. I felt continually criticized and anxious, and sometimes angry. I felt threatened by my own self-criticism and an ego ideal that had an exacting standard for performance and success. Mr. S feared my reactions to his aggressive and sadistic provocation. My own conflicts were stirred up by the patient. To the extent to which I acted under the influence of these internal motives and representations of my ego ideal, Mr. S found himself reexperiencing, or feared being confronted with, a reality reminiscent of his real and/or fantasied childhood—an angry, abusive, and rejecting parental figure. Perception of the countertransference reactions that are intrinsic to these interaction structures helps therapists to become conscious of the patient's ongoing transferences and interpret them rather than be unconsciously influenced by them.

Countertransference can affect the therapist's participation in a variety of ways. It can assist the perception of the patient's unconscious processes. The therapist's frustration and anger may help him, for example, to apprehend the patient's sadism and wish to defeat him. Many therapists today believe that their countertransference informs them about patients' mental states. Here is an instance from the case of Ms. M (see also Chapters 2 and 8) of the effective use of countertransference in an interaction structure. After a year of productive, twice-weekly therapy, Ms. M began to feel completely hopeless and depressed about her progress. She had difficulty remembering what she talked about in therapy and she worried that the therapist felt she was not serious about their work. The therapist responded by telling Ms. M that she was interested in her difficulties in working in therapy, by summarizing earlier sessions, and by repeatedly reminding Ms. M that she was not doomed to a tragic destiny. Ms. M either ignored the therapist's comments or became relentlessly argumentative. Her body posture, language, and tone of voice reflected an impenetrable, agitated despondency. The therapist in turn became increasingly concerned, discouraged, and frustrated, as well as irritated and aggravated.

The following illustration is from a session during this phase of the treatment. Ms. M is once again feeling helpless and depressed. She was not hired for a job for which she had applied, and she views this as negative feedback about herself. Ms. M says that a lot of the way she looks at herself depends on feedback from those around her. The therapist, in a way that has now become repetitive, attempts to reassure Ms. M. She points out that ordinary circumstances and events around looking for a job do not constitute negative feedback, and notes that positive responses from others seem not to count. Ms. M, in her now familiar way, brushes off the therapist's every comment.

Therapist: Your first point is the one that's operating now—the one where you need to lay claim to the misery.
Patient: Mm-hmm.
T: And perhaps even in response to me.
P: (*pause*) What do you mean?
T: Perhaps this feeling of needing to hold on to the misery while someone else is saying, "Yes, but what about this . . ." A refusal to recover in an interpersonal way.
P: (*pause*) Explain that again—refusal to recover in an interpersonal way. How does that . . .?
T: Well, you set up a situation where you can dismiss anything I say that is obviously positive, something that is obvious in the situations we have been discussing.
P: Yeah. (*pause*).
T: How do you imagine I feel? In the fantasy of what's going on when you dismiss or brush aside my comments and suggestions? How do you imagine that I feel?
P: I think you feel frustrated. (*pause*) I'm just like a wall, and you throw a ball, hoping to get through the wall, but it just bounces (*laughs*). What you say is just going to bounce off the wall and come right back. So I think you

would feel frustrated. You would feel, after doing that a few times, I think you would feel frustrated to the point of anger. "I've sat here and tried to say you are a worthwhile person, and the ball just keeps bouncing back. If I wasn't such a professional person (*laughs*), I would take another ball and throw it harder, in anger, throw it hard." (*pause*) That's what I think you feel.
(*Silence. Patient begins to cry.*)

T: What makes you cry?

P: It makes me cry 'cause it makes me feel crazy. It brings to light my craziness. To think beyond the initial frustrations, which is accurate, but to go beyond that, to the anger and wanting to hurt, feeling so frustrated you want to hurt. Turning things around seems crazy to me.

Ms. M and her therapist go on to link this interaction to how she felt about her depressed mother and her former husband, both of whom she wanted to help. She recalls her anger and frustration with them, and how it took all of her internal fortitude not to strike back. The therapist interprets the interaction structure as a reversal: Ms. M is doing to the therapist what the patient's mother did to her, hoping the therapist will not be as paralyzed as she herself was. In the subsequent sessions, the patient had a number of important insights.

Countertransference can, however, also distort and hinder therapists' perception. For example, the therapist's guilty need to help or to rescue the patient, combined with conflicts over his or her own aggression, may preclude the recognition of the patient's hostility. Another possibility is that the therapist's perception of the patient is accurate, but the countertransference may impair interpretive capacity. For example, the therapist observes the patient has made an erotized transference, but is inhibited from interpreting this because of his or her own anxious sexual conflicts. The countertransference, by affecting the analyst's understanding and behavior, can to some extent influence the form and expression of the patient's transference. Countertransference can affect the therapist's manner and behavior, which in turn influence the image the patient forms of him. It has been argued (Renik 1993) that the danger of the countertransference being repressed is greater the more these countertransference reactions are rejected as unthinkable by the therapist's ego ideal or moral sense.

The following illustration demonstrates a largely unconscious countertransference in which the therapist identifies with the patient's punitive internal mental representations and behaves as an angry and dissatisfied parent. The patient is talking about the problems in his unhappy marriage.

Therapist: Can you dance?
Patient: Sure. I didn't want to. She didn't ask me if I wanted to or not, it was just that I was being rude that I didn't ask her. She says, "Here, you didn't even ask your own wife to dance."
T: Yeah, I guess you make your choices and you take your consequences.
P: Mm-hmm.
T: Because there's certainly nothing wrong with you that would keep you from dancing, if you know how to dance.
P: Yeah, but I didn't even think of it, you know. It would have been nice to ask her to dance. It would have been nice.
T: Mm-hmm, it would have been.
P: But I just didn't even think about it.

T: You know, it's kind of funny because you just sort of say these things, like, "That's me."

P: But that frustrated me, too, because I allowed myself to be that way.

T: If you're going to be that way, then you ought to just take it as you, and say: "Well, that's me. I just don't ask people to dance. If I don't want to do something, I don't do it."

P: The thing is that it would have been a nice romantic thing to do.

T: It would have been. You say that but you also said, "I didn't want to dance."

P: Mm-hmm.

T: Now that's basically what you said. You remember how I talked to you early in therapy about an angry, hostile side to you?

P: Mm-hmm.

T: Well, this is an example of that. It's kind of like saying, "Hell, I didn't want to dance. I don't care whether you want to dance or don't want to dance. I'm not going to dance."

P: Yeah, but if she had looked at me and said, "Gee, why don't we get up and dance?" I would have probably said, "Yeah, okay." But it wasn't that way. I mean she just stormed off, furious at me.

T: Well, a woman does like the man to take some (*chuckling*) initiative.

P: It would have been nice. I know it.

T: I mean it's not really a (*chuckling*) bizarre request.

P: I know.

T: Uh-huh. You just go through life missing all these opportunities, apparently.

P: Mm-hmm.

T: Now what do you think you're going to do about that? I can't come there in the restaurant, tap you on the shoulder, and say, "Why don't you ask your wife (*P chuckles*) to dance?" I mean you're a bright man. You can think of these things.

Although the therapist may be correct in pointing out the hostility in the patient's behavior toward his wife, his reaction is contemptuous and punitive. His occasional chuckles betray his anxiety at the aggressiveness of his own response. The patient, having provoked this reaction, now submissively accepts the punishment that he no doubt believes he richly deserves. The therapist is enacting his punitive attitudes, which have been evoked by the patient's submissiveness and related self-punitive mental representations.

The next segment is drawn from the same case several weeks later. It demonstrates the repetitive nature of such interactions in which the therapist identifies with, and enacts, the patient's punitive mental representations. The therapist remains unconscious of the extent to which he is patronizing the patient. The patient is talking about his success at work.

P: I got plenty of clients.
T: Mm-hmm.
P: That is a plus; but I also see the fact that I can't just let all these things interfere . . .
T: Interfere with your personal relationship with your wife and trying to improve that.
P: That's right.
T: I mean you can still touch her or show interest in her, or at least you can try. And remember to take her danc-

ing occasionally. I mean, you said you knew how to dance.

P: Yeah. That was such a bad move. It was incredible. What an opportunity, I just blew it.

T: Like I said, someone should teach you how to court a woman.

P: That's true.

T: You know, with a few flowers . . .

Anxiety and guilt feelings in the countertransference also frequently cause a tendency to countertransference submissiveness (Racker 1968). The therapist may then overgratify or avoid frustrating the patient. The therapist's tendency to avoid frustration and tension will express itself in the effort to placate and reduce the intensity of the patient's transference by quickly deflecting it, for example, to a childhood experience. Or therapists might defensively attempt to rehabilitate themselves in the patient's eyes as the "good" or the "real" (undistorted) therapist. In the following illustration from a termination session, the therapist avoids by conciliation and flattery any negative transference reaction stemming from a forced termination of the treatment. In enacting her countertransference, the therapist misses the opportunity to explore more fully the patient's feelings about having to end the treatment.

Patient: But then we went to another store and I did buy a suit; it's quite close, I think, to the color of your suit.

Therapist: Oh, that would look good on you.

P: And it's real pretty. It's very bright. Brighter than almost anything that I have, and it's very expensive. I spent more on this than I've spent in any five-year period of time. (*laughs*)

T: Good, since you've been spending too little.

P: Yeah. So I sort of really made up for it all in one whack. But I haven't tried it on for anybody. I'm going to try it on for my husband and the kids.

T: What does it look like, what is it like?

P: Well, it's a silk suit. And it's got a long jacket that comes down to about right there and the skirt is short, you know, the skirt is just a short miniskirt underneath it. I really considered wearing it today, so you could see it.

T: Oh, that's too bad.

P: But I still have all my tags on it and everything. I don't want to take my tags off until I see if everybody likes this and so I thought, well, I think it would be sort of tacky to wear my tags. (*laughs*)

T: Send me a picture.

Another common form of countertransference involved in interaction structures is when the therapist somehow sees the patient in terms of his or her own conflicts or limitations. The therapist, for example, wishes to help the patient achieve an independence or assertiveness that the therapist does not possess; the patient should be able to act in a way the therapist cannot. This could be conveyed both directly and more indirectly, for example, by asking certain questions and offering suggestions.

In the following illustration, the therapist's indignant response to the patient's predicament seems at least in part determined by the therapist's wish for the patient to assert herself, especially in relation to powerful male figures. The reaction suggests that the therapist has a particular investment in this, since she introduces her own view of the persecuting object as "sociopathic." This condemnation is, of course, the therapist's interpretation of the patient's description. The patient's view is accepted as factual real-

ity, and the transference implications of the patient's representations of her employer are not addressed. She urges
the patient to be assertive without exploring the patient's
apparent long-standing difficulty in looking out for herself,
and the patient complies with the therapist's wish. The
patient is talking about her difficulty in obtaining payment
for work she performed for an attorney.

Therapist: And you won the case? I thought maybe you lost
the case.
Patient: No, no. We did really well.
T: This is devaluing yourself. This is saying, "I'm not worth
this."
P: Yeah, I think it is.
T: In an incredible way. I mean, they won the case?!
P: Well, I think what it's saying is I can live without the
forty-five hundred dollars but, H. can't, the attorney
can't. (*laughs*) I mean it's that same old silly stuff that
somehow here I'll just put this off a little bit longer—
and because your needs are . . .
T: You're going to allow him to treat you that way?
P: I know I really just can't—I'm just going to have to . . .
T: I would write the collection agency and carbon copy
him, period.
P: Yeah.
T: And tell them it's been two-and-a-half years. Tell all that
to the collection agency.
P: Yeah.
T: This is ridiculous!
P: Yeah, it is. It's ridiculous.
T: And it's the principle of it. I mean he's acting like a
criminal in a way. This is sociopathic, on his part. He's
manipulating you.

P: He is manipulating. I know that's right.

T: And he'll do it again to you and other people if he can keep getting away with it. You've got to fight for this; this lawyer thing is ridiculous! I mean, it's an insult to you.

P: Yeah it is.

The therapist apparently cannot tolerate the patient's helplessness, and is drawn into an authoritarian posture by the patient's inability to collect what is owed to her, and by her seeming nonchalance or willingness to suffer. The therapist exhorts the patient to behave more assertively, and perhaps deliberately overlooks her conflict in asserting herself. She emphasizes that the patient is being victimized, points out the moral correctness of the patient's position, and inpugns her employer's motives. In this way, the patient's own conscience-driven inhibitions and conflicts about entitlement, greed, and selfishness can, at least for the time being, be overcome, and she is able to act in her own behalf.

Interaction structures are the behavioral and affective expressions of the interplay of transference and counter-transference between therapist and patient. These slow-to-change two-person patterns actualize real, as well as unconscious, forces at play between patient and therapist. They represent how the patient's conflicts are represented in the transference, and the therapist's reaction to these conflicts. When transference reactions remain unanalyzed (not identified or understood) countertransference conflicts in the therapist are often the cause. Transference can be seen as the expression of internal object relations or mental representations in the interactive field. Understanding the transference will depend on the therapist's capacity to accept the patient's wishes, empathize with the patient's defenses, and remain conscious of identifications with the patient's internal objects.

The following illustration is from a lengthy and difficult therapy of an obsessional, passive-aggressive, and somewhat paranoid man. The patient has been relentless in his disavowal of any aggression, and the therapist has been experiencing a long-standing sense of frustration in relation to this patient. In the illustration, the therapist seems to consciously empathize and identify with the patient's anger and hostility, and is able to interpret this aspect of the patient's transference. But he also seems to unconsciously identify with the patient's punitive, rejecting internal objects or fantasies about authority figures, and enacts a kind of punitive contempt. The patient feels rebuked by the therapist, and resentful, which he expresses in his passive-aggressive response. The patient's transference is in a sense made real, or actualized, in the interaction. It is brought to life and intensified through the therapist's countertransference. An additional aspect of the therapist's countertransference is the therapist's need to discourage awareness of the more disturbed aspects of the patient's mental life, represented in the schizoid and perverse fantasies about humans/machines. The therapist reacts to the patient's detached attitude, calling it "peculiar for therapy talk." The therapist then goes on to make interpretations in terms that coincide with those of the patient's moralistic superego. The analysis of the patient's transference is made more difficult to the extent the therapist's punitive attitudes and introjects, incited by identification with the patient's self-punitive object representations in the transference, negatively influence the therapist's interpretations and conduct. The patient will more likely perceive as real his externalized self-object representations through his experience of the actual interaction with the therapist.

It should be emphasized that the therapist who conducted this treatment did not think this illustration captured an instance of countertransference enactment. He felt, instead, that this was an heroic effort on his part to confront the patient's entrenched character defenses.

Patient: (*two-minute silence*). (*sigh*) I'm afraid to start saying superficial things. I just feel as if . . . I came in last time and was talking up a storm, but like you said, it did seem to be kind of superficial for psychotherapy. All the things I've thought of so far are about the science-fiction books that I've been reading. There's this trilogy of science-fiction books by the same author. He's constantly trying to blur the line between organism and machine. There's also all this stuff in the books about sexuality; there are these creatures that are essentially centaurs, or part human, part horse, and they have three sets of sexual organs, one frontal, and two rear, and the rear genitals are both male and female for all the individuals. Um . . . it's a very kinky set of books . . . (*patient goes on in this vein for some time*).

Therapist: You know, it strikes me as you talk that there doesn't seem to be anything at stake in it for you. Which to me seems peculiar for psychotherapy talk.

P: Oh, yeah, I think that's true. On the other hand, it seems there is something at stake here. I'm not quite getting at it. You know, it's like . . . there's something, about . . . physicality and sex and . . . and, uh, machinery. There's something about these books that I find deeply disturbing on some level. What it's doing is like trying to, if not destroy, at least permeate the boundary

between human and animal and machine. I think I'm
uncomfortable with physicality to begin with. I mean, to
a certain extent, physical bodies do have a kind of
mechanistic aspect that's very frightening. It's something
about the body not being in your control, but your
being dependent upon it.

T: Why do you think that comes up now?

P: Well, I think it may relate back to fear of sickness. And
the whole thing I was saying about my work, and that
fear coming up at that same time. Especially with what's
been going on with P [acquaintance undergoing treatment for cancer]. And I think also just sexually, just not
feeling real sexually fulfilled in my relationship with
Alice, and not quite knowing what to do about it . . . it's
a relationship that works, it's about as good as it gets.
Um . . . maybe I'm kidding myself, but . . . (*pause*)

T: Do you ever think of yourself as mechanical?

P: (*sighs*) Not really. I definitely think of myself as material, sometimes. Just like, feeling like I'm completely
trapped by my body that, for that reason I'm completely
vulnerable. Sometimes I actually wish I were more mechanical, though. I found myself being fascinated by
gadgets lately, and really kind of obsessed by efficiency.
And sort of seeking for a technology that will work on
people, you know, like the right words to say, so that . . .

T: Exactly, that's the way you sounded at the beginning.

P: Yeah.

T: You are as phony as a three-dollar bill. And if you do
that with your bosses, they're going to see right through
you. It won't work. It looked like you were trying out a
technology to see if it would work on me, trying to think
of the right words to say. It seemed absolutely
ungenuine. I was taken aback, and if I were not in a
relationship with you, in which I can talk to you about

these things and try to help you with them, I would think ill of you.

P: Hmm. What are you thinking of in specific that I said?

T: When you said this stuff and that you really wanted to talk to me about it and, you know, had considered it—all of it was absolutely canned.

P: (*laughs*) Right. So I might as well do that anyway. (*laughs*)

T: Either that, or try to develop some actual interest in the way other people feel. And about your relationships with us. Or go and find dumber people.

P: (*laughs softly*) Right . . . (*sighs*) . . . (*pause*) I don't mean ill. (*short laugh*) (*pause*) Yeah, it's hard for me to take into consideration how other people are going to feel without becoming just completely tentative. And frightened, afraid of saying the wrong thing again. I mean, that's sort of the flip side of it, I guess. It's like, that sense of the mine field, like, you know, God, what am I going to say next? Or do next? And, uh, I get caught walking on eggshells with everybody. (*silence*) I don't know what to do. . . . Essentially, what you're saying is that, what you're calling ingenuineness, or whatever, is really sublimated aggression.

T: Well, maybe. Maybe. Not sublimated, but aggression.

P: Yeah, right, right, right, right. That's a different thing. That's what it's repressing anyway, maybe.

T: Or acting out, without taking responsibility for it.

This illustration captures an interaction structure. It is by far the most extreme example in a lengthy therapy; however, there were many milder examples of this kind of interaction. The therapist attempts to point out the patient's hidden aggression and sadism, while at the same time is enacting a punitive countertransference. The therapist has identified with the patient's moralistic, punitive inner mental representations; or, stated differently, the patient has provoked harsh superego aspects in the therapist, which find expression in a punitive attitude and a tone of contempt. In this respect, the form the patient's transference assumes is influenced by the therapist. A given therapist may unconsciously provoke a preponderance of certain transference reactions, or prolong them by failing to recognize his or her countertransference. In parallel fashion, the patient may evoke or engender certain countertransferences reactions, creating a bi-personal process—an ongoing interplay of internal mental representations and actual interaction.

Countertransference involvement is inevitable. The therapist's personal reactions to the patient, whether conscious or unconscious, real or fantasized, conspicuous or subtle, are continual and ever present. It could indeed be said that change processes cannot be set in motion without meaningful involvement on the part of both therapist and patient. The patient's transference reactions and the therapist's countertransference are mutually influencing and asymmetrically reciprocal. Often countertransference can further therapists' understanding of their patients. This section has emphsized the more problematic aspects of countertransference since these often lead to unmodified interaction structures and therapeutic stalemates. The extent to which countertransference reactions influence the therapist's conduct, stance, and interpretations makes more difficult the analysis of transference reactions.

Some of the most difficult countertransference reactions occur in response to patients' hostility, anger, and hateful destructiveness. In his research extending over two decades, Strupp (1998) has found that therapists' negative responses, especially to more difficult patients, are far more common and more intractable than has been generally recognized. He identified a particular type of repetitive interaction structure, which he termed "negative complementary interactions." In this kind of interaction, the patient's anger, hostility, or aggression exerted a strong influence on therapists, often evoking either hostile, ambivalent, or ambiguous verbal responses. Such repetitive interactions, he found, can begin early in treatment and are not easily rectified even if therapists are to some extent aware of their negative reaction. Significantly, even experienced therapists could be caught up in this kind of negative transference–countertransference interaction.

The active presence of subjective factors in the therapist cannot be denied. It is undoubtedly true that too much emphasis on neutrality and objectivity can lead to repression and blocking of awareness of the therapist's subjectivity and countertransference. However, it is also true that untrammeled and unexamined subjectivity is equally likely to obscure countertransference reactions. Excessive informality, too much self-disclosure, or using the therapist–patient relationship as a means of personal gratification promotes emotional overinvolvement. Poorly modulated personal involvement, coupled with an undervaluing of objectivity, can lead to countertransference–transference situations that present very real, if not insoluble, problems for therapist and patient. In particular, therapists will very often find it difficult to become fully aware of certain aspects of their reactions and to observe themselves and their impact on the process. Neutrality and objectivity are important aids in maintaining a stance in which the therapist can monitor his or her own countertransference fluctuations and deviations. Such a stance can only be maintained to a certain extent or for a certain time; it is never absolute and will shift in response to those same transference and countertransference pressures. Therapists' objectivity is fostered by making their own subjectivity and countertransference the object of ongoing observation and understanding. This is why it has always been considered absolutely essential for analytic therapists to undertake a personal analysis. Therapists' personal analyses contribute to the resolution of their own conflicts. And, among other things, personal analysis provides the empathy-enhancing experience of being a patient. It is also only through a personal analysis that therapists acquire the necessary capacities and habits of self-observation and -reflection, and the proper stance toward their own subjectivity.

6

Supportive Approaches: The Uses and Limitations of Being Helpful

The preceding chapters were devoted to describing insight-oriented, analytic approaches to therapy. The diverse orientations in psychoanalytic and psychodynamic therapy can been located on a continuum ranging from insight-oriented, or "expressive," approaches that promote self-reflection and greater self-understanding, to supportive strategies that strengthen the patient's capacity to defend against conflicts and disturbing affect. This chapter describes and illustrates supportive approaches, which comprise a broad set of interventions that many therapists use routinely in their clinical work. Although therapists are often inclined to support patients emotionally and in other ways, they are sometimes unclear about why and how they should go about being supportive.

The term *support* has very positive connotations to many therapists. It implies they are being helpful, and help is what therapists intend to offer their patients. It is consequently easy for many therapists to overlook the very real limitations of supportive, helping interventions. For example, rather than solving a problem for a patient, the therapist can work to build the patient's capacity to solve problems autonomously. In other words, there is another route available to analytic therapists, and this alternative is a defining feature of analytic therapies relative to the many other existing therapeutic approaches. Supportive interventions can be enormously useful at a given time for certain patients, and when they are applied in a conscious, planned manner, and with understanding and skill. However, very often supportive interventions are entered into almost reflexively, and without much thought. Supportive interventions applied in this fashion often represent interaction structures that actualize unconscious forces at play between patient and therapist. These repetitive patterns of transference–countertransference enactments are manifestations of the patient's conflicts in the transference and the therapist's reactions to these conflicts. In supportive approaches, it is more difficult for both therapist and patient to become aware of important aspects of their interaction and their inner experience in relation to each other. Significant meanings can remain hidden and not understood, and the patient's opportunity for acquiring self-knowledge and building self-reflective capacity is limited.

What Is Supportive Therapy?

Supportive approaches constitute a diverse array of interventions, and promote change through a variety of putative modes and mechanisms. Supportive therapy is not simply empathic, reflective listening. Nor do supportive interventions necessarily involve taking a supportive, even advocate-like posture in relation to the patient. Support is often erroneously construed as expressing direct approval of something the patient has done, encouraging the patient's self-assertion, agreeing with the patient's positive self-statement, or emphasizing the patient's strengths. In actuality, supportive forms can be quite complex, and are more appropriately identified by the extent to which therapists satisfy emotional dependency needs in the patient.

The therapist, for example, might deliberately gratify a lonely, isolated patient's need for human contact.

Supportive approaches are also defined by the extent to which therapists provide guidance to assist the patient's judgment about reality, or intervene in the patient's life situation when he or she is unable to cope with life circumstances. Another defining feature is the extent to which the therapist supports the patient's use of defenses, for example, the avoidance of certain difficulties, or reassuring the patient that all will be well. Supportive approaches often promote emotional catharsis to reduce affective distress. Although promoting affective experience may seem to be expressive in nature, it is considered supportive if the goal is to provide relief without necessarily achieving insight or self-understanding. The fundamental intent of supportive approaches is to help the patient regain emotional equilibrium by diverting, suppressing, or re-repressing awareness of anxiety, depression, and other disturbing affects, providing emotional release through affective expression, and distracting the patient from awareness of intense and painful conflicts.

Another process that may be considered supportive is that of providing the patient with a *corrective emotional experience,* or an experience that is contrary to the feared response the patient has come to expect. The patient, for example, expects to be judged and humiliated by the therapist for his shortcomings, just as he felt he was during his overly strict upbringing. However, the therapist receives the patient's confessions of imprudence and feckless behavior with calm interest, thereby presumably demonstrating to the patient that he need not always fear harsh criticism from others. Providing the patient with a corrective emotional experience has been controversial since the introduction of the construct by Alexander and French (1946). Its critics have argued that it requires the therapist to role play. However, the corrective emotional experience construct has proved to be an elastic one. Gill (1954), for example, held that an empathic, reality-oriented therapist who meets the patient's transference behavior with a genuinely nonjudgmental attitude can provide the patient with a corrective emotional experience without the risks attendant on taking a role opposite to what the patient expects.

A crucial distinction between expressive and supportive strategies revolves around how the patient's transference reactions are approached. Supportive techniques tend to use the patient's reactions to the therapist, and the therapist's authority, to achieve certain treatment goals. The therapist, for example, might suggest or persuade the patient to change some problematic behavior, and the patient complies to please the therapist or because he is obedient to authority figures. In insight-oriented approaches, the realistic interpersonal aspects of the therapist–patient relationship are explored to uncover hidden emotional and behavioral manifestations of transference fantasies. Supportive therapies and insight-oriented therapies are usually thought to have different treatment goals. Supportive therapies usually aim to achieve symptom alleviation, that is, the reduction of distress, anxiety, and depression. Insight-oriented therapies, on the other hand, hope to promote more enduring change in functioning or personality. Differences in the intensity, that is, frequency of treatment sessions, and duration also differentiate these approaches.

There is obviously an important role for such therapies. Supportive approaches can be very effectively used in crisis interventions that help patients who have suffered emotional trauma to suppress and manage overwhelming anxiety and distress, and to return them to previous levels of adaptive functioning. It is likely that most brief therapies conducted in the context of managed care are supportive in nature. Indeed, almost all brief, once-a-week treatments are supportive in nature, since they mostly do not create a situation in which transference–countertransference reactions can emerge and be explored and understood. In our study of the brief interpersonal (IPT) and cognitive-behavioral (CBT) therapies conducted as part of the National Institute of Mental Health (NIMH) Treatment of Depression Collaborative Research Program (TDCRP) (see Ablon and Jones 1999), we concluded that both of these treatments were predominantly supportive in nature. IPT and CBT were both conducted using manuals that guided and proscribed therapists' interventions according to each treatment's theory of therapy. The fact that these two presumably very different therapies were about equally effective in alleviating the symptoms of depression puzzled many observers. An initial reading of the verbatim transcripts from IPT and CBT treatments did seem to suggest they were different. However, when we studied the nature of the treatment *process*, using the Psychotherapy Process Q-sort (see Chapter 7 and Appendix), it quickly became apparent that these differences were rather superficial. There was a great deal of similarity in the therapists' authoritative stance and activity level, as well as their use of reassurance, their offering advice and counsel, and their focus on activities or exercises the patient was expected to conduct outside of the therapy session.

The following illustration is from an interpersonal therapy conducted as part of the NIMH study. The patient feels bad that she needs treatment, and has been too ashamed to tell family members that she is feeling depressed. The therapist attempts to persuade the patient that talking with others about her problems will be helpful.

Therapist: Well, if you had cancer, wouldn't your family want you to get help?

Patient: Yeah, yeah.

T: Or if you had a broken leg? You know, I think it's sometimes hard to remember that emotional problems are just as painful, if not worse, than physical problems. And everyone's enthused about you getting help for physical problems.

P: Mm-hmm.

T: And maybe if your son and daughter-in-law don't understand, they need to be educated a bit.

P: Well, I think that's it. I think that I'm afraid that they wouldn't understand how bad it really is with me. Because I have always tried to keep all of that to myself.

T: Mm-hmm. I think that's been a little bit of the problem. I think if you'd feel freer to talk about it, talk to them, talk to your husband, even your mother, or whomever, and say, you know, "I really feel down today." I think you found out that just talking to *me* has made a lot of difference.

P: Really, uh-huh.

T: It's probably the thing that's helped you feel better, finally being able to talk about your feelings. And that's something I hope you won't ever forget. Do what you feel good about doing, but it seems like your son and daughter-in-law care about you and make efforts to be with you and include you, and they might need to have a little educating on your part. And say, "Sometimes I've really felt bad, and I want to do something about it." It might make you feel a little easier around them.

P: Well, yeah. I wish I could talk to them. It's just that I'm not sure that I can explain it—like it should be explained.

T: Well, how *would* you explain it? You can maybe practice a little bit with me, if you would like. What would you like to say to them?

The therapist goes on to coach the patient on how to conduct herself with family members. The therapist reassures the patient that her emotional problems are nothing to be ashamed of, and suggests that she practice talking with her family about her difficulties. This approach is consistent with a focus on maladaptive communication patterns in interpersonal relationships that is advocated in the manual for IPT. The therapist's coaching of the patient is also consistent with the techniques of IPT, which include role-playing. However, in the process of reassuring and coaching the patient, the therapist also helps to suppress any awareness the patient might have of the self-punitive nature of her depression. In advising her that it will be helpful to discuss her problems with others, the therapist perhaps does not take seriously the patient's humiliation and wounded pride. The therapist suggests the patient override these feelings rather than think about them. From a psychoanalytic point of view, the therapist's strategy is clearly supportive in nature.

The next example, from a cognitive-behavioral therapy conducted as part of the NIMH study, contains many similar features.

Therapist: The fact that we're focusing on the depression, the fact that we're focusing on the negative thinking, the fact that we're focusing on the difficulty with activities, that we're focusing on, like a person with a cast on his leg, how much harder it is to do things when you're depressed.

Patient: That's going to make things worse? I mean, is that
what you're saying? You feel worse, but it helps you in
the long run?

T: Mm-hmm. Does that seem plausible to you?

P: I don't know. I suppose.

T: It's kind of hard to believe right now, isn't it?

P: I mean, I don't really know much about it.

T: And one of the reasons it's hard to believe is because
you don't know a lot about this therapy we're doing,
right? You're just starting to learn about it and so it is
kind of understandable that you would be skeptical
about something you don't know a lot about.

P: Well, I am basically skeptical anyway.

T: Are you? Okay.

P: (*chuckles*) I don't have faith in anything.

T: Okay. I don't mind your being skeptical. And let's put
this to the empirical test, okay? Let's see if it's worthwhile. Now, my belief in focusing on these issues and
working on them is that over the course of therapy,
you're going to feel much better. And you're going to
be actually coping with the depression rather than trying to hide from it. Okay? And coping with it, in my
experience, has led people to being able to conquer the
depression, okay? Being able to get on top of it and
being able to feel better.

P: Okay. Well, you know more about it than I do, so . . .

T: Okay, so we have two different opinions, right? You have
a skeptical one.

P: Well, it's just that I don't really know and I guess you
know. I, I hope you know more than I do.

T: Well, I hope I do, too. But not only do I have to know,
you also, eventually, are going to come to see it the way
I see it, but you've got to do that with some evidence,

right? And the proof of this therapy is in the doing and in the feeling better. Right?

The therapist is unabashed in his use of authority in his efforts to reassure the patient, and to persuade him that talking about his depression will be helpful. While initially expressing some skepticism, the patient compliantly assumes a deferential attitude. In both illustrations, the therapists make an analogy between their patient's depression and physical illness, thereby discounting any contribution by internal motives or conflicts to the patients' difficulties. Therapists in both IPT and CBT relied heavily on interpersonal influence; they offered advice and guidance, suggested patients change their behavior, and did not, as a rule, discuss features of their interaction with the patient. In spite of their different theoretical orientations, these two treatments are essentially supportive in nature.

Patients in this NIMH study began treatment meeting *Diagnostic and Statistical Manual* (*DSM*) criteria for major depression, which is often associated with poor self-image and low self-esteem. In our study, good outcome was associated with patients' experiencing a positive sense of self and idealized view of the therapists in the context of a compliant, deferential relationship to the therapists. Patients may have achieved this revised self-concept by identifying with desired attributes seen in the therapists. Alternatively, some of these depressed patients may have had relatively strong dependency needs. We theorized that they sought out authority figures with whom they developed deferential, idealizing relationships. Encouraged by their therapists, these patients may have been able to risk new, more adaptive behavior in the context of a positive, though somewhat passive and dependent relationship with a therapist who takes the role of a benevolent parental figure. It is likely that brief therapies, regardless of the theoretical perspective from which they are conducted, promote behavioral change and symptom improvement through these kinds of supportive processes.

Early analytic theorists held that the rapid amelioration of symptoms that can be observed early in treatment is due to transference factors and an increase in the effectiveness of repression. They conceptualized the process by which nonanalytic therapies promoted change as constituting a new symptom construction that depends on transference and the use of authority. The fact that patients' treatment gains in IPT and CBT in the study were not maintained at follow-up (Shea et al. 1992) seems to confirm the long-standing view that changes in brief therapy brought about by supportive interventions under the rule of a positive transference are not enduring.

Wallerstein (1986) has delineated mechanisms or processes of supportive therapy that are grouped into several categories. A number of them fall under the rubric of positive dependent transference, and include types of transference that, by remaining unchallenged and largely outside of awareness, can have a stabilizing effect on the patient. One of these is the well-known concept of transference cure. The term *transference cure* implies more than just a rapid, albeit unstable, patient improvement. Many clinicians have had the experience of a patient's symptoms quickly improving, and the patient declaring he or she was no longer in need of treatment. This can signify a flight from the dangers of transference feelings, positive or negative, or a retreat from the felt risks of the self-knowledge that might emerge through continuing treatment.

Another kind of process in this category is a patient's willingness to achieve certain changes or goals for the therapist's sake, in exchange for the gratification of needs within a positive and dependent attachment. Certain patients come to treatment because of the unhappy constriction in their lives and the wish to become stronger and more independent and assertive. New assertive behavior in their life can, for example, be encouraged if they are permitted to continue a dependent relationship with a therapist who takes on the role of a benevolent parental figure. The patient can become more assertive in his or her behavior on the basis of an unacknowledged, uninterpreted, new submission in the therapy relationship. The patient may become more assertive not because he or she has understood the nature and need for submissiveness and no longer needs it, but because of a fear of losing an important tie to a new object—the therapist. To maintain this tie, the patient is willing to risk being assertive in the world through obedience to the therapist.

In the following illustration, the therapist exhorts the patient, who is suffering from difficult medical problems, to become more assertive on her own behalf.

Therapist: Right? And another way of looking at it is that if it is too much for you to put up with it any longer, well, maybe the reason is that it is too much! And you ought to pay attention to that and maybe get a break. And ask the social worker for the renal dialysis unit to help you get some respite care. And you do this about everything. You can say, when you feel scared, there's something the matter with you, you're a scaredy-cat. Or you can say, well, maybe there's a *reason* why I'm scared. "What is it that frightens me?" And pay attention to it, and recognize that it is very frightening, what's going on.

Patient: Yeah, I can understand that.

T: You see that? Now, you have the tendency to put everything on yourself. You have this remarkable tendency to think that there is something the matter with you when you have such ideas. In other words, when you get angry, you think there is something the matter with you that you feel angry, rather than, "Hey, there must be something going on that annoys me. Something irritating. Let me see what this irritating business is." So my impression is that you keep your mouth closed too much.

To avoid displeasing the therapist, or perhaps even jeopardizing the relationship with the therapist, the patient overcomes his fearfulness, complies with what he experiences as the therapist's demands, and becomes more vocal in obtaining help for himself. The patient may eventually experience positive feedback and enhanced self-esteem when the new behaviors bring realistic rewards and gratifications. Wallerstein (1986) holds that in this way adaptive behaviors and other changes that are undertaken out of transference wishes toward the therapist can be reinforced by positive real-life consequences and can sometimes evolve into stable and enduring change.

Supportive Approaches and Interpersonal Influence

The means by which supportive interventions exert influence has been the subject of a great deal of discussion. Advice, information about reality, encouragement, and reassurance are presumably available in other relationships, for example, with parents, mentors, and friends. How is it, then, that educative or exhortative interventions in psychotherapy can influence behavioral change more effectively (at least usually) than in other human relationships? Many clinical theorists have argued that supportive approaches are a form of interpersonal influence, a type of indirect suggestion. The notion of suggestion as a form of interpersonal influence has had an important role in the history of psychoanalytic theorizing. In fact, both early (e.g., Glover 1931) and contemporary (e.g., Gray 1994) theorists have considered most psychotherapies to rely on a powerful component of suggestion bolstered by the use of the authority the patient invests in the therapist.

Psychoanalytic approaches place importance on uncovering psychological meaning and on personal change. Suggestion and the use of the therapist's interpersonal influence are usually seen as encouraging change without necessarily promoting self-understanding or insight, factors that contribute to the greater permanence of change. One of Freud's early unsuccessful experiments with therapeutic technique was to influence hypnotized patients through explicit suggestion. Since that time, therapies in which the patient is purposefully influenced in a manner that is outside of the patient's explicit awareness, and in a way that involves a deflection from the contents of the patient's mind, have been considered nonanalytic, or suggestion therapies. There is among analytic therapists a tradition that encourages caution about the purposeful or unwitting use of the therapist's authority to influence patients. One of the main objections stems from the concern that no matter how well intended, the therapist's solutions to the patient's problems may not adequately address the patient's conflicts. Only the patient can effectively achieve solutions and compromises to his or her unique conflicts, both conscious and unconscious. In fact, the extent to which a treatment refrains from relying on suggestive influence has long been considered a defining feature of psychoanalytic therapy. Supportive approaches, which do rely on the therapist's authority and which do not have insight or increasing the patient's capacity for self-reflection as a priority, have consequently been viewed ambivalently.

In the following illustration from the brief therapy of a schoolteacher, the therapist comments on her need to inhibit expressing any assertiveness or anger.

Therapist: And in a myriad of situations—I mean with me, and maybe at school with a parent or child—
Patient: Uh-huh.
T: —who says something to you that you feel is off the wall and none of their business.
P: Uh-huh.
T: And you say, "Hey I don't like that—it's not okay for you to ask me that."
P: (*whispering*) Oh God, I could never say that to somebody.
T: Well, that's what I want to talk about.
P: Yeah.
T: That's the thing.
P: Yeah.
T: Not who the lady is, and what's going on with her husband.
P: Yeah, no.
T: Ultimately, it doesn't matter. I mean what matters is what keeps you from saying, "Hey, I can't come over Wednesday. I really want to see you next week, and do you have any other time, and could you stay a little later, or could you come earlier because I have a really busy life and I want to see you." And instead you talk about what is convenient for them.
P: No, I'm a very accommodating person and . . .
T: Fix that. (*both laugh*)
P: I'd be happy to fix it. I really would be.

The therapist tells the patient to behave more assertively. The patient, who has noted how accommodating
she is, will make an effort to comply with the therapist's
directives. However, the motivations or conflicts underlying her need to be overly accommodating are left un-
touched, and will likely remain a force for inhibition.

Suggestive procedures can be classified according to
the amount and means of deflection from self-knowledge
(Glover 1931). These can range from simply ignoring the
patient's psychology and conflicts, to suggesting diversions
that might include doing something new, taking up a
hobby, or improving one's thinking. In many ways, this is
similar to the methods of some current cognitive-behavioral
treatments, which encourage the patient to increase pleasurable activities and alter dysfunctional cognitions. A related means of symptom relief without psychological knowledge or insight can occur when the therapist makes some
fairly accurate explanations about the nature of the
patient's difficulties that are nevertheless sufficiently inexact to serve a defensive function. Such inexact interpretations may continue to help ward off knowledge about some
threatening mental content, yet can promote adaptation,
since they remain distant enough from the actual source
of conflict to provide relief from anxiety. A good deal of
moral or rationalistic influence can be exerted in these suggestive procedures. Sometimes gestures and phrases reminiscent of obsessional, magical systems are used, such as repetitive exercises of a certain kind.

It is widely accepted that, all other things being equal,
electing a more supportive as opposed to expressive approach to therapy is determined by the patient's level of
psychological disturbance. Supportive approaches are considered to be indicated either for psychologically healthy

individuals suffering from acute reactive states, object loss, or acute anxiety, or for severe personality disorders, borderline disorders, and some overtly psychotic individuals. Expressive or insight-oriented psychotherapies are generally held to be indicated for those who have reasonable ego-strength and tolerance of anxiety, and who suffer from symptoms or character pathology. However, these loose guidelines have been blurred over the past two decades by new diagnostic and therapeutic conceptualizations, for example, Kernberg's (1975) application of object relations theory to thinking about borderline patients and Kohut's (1971) self psychology as a theory about narcissistic personality disorder.

Newer theoretical contributions have begun to raise the question of whether supportive approaches necessarily, or at least exclusively, effect change by relying on the therapist's authority to influence the patient in the context of a positive transference. Relational and intersubjective theorists have by and large discarded the distinction between supportive and insight-oriented therapies. The supportive-expressive distinction derives from ego psychological and drive/structural models, and a theory of therapy based on insight, or bringing unconscious conflict into awareness. Supportive approaches are defined by the extent to which they are based on covering up or re-repressing, and not on uncovering, conflicts and distress. Many interactional theorists argue that it is the experience of a new object relationship, a new kind of interpersonal experience, as much as the interpretive process, that promotes change. In a further challenge to these distinctions, Wallerstein (1986) argues that the presumed distinctive modalities of supportive therapy, expressive or insight-oriented psychotherapy, and psychoanalysis probably do not exist in pure form in the real world of clinical practice. Actual treatments reflect blends of expressive-inter-pretive and supportive-stabilizing elements. "All proper therapy is both expressive and supportive (in different ways), and the question at issue at all points in every therapy should be that of expressing *how* and *when*, and supporting *how* and *when*" (p. 689).

Supportive Approaches and Interaction Structures

Earlier chapters advanced a theory of therapeutic action centered around interaction structures—repeated, observable, mutually influencing interactions between therapist and patient (see Chapter 1). This construct provides another lens through which to consider the distinction between supportive and insight-oriented approaches. It captures the role of repetitive, mutually influencing interactions in facilitating the processes required to experience and represent certain mental states and patients' knowledge of their own intentionality. In this view of therapeutic action, insight and relationship are inseparable, since psychological knowledge of the self develops in the context of a relationship with a therapist who endeavors to understand the mind of the patient through the medium of their interaction.

Interaction structures inevitably play a role in supportive approaches, since the construct assumes that these interaction patterns emerge in every therapy relationship. Significant repetitive patient–therapist interactions that remain uninterpreted, not understood, and outside of explicit awareness most certainly can block greater self-knowledge and understanding and can lead to therapeutic stalemate. However, uninterpreted interaction patterns can in and of themselves have a supportive function. For example, a patient could form a defensive idealization of the therapist that provides greater emotional stability by strengthening positive self-other representations, and by repressing troublesome fantasy. The therapist does not interpret this overestimation, realizing the stabilizing function it serves, and hoping to use this idealization of his authority to influence the patient to make adaptive changes. All such interaction structures are at least in part unconsciously enacted by both therapist and patient. For example, when Mr. S (see Chapter 1) complained of not knowing what to do or what to think, Dr. H told him how to conduct his relations and what was in his mind. Since Mr. S did not achieve greater capacity for self-reflection, nor insight into the nature of his relationship to Dr. H, the defensive function of Mr. S's idealization remained intact, and the results of his therapy with Dr. H were unstable.

Supportive interventions are compatible with most therapists' defenses and needs. Therapists are inclined to defend against negative feelings they might have toward a patient. Very often, therapists need to feel helpful in a socially conventional sense. And while therapists ought to treat patients respectfully, they will often rely on social forms of behavior if they feel anxious, are unsure how to intervene, or if they do not have a clear theory about how therapy promotes change. For example, a patient was awarded, after some years of trying to overcome his inhibitions about success, a prestigious professional recognition. Should the therapist acknowledge and encourage his success, offer her congratulations? If the therapist offers her congratulations, this may foreclose an exploration of the patient's anxiety or guilt about his accomplishment, and his ambivalence about his ambitious striving. Or perhaps the patient has achieved this success to please the therapist, or to compete with her. Congratulations offered by the therapist could serve as a reassurance that no harm was done to her; alternatively, it could be experienced by the patient as patronizing, as if reassurance was needed. It could, of course, be argued that whether the therapist offers congratulations or remains silent, the therapist's actions have meaning to the patient and could be explored. The point being emphasized here is that therapists might respond in a socially conventional way because they fear negative reactions in patients, and that patients' reactions to such conventional, supportive responses often remain unspoken and unexamined.

Many therapists assume it is helpful to patients to maintain a continuity from session to session in the topics or themes that are discussed. This is particularly true in low-frequency, once-weekly treatments, where it is easy to assume it is supportive to recall for patients what was being discussed at the end of last session. One patient was repeatedly unable to remember what was discussed in the previous hour, and appealed to the therapist to remind her. At one point, the patient related that during a very upsetting experience between sessions, she had been unable to remember what she had understood about this problem, and consequently was unable to help herself in the absence of her therapist. The therapist commented that perhaps they could understand why the patient did not remember. The patient replied she had no idea, at which the therapist ventured an interpretation, saying perhaps the patient wanted the therapist to remember for her, to depend on the therapist to remember. The patient's response was to feel insulted and angry, as if to be dependent was terrible. The patient, by failing to remember, had been unconsciously forcing the therapist into a particular role; the therapist responded by being helpful, and remembering for the patient. This repetitive pattern constituted an interaction structure, which the therapist was under pressure not to notice. The patient began to explore the nature of her inner, hidden relationship to the therapist when the therapist recognized and interpreted the interaction pattern. Supportive interventions can represent interaction structures that actualize unconscious forces at play between patient and therapist. Significant meanings can remain hidden in the interaction and not understood, and the patient's opportunity for acquiring self-knowledge and building self-reflective capacity is limited.

Seemingly simple and deliberate supportive interventions, such as advice, reassurance, encouragement, or suggestions about how to conduct family relations can represent unacknowledged repetitive interactions that have significant transference–countertransference meanings. One of the limitations of supportive approaches, as Wallerstein (1986) points out, is that the therapist's understanding is constrained by a more psychologically defended interaction. It is more difficult for both therapist and patient to become aware of significant aspects of their interaction and their inner experience in relation to each other. The knowledge of the patient that guides the therapist's work is less complete, and must necessarily be based on a greater degree of inference; it is therefore less likely to emerge consensually or to be mutually validated. In contrast, insight-oriented approaches yield ever-increasing knowledge about patients, and the nature of their defensive processes, mental representations, and quality of object relations. This knowledge emerges in a manner that can be consensually validated between therapist and patient, and can ultimately lead the patient to a full and cogent self-understanding.

In the next illustration, the therapist, both directly and through her attitude, attempts to correct the patient's idea that she is a bad person and a bad daughter. The patient has become depressed during a visit by her mother of some weeks' duration. According to the therapist's formulation, the therapist is attempting, by providing an atmosphere of approval, to correct the patient's experience early in life of harshly critical and punitive parents.

Therapist: Try to remember what a good daughter (*laugh*) you are. And try to resist. Don't look at her. Find little things to do; I don't know what helps you. You know whether it's not looking at her when she's in this state. Or hold the phone away a little bit from your ear, or just something so you see a wider view. You're going to have your husband's family here. You'll probably get perked up, even if you're robot-like. You'll get perked up with the festivities.

Patient: Mm-hmm.

T: And remember how much worse your mother would be behaving had this break not happened.

P: Yeah.

T: And how awful it would be.

P: Oh yeah, I think that's right.

T: I mean you might tell her, "You constantly tell me that I hate you; even when you make a mistake on the plane arrangements, and you set it up so we can't possibly pick you up, you tell me that we hate you."

P: That's right.

T: "And then I break my butt trying to figure out how to juggle my entire family and [husband] was going to take the day off to go do this-and-that-and-the-other and you still tell me that I hate you."

P: Mm-hmm.

T: "I am totally frustrated. You don't allow us to please you at all. I'm sick of talking about this topic. This is a ridiculous topic."

P: Mm-hmm.

T: "And you're not going to make me hate you. I refuse to do it. If you keep provoking me." She is like trying to hold a red flag in front of a bull. She is trying to make you hate her. So that she can say, "You see, I'm not worthless because I *am* worthless, I'm worthless because you hate me."

The therapist reassures the patient and actively coaches her about how to think and how to behave. She urges the patient not to allow her mother to mobilize negative self representations ("Don't look at her; don't listen to her"). Negative mental representations are located outside of the patient. The therapist suggests that the patient is not hateful and worthless; instead, the patient's mother is. The patient's mother is construed as the source of hateful representations that the patient must fight off and resist. This example is an example of an interaction structure. This kind of interaction, which contains important uninterpreted transferences and countertransferences, occurs again and again during the treatment. The patient is able to use the therapist's more benign superego to modify her harsh self-punitiveness. The externalization of hateful negative mental representations also seems to allow for their partial modification. This illustration demonstrates how a therapist's supportive interventions comprise uninterpreted repetitive interactions. By allowing them to remain largely outside of awareness, the therapist deprives the patient of the opportunity to learn about, and to come to better terms with, her own aggression.

Using Supportive Interventions

When should a therapist intervene supportively? When patients are experiencing overwhelming affect, such as intolerable hopelessness and despair; when they are damaging themselves, or putting themselves in jeopardy; when they are endangering or hurting others; or when there is a possibility that they will break off the treatment. Supportive interventions should be used in a deliberate, conscious, planned way, not reflexively or defensively. A therapist might, for example, encourage a patient to treat his or her spouse with more consideration, or suggest that a patient who suffers from panic attacks enter phobic situations. A therapist might vigorously encourage a patient to seek a more suitable employment situation or, alternatively, argue against the patient's wish to withdraw from family or work responsibilities. The success of these kinds of interventions rests in part on the nature of the patient's emotional tie to the therapist. Supportive interventions represent a broad category, and such interventions can be applied in many different ways. The thoughtful, deliberate use of supportive approaches can be particularly challenging when such supportive interventions are consistent with therapists' defenses and needs, and with being helpful in a socially conventional sense. Supportive techniques can, in short, mask meaningful transference–countertransference interactions.

One supportive strategy is deliberately not challenging certain denials, or to form an agreement, tacitly or explicitly, to avoid discussion and exploration of particular areas of personality functioning or certain problems. Topics that might evoke anxiety or depression are then avoided by both the therapist and patient. In the following illustration, although the therapist addresses the patient's dependency

needs and wish to be cared for that are part of her interest in marriage, she avoids the patient's conflicts about
these wishes.

Therapist: So it's that you feel guilty about taking care of
  yourself, then. I was struck by what you said about marriage. You said, "It'd be okay if I got married and got
  myself taken care of." That's . . .
Patient: (*interrupts*) Well, that's what they [men] . . . want.
T: That's only one kind of a model of marriage. A very dependent model in which you become a child and the
  husband becomes a . . .
P: Right.
T: . . . parenting character for you. I mean, you can't allow
  yourself to think of a marriage in which you make an
  equal contribution.
P: Yes. Wait. I can't allow myself to? No! That's—I mean,
  I wouldn't want to get married for someone to take care
  of me if that's . . . although maybe I would. (*laughs*)
T: If you take a look at what you're saying . . .
P: Oh, maybe I am looking for someone to take care of me
  so I wouldn't have to worry about my problems or anything. I don't know. It's confusing.
T: It is confusing. And we're not going to solve it all in this
  hour . . .
P: (*interrupts*) No.
T: . . . but we're gonna make progress here. One thing's
  real clear—
P: (*interrupts*) What?
T: You know, it is confusing. You do feel very guilty doing
  things that are strictly for your own benefit. You felt
  guilty about coming to therapy, for that matter. You do
  feel you need it, but you feel guilty about investing time
  in yourself.

The therapist asserts her own views of marriage, and does not take up the patient's conflicts about dependency and wishes to be taken care of that underlie her difficulties in finding a suitable partner. Although the therapist does address the patient's guilt, what might be another important area for self-exploration is avoided, and the therapist forgoes an opportunity for the patient to learn about her conflicted wish to be dependent.

Re-education and Reality Testing

Other supportive interventions include reality testing and re-education. The therapist can take a directly educational role in the transmission of advice and information, particularly about normative and societal behavioral standards and expectations. The therapist might, for example, coach the patient about proper conduct with in-laws. This kind of intervention is particularly appropriate if patients' judgment or reality testing is poor, and they are not able to adequately protect themselves from the consequences of their actions. For example, a patient responded to a sexual advertisement in a newspaper using stationery of the company with which he was employed. The therapist initially tried to address the sexual conflicts surrounding this behavior. However, when the patient repeatedly used company letterhead in this way, the therapist finally commented that the patient seemed unaware of the trouble this might cause him, and insisted that the patient not use company stationery.

A 35-year-old woman, who seemed naive about sexual matters, asked her therapist whether a particular form of birth control would protect her from sexually transmitted diseases. The therapist, in an attempt to educate the patient, responded that it was not 100 percent safe. The patient misunderstood the therapist as giving her permission to continue her risky behavior. The therapist then had to forcefully repeat and clarify her earlier statement.

This exchange was a manifestation of a repetitive interaction in which the patient is naive and uninformed, and the therapist must take the role of explaining and providing information to protect the patient from the consequences of her denial and wish not to know. However, instead of exploring the patient's naiveté and need to rely on her therapist in this way, the therapist, to protect the patient, instead responds supportively by providing clear, unambiguous information in a forceful manner.

In the following illustration, taken from a brief therapy for a complicated grief reaction, the therapist attempts to educate the patient about the process of mourning. The therapist assumes that by providing this information, the patient will be less frightened and overwhelmed by the intensity of her feelings.

Patient: Mornings are the worst. Wednesday mornings are the hardest. He died on Wednesday; yeah, it feels like one huge pain in my whole body.
Therapist: Mm-hmm. I think that's a common reaction.
P: How long does it keep on . . . like this? (*laughs*)
T: Well, it doesn't last—you know, it's usually a matter of a few months . . . and somehow the mind is able to go through that.
P: Yeah. What happens? I mean, how do people, how does it change? Or why does it change?
T: Well, it changes for reasons that you said before, and you've already had moments of feeling it.

P: Mm-hmm.

T: It changes somehow with the acceptance. And the route to get to the acceptance is different for different people.

P: Mm-hmm.

T: And it involves struggling with different kinds of contradictions. But you know there is usually a way to get through to some feeling of reconciliation and then— and then the pain heals. I know that sounds a bit vague and I wish I could be more specific in helping you. I just kind of wanted to provide you with a bit of an overview . . .

P: Yeah.

T: . . . of the stages, because I think that is confusing to you and you don't know, are you going a little crazy or "What is this . . .

P: Uh-huh.

T: . . . and am I all alone in this?" and so on, and I think the answer is no, you're not alone, that this frequently occurs. It's frequently very intense, and it frequently gets better.

The therapist conveys that what the patient is experiencing is not unusual, implying that everyone must go through certain stages of grief, and that the painful feelings will be relieved with the acceptance of the loss. The effectiveness of this kind of supportive intervention is often determined by whether the therapist is able to convey such information in a way the patient perceives as nonjudgmental and as guided by the patient's well-being and interests.

Specific forms of reality testing and re-education include bolstering impulse control, clarifying reality, and helping patients achieve a realistic appreciation of the impact of their behavior on others. For example, the therapist might offer suggestions about how to improve relations with family members.

In the following illustration, the therapist actively coaches the patient about how she might more effectively relate to her mother, with whom she has a problematic relationship.

Therapist: I think you're kind of coaching her how to make this a dignified trip for herself. She was embarrassed last time she was here.
Patient: Mm-hmm.
T: She wrote you a letter apologizing, thinking . . .
P: Right.
T: . . . she was embarrassed. You're helping her to maintain her dignity by being clear on her limits, taking a little break, a little time out, you know, and coming back. And if she acts like a martyr you can just be kind and generous like you're being, you know. Even though you're feeling guilty and depressed, you didn't say to her, "Oh no, Ma, please come." And you still were able to be generous enough to say, "I'll pick you up and take you back and you can come see the children." And you can continue to act in ways that show that she's hell-bent on a martyrdom but that you're not participating in it. Actually you're a wonderful daughter to her. You know, I was thinking about what you said— you're probably the best daughter she could have. Really, the best daughter she could have. She would be this way with any daughter.
P: Yeah, she would. I think that's true.

This therapist urges the patient not to feel responsible for her mother's suffering, and helps relieve her guilt,

strongly reassuring the patient that she is a good and loving daughter. She also offers direct suggestions about how
the patient might conduct herself with her mother.

In the next illustration, the therapist provides direct
advice concerning a problem that this same patient is experiencing with a daughter.

Therapist: I would ask her. I would take this as a very positive move of her [daughter] toward you. And try, when
you're with her, to think only of her. You're a really
good mother. You really are. Okay, and she needs you
to feel with her. Feel empathy and understand and be
really interested in what she's feeling. We can deal later
with how you feel about how she's feeling.

Patient: Yeah, yeah, yeah, okay.

T: Be real encouraging. I think this is very, very positive.
She is coming to you and wanting to talk. As far as
therapy goes, you could offer it to her and tell her if
she . . . how old is she?

P: Ten.

T: You know, this is related to the divorce and to this issue coming up with her father that she'd like to work
out. But if I were you, I would offer myself since she
brought the communication to you as the open, avid
listener and encourage her to be positive about her communication of this beautiful, sad, sad poem and encourage her sad feelings to come out if you can.

P: I will.

T: You know that children of divorce have a lot of strong
feelings that they, you know . . .

P: . . . don't, don't go away.

T: And if she's bringing them to you it's a very good sign.

P: Yeah, that's good, that's very good advice. Yeah, I'll do
   that.

   The therapist reassures the patient she is a good
mother, advises the patient to encourage her daughter to
talk to her about her troubles, and to listen to her daughter sympathetically without blaming herself for the difficulties created by a divorce the patient sought. The therapist
actively helps the patient to ward off her own pain and sadness ("We can deal later with how you are feeling"), which
will presumably allow her to be more responsive and empathic to her daughter. These last illustrations are good
examples of uninterpreted interaction structures and the use
of suggestive influence in which the therapist uses her authority to directly influence how the patient feels and con-
ducts herself in relation to her mother and her daughter.

Sharing Guilt

One important means by which supportive interventions,
and suggestion therapies more generally, function is by
allowing the sharing of guilt with the therapist, and by
relying on the therapist's more benign superego or moral
authority. In essence, the therapist suggests that the patient
become more tolerant of threatening or unpleasant
thoughts and feelings. The therapist's tolerant attitude gives
the patient permission to consciously experience some
threatening emotion or idea ("You can allow yourself to
experience your hostility"). The patient relies on the therapist as a nonaccusatory moral authority, a kind of auxiliary
superego that the patient borrows that is less harsh and
punitive. Patients are then able to share guilt with the
therapist and accept new or more adaptive symptoms or

strategies through identification with the therapist as a benign moral authority (Strachey 1934).

The following example, from a brief therapy for a patient suffering from a complicated grief reaction, illustrates a supportive intervention that eases the patient's guilt and self-punitive attitudes. There are unrealistic cultural expectations about recovery from the loss of a close loved one, and a corresponding minimizing of the painful working through that is required. The patient's husband of many years has recently died, and she is feeling troubled and guilty about the emotions she is now feeling. The therapist attempts to help the patient accept her feelings, in part by "normalizing" the patient's painful emotional reactions to her husband's death, including her suicidal thoughts and her murderous impulses toward her daughter, about which the patient feels extremely guilty. The therapist allows the patient to use his own benign, nonjudgmental authority to ease the patient's self-recrimination and related self-punitive and self-destructive thoughts.

Patient: Whenever I think of dying myself, the thing that I'd trip over was my daughter. And I found myself beginning to have fantasies that something had happened to her, and my fantasies would always be just of the worst sort of . . . horrible . . . things. You know, kidnapped by a maniac who does horrible things and ends up killing her—that kind of stuff—which would *leave me free.* Not only would leave me free, but would be one more enormous reason why life would be so painful that I could just end it all. And those fantasies are just so horrible, and felt like such a punishment of myself in some way that I stopped those.

Therapist: Uh-huh. Well, I'm sure you feel bad about those fantasies.

P: Uh-huh, oh yeah.

T: "That's horrible, that I have those kinds of thoughts," kind of feeling. But again, it's understandable that you feel that way.

P: Um-hmm.

T: Well, maybe we could try to look at that in a less judgmental way.

P: Yeah (*laughs*).

T: And try to understand what that's about. One of the things that you had told me was that you have been in a great deal of pain and suffering, and that at times you sort of felt suicidal.

P: Um-hmm.

T: And that the thing that stopped you was your commitment and love toward your daughter.

P: Uh-huh.

T: And at the same time you might have felt as though in a way she was trapping you into your pain in that way.

P: Yeah, sometimes she feels like a responsibility that I wish I didn't have.

T: So you might resent that.

P: The awful thing that I felt coming into my mind when I stopped the fantasies was, well I'll do something that will kill her and kill me at the same time, and that'll solve the problem. And I carried that around with me for a few days last week and finally admitted it to somebody. I mean, I recognize it as part of an emotional despair, not as something that I'm sitting down and thinking about how to do.

T: Uh-huh.

P: Still, that it should even go into my head feels ... I mean it's horrible, you know? It's something I know I'm not capable of doing, but that I would be burdened with that kind of a thought . . . it makes no sense! I mean, it just amazes me how far my own pain, and the idea that I could just simply wipe it all out, and that the only way that I can conceive of doing that is by dying. How far that would take me, you know.

T: Um-hmm. Well, that's a measure of how profound your pain is, rather than how evil a person you are to have such thoughts.

P: Yeah.

T: I think that gets confused in your mind. I think your pain is profound.

P: Uh-huh. Yeah.

T: So one gets into the kind of false logic of thinking that the only loving thing to do is to do . . . these horrible things.

P: Um-hmm. Yeah. (*sighs*) I guess what I'm feeling is that on top of all the other burdens I have in dealing with my loss, it seems too hard for me to also have to carry all this self-reproach and hatred for having all these thoughts. That's too much.

T: Yeah. You know, perhaps you need to be more accepting of yourself, and that this is an intense time.

P: Yeah. See those are also things that I don't burden myself with when I'm in a more accepting frame of mind about what the feelings are because A. [husband] died, no matter what they are. Being accepting of those means I don't have to take anything else on myself. It simplifies things a whole lot for me to just say, "Uh, yeah, I feel very badly and that's understandable."

The patient, through a process of identification with the therapist's tolerant attitude, begins to become less judgmental toward herself. She accepts, at least in part, the therapist's view that she is not evil, and complies with the therapist's admonition to become more accepting of herself.

T: Yeah. Well, that comes back to your wish for something like a widow's support group or an opportunity to find out from other people, other women perhaps . . .
P: Uh-huh.
T: . . . that they're having similar kinds of thoughts.
P: Hmm.
T: And that, you know, you're not all alone, and you're not crazy for having them. And that other people have these deeply troubled feelings, and I think they do.
P: Uh-huh.
T: I know they do from my experience in helping other people and so on.
P: Uh-huh.
T: And that one of the difficulties of your being in individual treatment here with me is the feeling that somehow that's a statement that this is . . . that your grief is wrong or pathological or something like that.
P: Yes.

The therapist relies on his authority as someone who has experience helping people with similar problems in suggesting to the patient she is not crazy or evil. The therapist then reinforces the patient's wish to join a support group for bereaved widows to help further with her guilt about her feelings. The group would presumably offer the patient an additional auxiliary superego that is less harsh and accusatory. The group would allow the patient to share her guilt by demonstrating to the patient that her feelings are not unusual, and she may then be able to feel less disturbed by them. Some patients may benefit from a grief group; others may not. A thoughtful assessment of the patient's needs, capacities, and conflicts should precede a recommendation of such support groups.

Reassurance

Reassurance is another common, yet deceptively simple, supportive strategy. Reassurance can be defined as the therapist making a direct effort to allay the patient's anxieties, and instill the hope that matters will improve: "Don't worry, your problems can be solved." Although therapists may intervene in a way that intends to be reassuring to the patient, the effect of reassurance can be complex. Patients may feel that the significance of their problems is dismissed or not really understood. Indeed, an attempt to reassure the patient may paradoxically increase the patient's anxiety. For example, a patient may worry about how well he will perform on an upcoming examination. The therapist reassures him that because he has studied so diligently, he will surely succeed. Although the patient consciously wishes to do well, the therapist's reassurance may stimulate his unconscious worries about competing successfully, or the patient may fear he will disappoint the therapist if he does not do well.

Reassurance can also be defined as not challenging the patient's particular perceptions of a relationship, or a situation that serves an important defensive function. This is an interactive conceptualization of reassurance. The therapist acts in a way the patient wants the therapist to act as, for example, an accommodation to the subtle but sometimes powerful pressure or invitation to enact a benign tolerant relationship. The patient's wish to reassure himself can appear in many forms, including the need to perceive the therapist as a certain kind of person, for example, kind and permissive or critical and demanding, and needing to maintain a certain kind of relationship (Feldman 1997).

In the following illustration, the patient is talking about what she thinks was her father's punitive response to her having a boyfriend at age 16, when she was sent off to boarding school. This vignette could be interpreted as the patient attempting to reassure herself that she is not a bad, immoral person. The therapist takes the role of standing up for the patient, protecting her from this internal accusation, and helps externalize the charge of immorality onto the patient's father. The therapist can also be seen as reassuring himself by being a certain way that is consistent with a version of himself with which he is relatively comfortable.

Patient: I'm confused as to what extent . . . this sort of unhealthy stuff going on in my family accounted for my being punished, and to what extent that would have happened in nine out of ten families, because that was the accepted thing.

Therapist: You're protecting him, completely.

P: You don't think that would have happened?

T: That's ridiculous!

P: I guess in a way I do think that in religious families, that sex was a punished thing. I mean you got punished for it. But I don't have a religious family. (*laughs*)

T: And your father was not a moral man.

P: No, he wasn't.

T: He was having affairs with women in your mother's bed.

P: Yeah, I know it doesn't exactly fit.

T: No.

P: I think maybe at the time I thought it made sense.

T: Right. This is a very benevolent interpretation of your father.

P: Mm-hmm.

T: I mean, this borders on being completely ridiculous.

P: Mm-hmm.

T: Because here is this raging alcoholic [patient's father], at the time, who is behaving in such a way that important people in the town are removing their children from your presence, because of this behavior. They feel terrible about it; he's behaving scandalously with women inside your mother's house. There is not an ounce of morality in this; it's all insane possessiveness.

The therapist becomes the patient's champion against her self-recrimination and guilt about her sexual feelings, and helps her externalize her bad feelings onto her father. It is a reassurance that consists of reducing the patient's anxiety by emphasizing and making central a version of the patient, her object (father), and their relationship that has been achieved through the externalization of disturbing elements of herself. It was the patient's father, not the patient, who engaged in sexually immoral behavior. The therapist may be under considerable conscious and unconscious pressure to participate in this. The patient's projections (e.g., of a harsh, punitive parent) can mobilize anxieties and conflicts within the therapist (e.g., about being aggressive or judgmental). Moreover, therapists may also have their own reasons for wishing to disown self representations that are harsh, seductive, or ineffective, and to emphasize a self-image that is benign, loving, and helpful. The patient's projections and transference wishes may recruit the therapist's own difficulties, and lead to interventions that are reassuring to both. In this sense, supportive approaches, whether self-conscious and deliberate interventions or unconscious enactments, can be viewed as transference–countertransference interactions (see Chapter 5).

Supportive approaches can be enormously useful if they are applied in a deliberate and thoughtful manner. Most treatments require supportive interventions by the therapist at some point, and to some degree. It is, however, easy for many therapists to overlook the very real limitations of supportive, helping interventions. Seemingly simple supportive interventions, such as advice, reassurance, encouragement, or suggestions about how to conduct family relations, can be used defensively, and can be expressions of unacknowledged interaction structures that actualize unconscious forces at play between patient and therapist. In these interactions, the therapist usually assumes a more authoritative, less collaborative stance. The therapist's understanding is limited by a more psychologically defended interaction, and it is more difficult for both therapist and patient to become aware of significant aspects of their interaction and their inner experience in relation to each other. The therapist's knowledge of the patient is less complete, and is necessarily based on a greater degree of inference.

In contrast, in analytic approaches, there is an emphasis on understanding the therapist–patient relationship. The extent to which the patient becomes aware of a distinction between his fantasy object and the real external object in a sense defines the extent to which the intervention is insight oriented rather than supportive. Insight-oriented approaches yield ever-increasing knowledge about patients, and the nature of their defensive processes, mental representations, quality of object relations, and the meanings of the therapist–patient interaction. This knowledge emerges in a manner that can be consensually validated between therapist and patient, and can ultimately lead the patient to a greater capacity for self-reflection and sense of agency and autonomy.

7

Studying Psychoanalytic Therapy

Formal research in psychoanalysis and psychotherapy is difficult to pursue because of the problems in operationally defining and quantifying clinical psychoanalytic constructs. How does one define and measure unconscious processes, defenses, transferences, or changes in patients' capacity for intimate relationships? The research strategy described in this chapter offers answers to some of these problems, and allays doubts about the potential value of empirical research on psychanalytic therapy. This chapter describes a model for single-case quantitative research that is the basis for the interaction structure construct. The model uses information derived from the therapist–patient interaction over the course of a therapy, and offers the potential for planned, systematic research through the replication of findings over a succession of individual treatment cases.

How Should Analytic Therapies Be Studied?

Many psychoanalytic clinicians remain unaware that since the 1940s there have been perhaps as many as two thousand controlled experiments, mostly conducted by psychologists, attempting to determine the validity of psychoanalytic concepts (see Hornstein 1992). Although a good deal of this research seems to support psychoanalytic constructs, much of the content of these laboratory-based, experimental studies bears only a distant relation to what psychoanalysts have demonstrated in clinical work, for example, the use of subliminal stimuli to evoke libidinal and aggressive wishes in study subjects.

Formal quantitative research that has attempted to assess the effectiveness of psychoanalytically based treatments has similarly seemed removed from important questions of theory and technique. Randomized clinical trials have been touted as the "gold standard" for research that attempts to demonstrate the effectiveness of psychotherapy. Such studies contrast a treatment to a comparison group under controlled conditions. These conditions include (1) patients meet criteria for a single *DSM-IV* diagnosis; (2) patients are randomly assigned to the treatment and the control conditions; (3) patients are seen for a specified number of treatment sessions, usually an average of sixteen hours; (4) therapies are conducted according to a treatment manual, and therapist adherence to the manual is monitored using videotaped sessions; and (5) the criteria for successful outcome are clearly spelled out, for example, a particular score on a depression self-report inventory, or a decrease in the number of dysfunctional cognitions.

Several controlled studies have in fact demonstrated the benefits of short-term psychodynamic therapies (Crits-Christoph and Connolly 1998). However, there have been very few outcome studies of longer-term therapies, and it is difficult to imagine the controlled clinical trials paradigm being realistically applied to the study of analytic therapies. What patient, for example, would be willing to be assigned to a waiting list or placebo condition for months or even years so that researchers could maintain the necessary control condition? The limitations of controlled outcome studies have, as well, become more apparent (Seligman 1995).

Such studies are conducted with carefully selected patients, while possible subjects who have multiple (or comorbid) diagnoses or have not been treated effectively in previous studies are screened out. Most patients seen by analytic therapists have multiple, often related, problems, and many of our therapy patients have been treated by other means, including medication, without success. In real-life settings, moreover, the goals of therapy include not only symptomatic relief, but also improvement in general functioning, the sense of well-being, the quality of personal relations, self-understanding or personal growth, and structural or personality change. In naturalistic settings, therapists shift their approach or technique flexibly according to the patient's needs, rather than adhering to a fixed application of manualized procedures. In short, the generalizability of the results of randomized clinical trials to actual, realistic clinical conditions is very limited. As a consequence, there lingers an understandable skepticism about the value of quantitative research within the psychoanalytic tradition and its potential for meaningful contribution to psychoanalytic theory and practice. Indeed, some therapists question the relevance of the research enterprise altogether, noting that much of what occurs in psychoanalytic treatments is unconscious and cannot be effectively operationalized and measured. They feel that any attempt to quantify clinically and theoretically significant constructs inevitably distorts them to the point of unrecognizability (Green 1996).

Many analytic clinicians no longer share this extreme view. They are nevertheless unsatisfied with studies of psychodynamic treatment outcome aimed at determining whether analytic approaches yield measurable therapeutic effects. There is a greater interest in understanding *how* psychoanalytic therapies work by examining the process that underlies therapeutic change. If psychoanalytic research is to move forward, it must be firmly grounded in the phenomena considered important to the analytic clinicians. Some critics of psychoanalysis (e.g., Grünbaum 1984) have asserted that clinical data derived from the consulting room, which are usually in the form of process notes, are not useful for establishing the validity of psychoanalytic ideas because the data are likely to be contaminated by suggestion, circular reasoning, and theoretical preference. However, valid data can be acquired by means of audio-recording therapy sessions. Tests of psychoanalytic hypotheses outside the treatment situation, or those limited to controlled clinical trials and experimental studies, do not permit study of those aspects of the theory that are related to the immediate clinical situation, such as interaction structures, transference-countertransference, containment, or intersubjectivity. Psychoanalytic practice is the crucial place in which proof of its explanatory theories must be derived. There is an emerging consensus about the central importance of clinical data, or data derived from the therapeutic process, for the study of psychoanalytic hypotheses because they are the necessary, ecologically valid context for meaningful inquiry.

The Psychotherapy Process Q-set

To use clinical data to test psychoanalytic constructs, it is necessary to first establish that certain kinds of observable phenomena co-occur, and then assess the strength of their relationship. Clinical phenomena must be intersubjectively observable, which is to say that different judges can independently agree about whether they occur and about their characteristics. Disagreements about the interpretation or meaning of the same case material are commonplace in clinical work, and constitute important grounds for criticism about the scientific status of psychoanalytic methods for acquiring knowledge. It is crucial that any research methodology establish the extent of consensus among judges about the presence and nature of a clinical phenomenon, that is, establish reliability. It seemed that the direct study of the analytic process would be aided by a comprehensive classification system, a method that would describe and define process and that would form the basis for an observationally grounded research. After much thought about what should constitute such a system, and according to what principles it should be constructed, I developed the Psychotherapy Process Q-set (PQS) (see Appendix) to provide a basic language for the description and classification of intervention processes in a form suitable for quantitative analysis.

The method is designed to be applied to an audio- or video-taped record or verbatim transcript of treatment sessions. In clinical data recorded by conventional means (process notes and case reports), what is retained is selective. It is often impossible to discern what the data are and on what data the inferences are based. Accurate and reliable records of the therapist's and patient's utterances are essential in attaining intersubjective agreement about processes that require inference. Recordings also have the enormous advantage of opening the door of "privileged access" to psychoanalytic data and fulfilling the cardinal requirement of science: publicly verifiable data.

The PQS comprises 100 items describing patient attitudes, behaviors, or experience; the therapist's actions and attitudes; and the nature of their interaction. A coding manual (see Appendix) provides the items and their definitions along with examples to minimize potentially varying interpretations. After studying a record of a treatment

session, clinical judges proceed to the ordering of the 100
PQS items, each printed separately on cards to permit easy
arrangement and rearrangement. The items are sorted into
nine piles ranging on a continuum from least characteristic (category 1) to most characteristic (category 9). The
number of cards sorted into each pile (ranging from 5 at
the extremes to 18 in the middle or neutral category) con-
forms to a normal distribution, which requires judges to
make multiple evaluations among items, thus avoiding either positive or negative halo effects. The special value of
the Q-method is that it provides a way of quantifying the
qualities of the analytic or therapeutic process, and can
capture the uniqueness of each session while also permit-
ting the assessment of the similarities or dissimilarities between sessions and patients (see Block 1961). The instrument addresses key questions concerning unit of analysis,
content and coverage, questions of sampling, the use of
inference, and the role of theoretical perspective (see Jones
et al. 1991). Q-methodology (among other sophisticated
techniques now available) addresses the long-standing problem of how to achieve agreement about the nature of clinical phenomena, and judgments requiring relatively high
levels of inference can now be made reliably.

The PQS and the Unit of Observation

In process research, the question arises as to what time
frame or segment should be studied. A self-evident characteristic of the ongoing therapy process is that it has a temporal sequence, or "stream," that consists of the interdepen-
dent and meaningful relation between the actions and
intentions of therapist and patient. The usual approach for
taking into account time and rendering it amenable to

study is to restrain it through some form of sampling. The sampling may consist of arbitrary time periods, such as 10-minute segments, or specific behaviors or events that constitute a theoretically linked phase. It has become increasingly clear that aggregate data analyses that use rates, frequencies, or ratios of units across time segments (e.g., 5-minute segments within a session or across several sessions) without consideration of meaningful factors of context and timing cannot capture change processes. Aggregations obliterate the context; it is more the patterning of variables than their simple concurrence that indicates their significance as therapeutic process. With the Q-technique, an entire session, not just a small segment, is rated. The therapy hour might be termed a "natural" time frame; it is a segment of time that has practical utility for researchers as well as inherent meaning for therapists and patients.

What should be the unit selected for study—interpretations, dreams, or turns of speech? In process research there are potentially as many different units of observation as there are theoretical or empirical constructs, and each may require a different kind of measurement. The choice of level or unit of analysis refers to the degree of generality or specificity. If one selects a grain of analysis that is too fine, there is a risk of separating variables that function together, the "artificial untying of variables"; likewise too global a level of analysis may lead the investigator to make the error of the "artificial tying of variables," where variables are clumped together that do not occur together in the phenomenon under study. The unit chosen, whether a symptom, for example, Luborsky's (1967) "momentary forgetting" or a "patient test" (Weiss and Sampson 1986), depends on the construct or the particular research question being investigated. The "therapeutic alliance" construct, for example, refers to a wide range of therapist and patient behaviors and is at a general level of analysis, while a turn of speech is relatively specific.

Most observational systems have involved ratings of relatively narrower dimensions of process that are tied to particular theoretical constructs, for example, transference interpretations. Our own studies have shown the value of measuring multiple interventions and interactions of the kind contained in the PQS in revealing clinically meaningful patterns or configurations. In one study of brief psychotherapy of patients suffering from posttraumatic stress responses and complicated grief reactions, a therapeutic process emphasizing evocation of the patient's feelings, the linking of memories with current experience, the examination of views of the self in relation with others, and the frequent use of transference interpretations was associated with successful outcomes in less disturbed patients. In contrast, patients who suffered greater psychological distress were helped more by therapists who provided encouragement, reassurance, and advice about reality-based problems, and who supported patients' defenses (Jones et al. 1988). In another study comparing brief psychodynamic and cognitive therapies, we demonstrated that the extent to which each of these very different treatment approaches contained elements of psychodynamic technique (e.g., emphasis on affective experience, interpretation of unconscious wishes and ideas, interpretation of defenses, and attending to the therapist–patient interaction during treatment sessions) was consistently associated with positive outcome in both therapy modalities (Ablon and Jones 1998, Jones and Pulos 1993). The PQS has been able to provide difficult-to-obtain confirmation of the usefulness of technique derived from psychoanalytic principles by studying the patterning of many different aspects of process.

The PQS and Single-Case Research

Research strategies relying on group data have significant limitations as a means for assessing patient change. Process research that derives its data from samples of patients and therapists rests on two assumptions: (1) that the interpersonal processes that occur have fixed meanings that are context independent; and (2) that such processes discretely and uniquely contribute to outcomes. An illustration will help clarify this problem. It has been argued by some theorists (e.g., Malan 1976) that the frequency of transference interpretations in brief, psychodynamic psychotherapy is related to outcome. This is a classic example of a "decontextualized" conception of process, in which all transference interpretations are assumed to have a fixed meaning, that is, the same significance regardless of accuracy, timing, or importance, and that they contribute to patient change in a direct way regardless of what else is occurring between therapist and patient. There are problems with framing the hypothesis in this fashion, since it assumes that an isomorphism exists between outcome and the relative frequency of a particular therapist intervention. However, therapists may interpret the transference relatively infrequently, but when they do, it may have an important impact. In this case, simply counting the relative frequency of specific therapist actions in samples of treatments will not allow us to detect any relationship to patient change. Each therapeutic technique or action derives its meaning only from the impact it has on the ongoing therapist–patient interaction. The context-determined meaning of events makes it difficult to identify simple, direct associations between particular therapist actions or patient behaviors and treatment outcomes in group data or samples of treatments.

Studies of the analytic or therapeutic process, which remain closer to the subjective experience of therapist and patient and retain a complexity of context, are more likely to yield useful findings. The PQS, which can be effectively applied in single-case research designs as well as in studies of samples of patients, can take into account the interaction of multiple influences in psychoanalytic treatments. Specific processes are conceptualized as simultaneously and conjointly defining the meaning of an event; one element becomes more fully understood in relation to others. Within this framework any given interaction is best understood when viewed within a sequence of actions that extends over time. A longitudinal approach, that is, one that takes into account time, context, and the effect of previous sessions on subsequent events in therapy, then becomes a natural framework for the study of process. Therapy process is then studied as interrelated configurations or patterns of relationships (or Q-items) along temporal dimensions.

It is here that single-case research, which more naturally captures the context in which therapist and patient actions occur, has important advantages. The primary means of clinical inquiry, teaching, and learning has been, and still remains, the case study method, grounded in the tradition of naturalistic observation. Statements about psychotherapy that are derived from group data typically have little direct relevance for the clinical problems that are presented to the psychotherapist. In fact, many analysts implicitly view their clinical work as scientific, as a form of single-case research, and are not fully aware of its limits as a methodology. There are, however, long-recognized difficulties in using data from the clinical psychoanalytic method for hypothesis testing or the verification of clinical constructs: the problem of assessing the reliability of case study data, that is, the manner in which observations are selected and recorded; the difficulty in choosing among alternative interpretations of the same observations; the sources of uncontrolled variation; the problems in comparing one case study to another; and the difficulty in replication. These limitations have led to a widely shared view among researchers that the single-case study is important primarily as a source of new information, or as the basis of a new principle and as an illustration of an approach—in short, for hypothesis generation rather than testing.

Advances in quantitative methodology in single-case research has led to a resurgence of interest in single-case designs. In fact, almost all of the research on psychoanalytic process has used one or another kind of single-case methodology. Most criticisms of single-case research apply to the uncontrolled, informal case study, and it is important to distinguish between these and the more formal and systematic study of the individual case. Single-case research can be considered a subclass of intrasubject research that avoids averaging across cases. A factor (e.g., the analyst's interpretive activity) will fluctuate or vary; such a variable can only take one value or score at a specific point in time, and repeated measures of the variable(s) over time are conducted. This approach, then, involves the repeated measure of a set of variables over time within the individual case, and focuses on the temporal unfolding or change of these variables and the attempt to understand this change as a function of other variables. The Berkeley Psychotherapy Research Project has developed methodologies that might be termed "single-case quantitative analysis"; they use longitudinal analysis of data derived from observer-based ratings of audio- and video-recorded process.

In an initial study of psychoanalytic process using the PQS, the audio-recorded sessions of the oft-studied six-year analysis of Mrs. C were transcribed, and blocks of ten sessions were selected at regular intervals throughout the course of the analysis (see Chapter 1). Transcripts of these sessions were then rated in random fashion by clinical judges with the Q-set. The resulting Q-data provided a chronicle of the course of the analysis based on reliable descriptive categories and showed striking changes over time on different sets of Q-sort ratings. Over the years the patient's discourse was less intellectualized and dominated by rationalization, and increasingly reflected greater access to her emotional life and her developing capacity for free association. The data also allowed us to characterize particular stages in the analysis, and in the later phase captured the resolution of transference resistances, signaled by the patient's greater openness about her desires and fantasies, including sexual desires and the need for intimacy, as well as a significant alleviation of the patient's long-standing feelings of inadequacy, guilt, and anxiety.

Single-Case Research: Causal Effects and Generalizability

A limitation of this initial study was that it did not provide evidence of causal relationships. The data were silent on the question of to what these evident changes in the analytic process and in the patient might be attributed. A skeptic could argue that these changes could have resulted simply from the passage of time. One of the crucial problems for psychoanalysis as scientific endeavor is identifying causality. Testing hypotheses about causal relations in analytic process can contribute to verifying or refuting broad psychoanalytic principles. Q-sort ratings of the analytic process in the single case can be studied over time in ways that begin to identify causal relations. Establishing the facts of chronology is especially important in demonstrating causality effect. Quantitative analyses that make use of temporal sequence include time-series analysis, or sequential analysis (see Chapter 8).

In a second study of the Mrs. C case (Spence et al. 1993), time-series analysis was used to attempt to identify causal relations. The transcripts of the analytic sessions were scored by computer with a measure of free association based on the co-occurrence of words that are highly associated in normal language usage. Findings showed that the analyst's interpretations had a greater influence on the associative structure of the patient's language in the latter phase of treatment. Using the Q-items that scored the analyst's activity, it could then be demonstrated that particular categories of intervention, such as interpretation of defenses, identification of a recurrent theme in the material, and discussion of dream or fantasy material, led to an increase in the patient's associative freedom, and that this effect carried over into at least the following three analytic sessions. Using time-series analysis, it is possible to look at delayed effects. Such findings may be relevant to the question of whether more frequent sessions are more effective than fewer, since the former tends to facilitate more continuity in treatment, and provide for greater delayed effects.

Time-series analysis stands in contrast to the more usual procedure in therapy process research of segmenting a record of the process, usually transcripts of therapy sessions, into sections of comparable length. In that method, the conjunction of two purportedly causal events is identified. Luborsky's (1967) symptom context method, for example, identifies the relationship of the occurrence of a symptom and its determinant; Weiss and Sampson (1986) use the critical events approach, selecting patient transference "tests," and the patient's subsequent reaction to the therapist's response to such tests. The idea is to identify the co-occurrence of two phenomena of interest by extracting samples of segments representing the two events. If a time-bound association between the two can be demonstrated by contrasting these to randomly selected segments, this association may constitute evidence for a causal relationship. This strategy of replication through segmentation has the difficulty of missing processes that change at a slower rate. It has the additional limitation of overlooking reciprocal influence, that is, the patient's influence on the therapist's attitude and behavioral response. Time-series approaches preserve the sequential dependencies in the analytic process and can identify relationships over a long period of time.

Time-series analysis can be used to study the relations between many kinds of variables within a single analyst–patient dyad. Briefly summarized, it examines the causal relation between one series of data points (e.g., scores on a dimension of therapy process, such as a class of interventions [series A]) and a second series (e.g., a measure of the patient's affective state [series B]) that have been collected over a period of time, say during the course of an analysis. Time series requires data to be extracted at equal intervals over a relatively large number of measurement occasions (minimum $N = 50$). The essential idea is to first control for the correlation inherent in the repeated measure of any variable, and then apply a model to determine whether series A can predict series B. The time-series analysis of single-case data could then provide evidence of causal relationships in the therapy process by demonstrating that we can reduce the uncertainty in predicting the patient's affective states (B) from a knowledge of the therapist's past activity (A), over and above our ability to predict simply from the patient's past affective states (see Gottman 1981, for a discussion of the more technical aspects of this approach).

In a further application of time-series analysis in single-case research, we began to study bidirectional effects. The conventional manner of studying process attempts to identify the ways in which therapist actions or techniques influence patient change. Causal influences are assumed to flow principally in one direction. In one study (see Chapter 8), a patient suffering from a severe depression was seen in a twice-weekly psychoanalytic therapy for two-and-a-half years. Each session was audio- and videotaped, and assessments of patient change were obtained at regular intervals; videotapes of therapy sessions were Q-sorted in random order. We applied a form of sequential analysis that can also capture processes in which causality is reciprocal rather than unidirectional. This analysis of causal effects in therapy showed that therapist and patient mutually influence one another. Our data showed that during the early phase of the treatment, the therapist was neutral, facilitative, and nonjudgmental. As the treatment continued, the patient's self-punitiveness and depressive affect seems to have gradually drawn the therapist toward a more actively challenging and emotionally reactive and involved posture. This change in the nature of the process was predictive of the patient's gradual reduction in symptom level. Such findings provided formal evidence for the validity of the interaction structure construct. Chapter 8 provides further examples of this strategy for studying psychoanalytic therapies.

Newer theories about the psychoanalytic process have begun to emphasize an interactional perspective, that is, an appreciation of mutual influence processes between analyst and patient. The recognition of reciprocal influence would move closer to contemporary interactive conceptions of process, which emphasize the subjective experience of the therapist and related notions about enactments. It is consistent, too, with the current greater attentiveness to countertransference and the role of the analyst's emotional interaction with the patient, both unconscious as well as intentional, in the change process. In time series and other sequential models, the influence of patient characteristics and behavior on the therapist, on the therapy relationship, and on the evolving process can also be identified and assessed, offering a more adequate research model for psychoanalytic therapies.

An important criticism of single-case research is that its results are not generalizable. This view reflects a lack of understanding about the inferential possibilities offered by single-case data. Chassan (1979), among others, has argued that the intensive study of the single case can provide more operationally meaningful information that has more direct implications for analysis and psychotherapy than observations extended over a relatively large number of patients. The heterogeneity of characteristics in larger samples and the reliance on averages results in a lack of specificity and a vagueness about patient characteristics and other variables from which inferences are drawn. Applying findings derived from group data directly to the individual case violates the logic of inference.

A single-case research model, based on frequent observations of the individual patient over longer periods, addresses some of these limitations. It attempts to establish the generality of its findings through replication on a case-by-case basis rather than through group averages. A focus on the variability within the analytic dyad is the very core of process research. Establishing the presence of certain patterns or configurations of variability across a series of cases would begin to form the basis for generalizability. The scientific base for clinical psychoanalysis would be greatly strengthened by a programmatic research effort that attempts to replicate findings over a succession of studies of individual cases.

Summary

The complex processes of psychoanalytic treatments are more validly and usefully captured in the formal, quantitative study of the single case than in experimental or other means that do not derive data from the consulting room. Sophisticated descriptive coding systems, such as the Psychotherapy Process Q-set, now make it possible to achieve agreement among clinical judges about the nature of clinical phenomena. Accurate and reliable records of therapists' and patients' speech, in the form of verbatim recordings, are essential in attaining agreement about clinical processes that require inference. This makes it necessary to introduce research procedures into psychoanalytic treatments.

Single-case quantitative research has the unique potential for studying change and variability within the individual patient. Single-case research models are closer to traditional methods of psychoanalytic investigation, and are likely to have more direct relevance to theoretical questions as well as to clinical practice. Research on the single case is more scientifically persuasive if certain features are included in its design. First, such studies should use methods such as the PQS that can track and quantify various aspects of the interaction, so that the effect of multiple influences in analytic process can be taken into account. Second, they should be longitudinal, following the process over longer periods of the treatment, so that relationships developing over longer periods of time and processes that change slowly can be identified. In addition, if such models are interactional, they can potentially identify reciprocal influence processes between patient and therapist. Finally, such research should be programmatic, that is, represent an organized, systematic attempt to replicate findings over a number of individual cases. Intensive, quantitative studies of individual psychoanalytic treatments are more likely to uncover causal links that could verify or refute competing theories about how the therapy process effects change.

8

Case Studies

Studying How Patients Change in Therapy

The interaction structure construct introduced in earlier chapters emphasizes the presence and meaning of repetitive patterns of interaction in the therapy relationship. It is a theory about therapeutic action that attempts to address the roles of both psychological knowledge through uncovering meaning and interpersonal interaction in patient change. Patient and therapist interact in ways that are repetitive and mutually influencing. These patterns of interaction likely reflect the psychological structure of both patient and therapist, whether psychic structure is conceptualized in terms of object representations or compromise formations and impulse-defense configurations. It is not assumed that influence flows only in the direction of therapist to patient. Instead, the nature of the patient's influence on the therapist and on the emerging patterns of relationship are considered along with the manner in which the therapist's interventions influence patient change, providing a framework in which mutual or reciprocal influence processes between patient and therapist can be taken into account. Interaction structures allow the consideration of both the intrapsychic and interpersonal by recognizing that what is internal is an important basis for what becomes manifest in the interpersonal or interactive field. Interaction structures refer not only to how the patient's conflicts are represented in the transference, but also to the characteristic manner in which the therapist reacts to these conflicts. These patterns of interaction are the observable behavioral and emotional components of the transference-countertransference. While more than one such interaction structure may occur in a therapist–patient pair, one dominant pattern usually emerges.

This chapter describes a study of the psychotherapies of three patients diagnosed as suffering from major depressive disorder. The aim was to identify the presence of interaction structures and to determine how they might be causally linked to patient change. These cases were selected because they had contrasting outcomes: two had a successful outcome and in the third the patient reported only modest change. The research questions were threefold: (1) Were there meaningful structures of therapist–patient interaction? (2) Did these structures differ across the three treatments? and (3) How are changes in structures of interaction associated with patient improvement?

Interaction structures can play a mutative role through several modes. The first case, Ms. A, represents a mode of therapeutic action in which repetitive, mutually influencing interactions facilitate the patient's experience and representation of certain mental states and the knowledge of her own intentionality. These slow-to-change patterns of interaction, which therapist and patient gradually come to understand, are the expressions of the transference and countertransference. When the therapist can bring unconscious countertransference associations and reactions into awareness, this may also bring them, along with the patient's transference reactions, into a mutual sphere of consciousness that the patient alone can not do. In this mode of therapeutic action, insight and relationship are inseparable, since psychological knowledge of the self develops in the context of a relationship with a therapist who endeavors to understand the mind of the patient through the medium of their interaction.

In the second case, Mr. B, significant repetitive therapist–patient interactions remained uninterpreted, not understood, and outside of explicit awareness. This interaction pattern, whose meaning was not sufficiently understood and interpreted, served as an impediment to Mr. B's greater self-knowledge and understanding, obstructed progress in the treatment, and led to what appeared to be a therapeutic stalemate. However, interaction patterns that remain unacknowledged and not interpreted do not necessarily signal that therapy is not helpful to the patient. Uninterpreted interaction patterns can in and of themselves have a supportive function. For example, a patient could rely on the therapist's accepting, nonjudgmental attitude to ward off harshly self-punitive introjects, relieve guilt, and bolster a threatened self-regard. Whenever the patient becomes caught up in irrational self-blame, the therapist, through his attitude and interventions, repeatedly conveys that the patient is not the worthless person she feels herself to be. However, the therapist does not interpret the patient's need to rely on him for this important function, and this vital interaction and its meaning is not understood. The patient, for example, can remain unaware of a wish to treat others cruelly, and the therapist can fulfill the need to see himself as a compassionate rescuer. The interaction structure construct implies that the therapist is not simply deliberately and self-consciously providing the patient with an experience that is new and contrary to the response the patient has come to expect (a corrective emotional experience). It implies, in addition, that the therapist is also involving him- or herself in a partially unconscious transference–countertransference interaction pattern.

Interaction structures that remain uninterpreted and outside of awareness may not necessarily serve only a defensive function. There may be a means through which unacknowledged interaction structures can also promote patient change in a way that modifies psychic structure. The third case, Ms. M, represents this mode of therapeutic action. In this mode, unconscious interaction patterns are mutative by creating opportunities for the modification of the patient's problematic mental representations of self and others that had been largely outside of consciousness. Certain kinds of uninterpreted transference–countertransference interactions, despite remaining unacknowledged, nevertheless seemed to promote this patient's capacity for self-reflection and insight into certain aspects of her mental life. In the case of Ms. M, much of the work of therapy occurred, at least explicitly, outside the transference–countertransference matrix.

The Study Design

Studying psychoanalytic constructs requires innovative research strategies, particularly new quantitative methods for the study of single cases. The renewed interest in research case studies has been prompted by a confluence of several influences in clinical practice and research. First, there has been a growing recognition that controlled clinical trials (in which patients are randomly assigned to types of treatment and therapists) do not inform us about *how* patients change. Understanding the processes that promote therapeutic change requires a close analysis of the therapist–patient interactions. A second reason is the need to test clinical theoretical models. Although comparative treatment outcome studies can confirm the efficacy of the treatments under investigation, the value of such studies for testing the treatment models' underlying clinical constructs is indirect and limited. Treatment research has had little influence on either psychoanalytic theory building or clinical practices. Statements about psychotherapy that are derived from group data typically have little direct relevance for the clinical problems that are presented to analytic therapists, so that much of the therapy research enterprise has remained peripheral to clinical practice and to the major theoretical and intellectual currents in psychoanalysis.

Chapter 7 described a longitudinal model for the study of single cases using quantitative methods while retaining clinical relevance. This research applies an innovative set of methods in intensive single-case designs to identify the presence of interaction structures and to determine how they are linked to patient change. The strategy is to focus on patterns of therapist–patient interaction within and across therapy sessions and to explore their association with patient change. Specific processes are viewed as conjointly defining the meaning of an event; one element (e.g., transference interpretation) becomes more fully understood in relation to others. Therapy process is considered as a sequence of actions and events that extend over time.

Assessing Therapy Outcome

The three treatments studied were conducted as part of an investigation of longer-term psychotherapies for major depressive disorder. Patients referred to the study were assessed through the following intake procedure: (1) a videotaped semistructured interview based on the Schedule for Affective Disorders and Schizophrenia (SADS-I; Endicott and Spitzer 1977) and resulting in a Research Diagnostic Criteria (RDC) diagnosis (Spitzer et al. 1979); (2) a second, 90-minute videotaped life-history interview covering areas of distress and symptomatology, current life circumstances, and history of interpersonal relationships; and (3) a battery of pretherapy self-report measures. Patients met the following inclusion criteria: (1) a definite diagnosis of major depressive disorder on the RDC; (2) a score of 16 or higher on the Beck Depression Inventory[1] (BDI; Beck et al. 1961); and (3) a score of 14 or higher on the Hamilton Rating Scale for Depression (HRSD; Hamilton 1967). Therapies were conducted over a two- to two-and-a-half-year period, twice weekly; all treatment hours were video and audio recorded. Assessments were conducted every sixteen sessions. Follow-up assessments were conducted, when possible, at six months and one and two years posttreatment in order to track whether levels of improvement remained stable. Therapists were experienced practitioners, whose routine and preferred approach to treatment was longer-term psychoanalytic psychotherapy.

The assessment of change in psychotherapy has focused almost exclusively on the measurement of symptomatic improvement. However, for most psychoanalytically oriented clinicians, an important goal is change in *psychological structure*, that is, long-term symptom relief coupled with enduring change in the patient's mental functioning and personality. Psychological structure has been variously defined. It has been used to refer to the structural model of the mind; to impulse-defense configurations; to the grouping and organization of functions that lead to object-

and self-constancy, which serve the regulation of relationships and sense of self; to unconscious fantasies and wishes (e.g., structures of meaning); to core conflicts; and to changes in the level of organization of internalized object relations as reflected in transference manifestations (Kernberg 1988). In this study, changes in patients' psychological structure were assessed using the Structural Analysis of Social Behavior measure (SASB; Benjamin 1993), which captures mental representations of self and other. With the SASB, patients are asked to rate items for applicability to themselves at their best and worst, and their relationship with important others at their best and worst. Respondents are then classified along two basic dimensions of control and affiliation. Depressed patients tend to have high scores for self-punitive, attacking, and controlling introjects (Jones 1998) on the SASB.

Constructing Case Formulations

Disagreement about the validity of differing psychodynamic formulations of the same case material are commonplace in clinical work, and constitute important grounds for criticism about the scientific nature of clinical psychoanalytic methods for acquiring knowledge. It is crucial that any research methodology establish the extent of consensus, or reliability, among judges about the nature of a clinical formulation. To summarize each case in a reliable way, we used a method based on agreement among a set of clinical judges to construct case formulations. After the three treatments had been completed, several psychoanalytic clinicians viewed the 90-minute intake interviews of the patients and were asked to create a case formulation for each. They were blind to treatment outcome and had no other

information about the case beyond that contained in the
initial interview. Using a variant of Caston's (1993) consensus method for developing case formulations, the clinical
judges were asked to group their inferences about the case
in five theoretically relevant domains: (1) conflictedness,
(2) defense-impulse configurations, (3) historical anteced-
ents, (4) wishes, and (5) transference. The resulting array of
clinical propositions about the case generated by each judge
was then divided into thought units and listed. Only those
propositions that appeared in the material of a majority of
the judges were included in the case formulations, which are
rendered in narrative form below. This method provides the
basis for consensually derived case formulations.

Studying the Therapy Process

The Psychotherapy Process Q-set (PQS; see Chapter 7 and
Appendix), constructed to provide a basic language and
rating procedure to describe therapy process in a form
suitable for statistical analysis, was used to rate the videotaped therapy sessions. Raters were a group of research-
oriented clinicians and advanced graduate students in
clinical psychology who received training in the application of the Q-sort method. Videotapes of the three cases
were completely randomized, and independent Q-ratings
were made by two judges who were blind to one another's
ratings; when agreement was below .50, a third rater was
added. Interrater reliability was calculated using the
Pearson product-moment correlation coefficient; average
interrater reliability achieved $r = .80$ (Spearman-Brown
corrected; range, .66 to .94). Q-sort composites (i.e., Q-
ratings averaged across judges) were used in all subsequent analyses.

A statistical analysis called a P-technique (Luborsky 1953, 1995) was applied to the Q-sort ratings of therapy process. The P-technique is a factor analysis of repeated measures within the same therapist–patient pair to identify potential underlying structures of interaction. Time-series analysis (Gottman 1981), a quantitative technique that is now gaining popularity, is used to assess changes over time by analyzing the temporal unfolding of variables. Time-series analysis requires the repeated measure of a set of variables over time within the individual case and attempts to understand temporal variations or change in the scores of certain of these variables as a function of other variables.

Ms. A: An Interpreted Interaction Structure

Ms. A, a college student, was 21 years old at the beginning of treatment. She was seen by a male therapist twice weekly for 126 sessions over a period of 21 months. She became depressed and sought therapy after the sudden onset of an apparently serious mental disorder in an older sister with whom she had a close relationship. A case formulation was derived from the statements about Ms. A made by clinical judges after viewing her intake interview (see above). They saw Ms. A as conflicted about autonomy and independence, and guilty and inhibited about self-assertion, aggression, and competitiveness. She avoided conflict, and relied on denial, especially of her anger and defiance, as her primary psychological defense. She was fearful of authority figures, and generally compliant and eager to please. Ms. A wished for both a greater sense of independence and more closeness with her parents. She also wanted to have better relationships with men.

The clinical judges agreed that Ms. A had suffered significant trauma in early life. Her childhood was characterized by frequent relocations. She lived with her parents and older sister until age 7, at which point her parents divorced. Her father remarried shortly thereafter and she then lived with her father, siblings, and a stepmother, along with the stepmother's children. The stepmother became the dominant figure in her life while her father withdrew emotionally, becoming preoccupied with work. Ms. A describes a bleak existence in which she had a heavy load of chores and her stepmother was frequently physically abusive. Ms. A blamed herself for the difficulties, and believed that if she continued to work hard she would eventually be accepted into the family. She also reported being sexually abused over a period of years by her stepmother's sons. Finally, in her mid-teens she left to live with her mother.

Ms. A: Therapy Outcome

Ms. A's treatment was successful by all indices of patient change. Figure 8–1 plots scores on several symptom measures over the course of treatment. Evaluating change in the single case does not allow researchers to compare such change directly to that of other patients, as is possible in large sample studies. This problem was addressed by estimating the clinical significance of patient change using the method suggested by Jacobson and Truax (1991), which determines whether the patient achieves a postscore on a measure that is more likely to belong in the functional than the dysfunctional population. A cutoff score was calculated using the means and standard deviations from normative data for functional and dysfunctional populations for the outcome measures, and it was then determined if

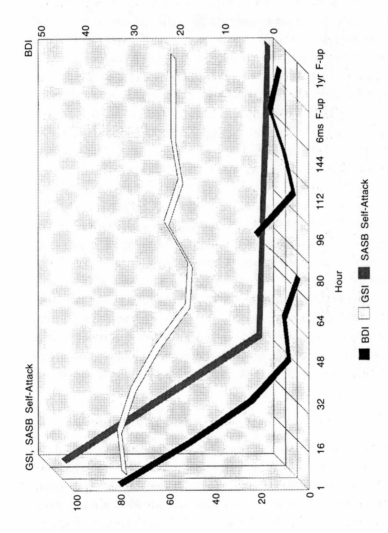

FIGURE 8–1. Plot of scores on Ms. A's symptom measures over the twenty-one-month treatment and at six-month and one-year follow-ups. (BDI, Beck Depression Inventory; GSI, General Severity Index of the Symptom Checklist 90-Revised; SASB, Structural Analysis of Social Behavior.)

Ms. A crossed the cutoff point in the direction of a functional sample from pre- to posttest. Her symptom scores and problem indices demonstrated clinically significant change, and she maintained these gains at six-month and one-year follow-ups (see Table 8–1 and Figure 8–1). Ms. A met criteria for clinically significant change both posttherapy and at one-year follow-up on the BDI, the General Severity Index (GSI) of the Symptom Checklist-90-R (SCL 90-R)[2] (Derogatis et al. 1974), the Automatic Thoughts Questionnaire (ATQ)[3] (Hollon and Kendall 1980), the Depression scale of the Minnesota Multiphasic Personality Inventory (MMPI)[4] (Dahlstrom and Welsh 1960), the Social Adjustment Scale (SAS)[5] (Weismann et al. 1978), and the Inventory of Interpersonal Problems (IIP)[6] (Horowitz et al. 1988). There was a large correlation of the GSI with treatment session number, $r = -.82$, demonstrating a significant association between patient improvement and length of treatment. Ms. A's SASB sores reflected a marked decrease in her propensity for self-accusation, self-blame, and self-punishment; in short, harsh, self-critical mental representations had apparently been altered. Note that the decline in Ms. A's symptoms is closely associated with a decrease in her "self attack" score on the SASB.

Identifying Interaction Structures in Ms. A's Therapy

To determine whether structures of interaction could be identified, the Q-ratings for treatment hours ($N = 63$) were subjected to an exploratory factor analysis (principal components method). The factor analysis yielded three interpretable clusters. Factor 1 was labeled *Collaborative Exploration*; factor 2, *Ambivalence/Compliance*; and factor 3, *Provoking Rescue*. Factor scales were constructed by averaging the relevant PQS items for each of the three clusters. Only factor 3, Provoking Rescue, was correlated with patient improvement. The items that define factor 3 are listed in Table 8–2 (see Jones and Price 1998 for details about the statistical analysis).

We hypothesized that decline in the intensity and frequency of certain interaction structures were related to patient improvement. It is, of course, more difficult to make causal inferences from quantitative single-case designs than from randomized clinical trials. However, single-case designs have an advantage in affording multiple observations of the same variables taken at regular time intervals (i.e., time-series data). In addition to knowing the magnitude of change in a variable, we also know *when* that change occurred relative to changes in other variables. Causality can therefore be inferred using time-series analysis. The basic logic is as follows: If, for example, the factor labeled Provoking Rescue influenced symptom improvement, then a score on the SCL-90-R at a given time should be predictable from past levels of Provoking Rescue above and beyond what is predictable from knowing previous SCL-90-R scores alone. Furthermore, the influence should be unidirectional, that is, SCL-90-R scores should not predict future Provoking Rescue above and beyond what could be predicted from past levels of Provoking Rescue.[7] Time-series analysis demonstrated that shifts in Provoking Rescue influenced changes on Ms. A's symptom scores.

We concluded that therapeutic action for Ms. A was located in the case-specific interaction structure, Provoking Rescue. This interaction structure of Ms. A and her therapist was captured by the Q-items in Table 8–2. This repetitive interaction was characterized by the patient's passivity and lengthy silences accompanied by depressed affect; a

TABLE 8–1. Patient Scores on Assessment Measures

Measure	Patient	Pretherapy	Post-therapy	One-Year Follow-up
SADS-RDC	A	Major depressive disorder	—[a]	—
	B	Major depressive disorder	—[a]	—
	M	Major depressive disorder	—[a]	—
Hamilton Rating Scale for Depression	A	30	—	—
	B	23	—	—
	M	22	1[b]	—
Beck Depression Inventory	A	40	3[b]	4[b]
	B	18	12[b]	17
	M	24	1[b]	0[b]
SCL-90-R (GSI)	A	71	50[b]	50[b]
	B	81	74	75
	M	70	32[b]	30[b]
Automatic Thoughts Questionnaire	A	107	32[b]	32[b]
	B	68	54[b]	64
	M	61	30	30
MMPI-2 Depression Scale	A	62	42[b]	47[b]
	B	92	77	73
	M	75	46[b]	43[b]

Social Adjustment Scale	A	2.65	1.42^b	1.69^b
	B	2.33	1.56^b	1.78^b
	M	2.10	1.40	1.2
Inventory of Interpersonal Problems	A	2.64	$.34^b$	$.79^b$
	B	1.41	1.62	1.39
	M	1.27	.29	0
Patient Change Rating (–4 to +4)	A	—	4	3
	B	—	3	2
	M	—	4	4
Therapist Change Rating (–4 to +4)	A	—	2	—
	B	—	2.50	—
	M	—	4	—

SADS-RDC, Schedule for Affective Disorders and Schizophrenia-Research Diagnostic Criteria; SCL-90-R (GSI), Symptom Checklist 90-Revised (General Severity Index); MMPI-2, Minnesota Multiphasic Personality Inventory-2. Dashes indicate data were not available.

[a]Patient did not meet criteria for major depressive disorder or minor depressive disorder.

[b]Patient met criteria for clinically significant change.

TABLE 8–2. Provoking Rescue

Q 12   Silences occur during the hour.
Q 13   Patient is (not) animated or excited.
Q 15   Patient does not initiate topics; is passive.
Q 61   Patient feels shy and embarrassed (vs. unselfconscious and self-assured).
Q 54   Patient is (not) clear and organized in self-expression.
Q 41   Patient's aspirations or ambitions are (not) topics of discussion.
Q 25   Patient has difficulty beginning the hour.
Q 74   Humor is (not) used.
Q 94   Patient feels sad or depressed (vs. joyous or cheerful).
Q 59   Patient feels inadequate and inferior (vs. effective/superior).
Q 56   Patient (does not) discuss experiences as if distant from his or her feelings.
Q 52   Patient relies upon therapist to solve her problems.
Q 69   Patient's current or recent life situation is (not) emphasized in discussion.

Note: Items in which the term (*not*) appears indicates this item was rated in the uncharacteristic or negatively salient direction.

strong sense of inadequacy, inferiority, and humiliation; and a wish to rely on the therapist to solve her problems. Reduction in the intensity and frequency of this interaction was strongly correlated with length of treatment ($r = -.71$, $p < .05$).

Here is an illustration of this kind of interaction pattern, taken from a verbatim transcript that contained some striking examples of the Provoking Rescue. Earlier in the session, Ms. A brought up her feeling of frustration that she's not doing anything, although she knows she is taking all the necessary steps to pursue her goals. There are many lengthy pauses and silences during this hour. The therapist is identifying Ms. A's wish to be rescued.

Therapist: You'd mentioned something to the effect of being frustrated in here, but you haven't said a whole lot about what that's about or what's behind it.

Patient: (*pause*) I just wonder why . . . I wonder if . . . y'know (*pause*) if I'll ever resolve all these issues, or if I just bring them up. I guess I wonder if it's worth it or how it's worth it.

T: Is it related at all to what you said earlier today about maybe wanting something more in terms of support from people? Perhaps I'm in that category.

P: Yeah, I don't say very much. (*pause*) I don't say anything.

T: So maybe part of what you were saying earlier today was indirectly related to me, in terms of perhaps wishing and wanting someone might be giving you more advice and being supportive or kind of giving you that guidance that you feel that you'd want. Even though you're taking all these steps, doing all these things.

P: (*silence*) Hmm. It's like . . . all the steps aren't recognized. They're seen as things.

T: As opposed to?

P: (*pause*) Steps! Steps that get somewhere.

During these repetitive interactions there was a strong implicit, and often explicit, demand on the therapist to fill the painful silences and to deliver transformative explanations. The therapist, on his part, often felt ineffective, and was prompted to become more active in drawing the patient out and rescuing them both from her tortured silences. The therapist was nevertheless able to interpret this pattern as, among other meanings, a way of avoiding the pain associated with talking about herself, reflecting on past traumas, and the fear of making herself vulnerable by revealing herself. This interaction structure also represented an unconscious effort to provoke the therapist into pursuing her, which repeated in the transference the traumatic sexual abuse the patient had experienced in childhood and early adolescence. Time-series analysis demonstrated that the slow decline in frequency and intensity of this interactive pattern predicted Ms. A's improvement in both her depression and her daily functioning. We attributed the eventual fading of this interaction pattern to the therapist's interpretation, and the patient's gradual understanding, of Provoking Rescue.

Mr. B: An Uninterpreted Interaction Structure

Mr. B was a 29-year-old single man who had an advanced degree in a business-related field. He was seen for a total of 208 treatment sessions, twice weekly, over a period of two-and-a-half years. His presenting complaint was a long-standing depression and anxiety, which had recently become particularly acute. Mr. B felt isolated and lonely, and pressured by his job, where he felt he had to work under uninterested authority figures. He felt he lacked self-confidence, and was deeply pessimistic about his future. He also reported a variety of somatic complaints, which he believed were related to stress and anxiety.

In their case formulation, clinical judges viewed Mr. B as conflicted about closeness, intimacy, and commitment. He was seen as using primarily cognitive defenses, such as intellectualization and isolation, as well as somatization, to ward off feelings of sadness and anger. They understood the origins of Mr. B's difficulties to stem from the death of his mother when he was 12, unresolved grief at her loss, and his identification with a depressed, pessimistic, and emotionally withdrawn father. The patient was also thought to have difficulty in regulating affect; he tended to shut off or repress his feelings. Mr. B was seen as wishing to repair the loss of his mother, to achieve intimacy with women, and to be strong and successful. The clinical judges predicted that his primary transferences toward the therapist would be a yearning for a mother figure, and struggles around submitting to, or defeating, authority figures.

Mr. B: Therapy Outcome

Mr. B demonstrated only modest symptom change after more that two years of twice-weekly psychotherapy. His symptom scores fluctuated considerably, and at termination he was somewhat improved, although at one-year follow-up he had returned to pretreatment levels (see Table 8–1). Figure 8–2 plots some of the symptom measures and on the SASB over the course of treatment. Mr. B met criteria for clinically significant change at posttherapy on the BDI, ATQ, and SAS, but not on the SCL 90-R, the IIP, the Depression scale of the MMPI, or the "self attack" index of the SASB. At the one-year follow-up, Mr. B met criteria for clinically significant change only on the SAS. There was no correlation between session number and score on the GSI Total Score of the SCL-90-R, $r = .00$.

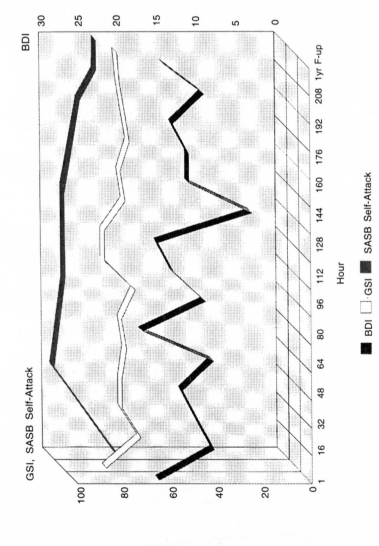

FIGURE 8–2. Plot of scores on Mr. B's symptom measures over the two-and-a-half year treatment and at one-year follow-up. (BDI, Beck Depression Inventory; GSI, General Severity Index of the Symptom Checklist 90-Revised; SASB, Structural Analysis of Social Behavior.)

Identifying Interaction Structures in Mr. B's Therapy

As with Ms. A, Q-sort ratings were made for every other treatment hour ($N = 104$) in completely randomized order, and subjected to a factor analysis. The factor analysis yielded three interpretable clusters: factor 1, which was similar in content to the first factor for Ms. A, was identically labeled as *Collaborative Exploration*; factor 2 was labeled *Resistant and Withdrawn*; and factor 3 was labeled *Angry Interaction*. The items that best define Angry Interaction are listed in Table 8–3.

TABLE 8–3. Angry Interaction

Q 14	Patient does not feel understood by therapist.
Q 9	Therapist is distant, aloof (vs. responsive and affectively involved).
Q 31	Therapist (does not) ask for more information or elaboration.
Q 42	Patient rejects (vs. accepts) therapist's comments and observations.
Q 77	Therapist is tactless.
Q 87	Patient is controlling.
Q 65	Therapist (does not) clarify, restate, or rephrase patient's communication.
Q 39	There is a competitive quality to the relationship.
Q 24	Therapist's own emotional conflicts intrude into the relationship.
Q 30	Discussion centers on cognitive themes (i.e., about ideas or belief systems).

The scores on the clusters for each rated treatment hour and the GSI of the SCL-90–R collected at regular intervals over the course of the treatment were subjected to a time-series analysis to determine if one series of scores was partially predictable from another. This analysis showed that symptom scores on the SCL-90-R predicted the factors Collaborative Exploration and Angry Interaction. Changes in patient symptom level signaled changes in the structure of the interaction, rather than changes in process predicting patient symptom improvement, as with Ms. A. When Mr. B was more symptomatic and depressed, this signaled that he and his therapist would be less involved and collaborative, and more inclined to become caught up in angry interactions, in the next sessions.

Here is an illustration of this kind of repetitive interaction, taken from the verbatim transcripts of a session that had one of the highest scores on this factor. Mr. B was often provocative in a way he was not able to acknowledge. Earlier in this session, Mr. B had asked his therapist to reduce his already low fee even further.

Therapist: What seems to start that? That process of disavowing intent? They ... *they* have put me here in this situation. They've put me in the awkward situation that I have to say to you that the arrangement that I said would be temporary may need to endure. You know, yesterday you were fine, but it's like, sorry I'm late, I missed the bus. If the bus hadn't come so early I would have been here.

Patient: But, yeah, on another occasion, when I just said sorry I'm late, you said, well, you didn't even bother to say why you were late this time. It was like, well, what do I do? You know, it was, like, that's a nicety, that's what people say. That's just what you do. I mean, what's the alternative?

T: What we're talking about, the issue you raise is about your aggression. And what we're talking about, I think, is the difficulty you have in taking responsibility for your aggression.

P: Mm-hmm ... Can you say more about that?

T: And that comes out either in a kind of what you called yesterday an "obtuseness."

P: Mm-hmm. Mm-hmm.

T: As you provoke other people, hurt other people's feelings, it comes out in a disavowal of responsibility. Things conspire to put you in a situation where you can't do what you've agreed to do or what other people want you to do. I was thinking of the way yesterday's hour began with your being late and then forgetting your checkbook. We talked about it later. You said, "Yeah. It's just like, if it's not one damn thing, it's another." Your father's phrase. Afterward, it occurred to me that you don't think: if *I* don't do one damn thing, *I* do another.

P: Mm-hmm.

T: Well, it's externalized.

P: Right.

T: It's not something you're doing. Something else has put you in this situation of having created with me a false agreement.

P: Mm-hmm.

T: It isn't that you failed to get the details right.

P: I see. So, in other words, it's that you would say it differently. That would constitute taking responsibility?

T: That's the business about finding a technology (to find the right words to say to others). I don't think it'll work to try to learn the words that I would use.

P: Well, other than punching my boss in the nose, what would constitute being responsible for my aggression?

T: Well, say more.

P: Well, I mean, say excuse me, but I'm a very aggressive

person. I'm going to have to punch you in the nose, you know. I don't think that's going to be socially acceptable. You could say it's a technology not to punch my boss in the nose. However, it's not something I'm going to do. Ergo, it makes me wonder what would constitute being responsible for my own aggression?

These repetitive interactions were tense, competitive, and intellectualized exchanges in which the patient attempted to control the therapist, and in which the patient did not feel understood and rejected the therapist's attempts to help. The therapist, in turn, was less tactful, and had to struggle with angry, contemptuous countertransference reactions. In our example, the therapist attempts to interpret the patient's evident hostility and simultaneous disavowal of such feelings. However, in the face of the patient's rigid defenses, the therapist responds with annoyance and perhaps some punitiveness.

The causal direction of the relationship of interaction structures to symptom change was different from those with Ms. A and her therapist, with symptom scores predicting levels and frequency of interaction patterns. With Mr. B, lower levels of depression and symptom scores predicted higher levels of Collaborative Exploration, and higher symptom scores predicted more frequent and intense Angry Interaction. Mr. B was more capable of working in collaboration with the therapist, and less likely to provoke tense, angry exchanges, when he felt less depressed and anxious. There was no decline in the intensity and frequency of this interaction structure during the therapy (correlation between therapy session number and this factor was $r = -.06$, not significant). This Angry Interaction structure was likely insufficiently interpreted and understood, and we conclude that this unanalyzed, and relatively unchanging interaction pattern was associated with the fact that the patient reported only little improvement at termination. It is an illustration of a largely unconscious pattern of interaction that may have led to a stalemate in the treatment.

Ms. M: A Supportive Interaction Structure

The case of Ms. M was described in Chapter 2, and will only be summarized briefly here.

> Ms. M was a 35-year-old divorced mother of three. She became depressed when her eldest son, age 16, expressed the desire to live with his father, her former husband. Ms. M's first episode of severe depression had occurred six years earlier when, in the course of a year, she underwent two abortions. She was treated by a psychiatrist through a regimen of antidepressant medication and some psychotherapy. Ms. M's older brother was killed in an accident when she was 7 years old. Ms. M's mother then became depressed and her father began to drink excessively; her parents eventually divorced. (A case formulation for Ms. M is presented in Chapter 2.)

Ms. M: Therapy Outcome

The treatment was, by all indices of patient change, successful. At termination, Ms. M no longer met criteria for either major or minor depressive disorder on the SADS-C (change). Her symptom scores and problem indices decreased markedly, and she maintained these gains at six-month and one-year follow-ups (see Table 8–1). Figure 8–3 shows Ms. M's scores for her punitive introject, along with her symptom scores, over the course of treatment and in the follow-up assessments. It depicts the initially relatively rapid, and then steady, decline in Ms. M's depressive symptoms. The striking, short-lived increase in symptoms at session 176 coincided with a visit of some weeks' duration by her mother. Ms. M met criteria for clinically significant change on the BDI, General Severity Index (GSI) of the SCL-90-R, and the Depression scale of the MMPI and the HRSD; on the ATQ, Ms. M was already in the normal range at pretest. The SASB self-attack scores reflected a marked decrease in Ms. M's propensity for self-accusation, self-blame, and self-punishment. It is interesting to note that her depressive symptoms, as indexed by the BDI, were alleviated long before a change occurred in her tendency to attack and torture herself. At session 192 there was a precipitous change in her level of self-attack. Ms. M's capacity to see herself more benevolently and as deserving of care and self-protection increased, and harsh, self-critical mental representations had apparently been altered, all of which could be construed as a change in psychological structure.

Identifying Interaction Structures in Ms. M's Therapy

The Q-ratings for 53 treatment hours (every fourth hour) were subjected to the same kind of statistical analysis as were the process ratings for Ms. A and Mr. B. The factor analysis yielded four clusters. Factor 1, which was labeled *Therapist Neutral Acceptance*, reflected the therapist's nonjudgmental acceptance, her empathy and facilitative activity, and her accurate perception of Ms. M's experience of the therapy relationship, as well as her degree of neu-

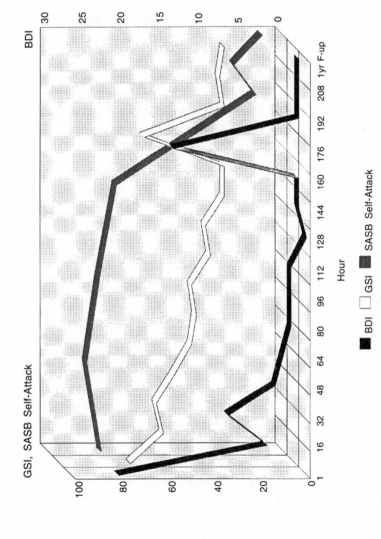

FIGURE 8–3. Plot of scores on Ms. M's symptom measures over the two-and-a-half-year treatment and at one-year follow-up. (BDI, Beck Depression Inventory; GSI, General Severity Index of the Symptom Checklist 90-Revised; SASB, Structural Analysis of Social Behavior.)

trality. Factor 2, labeled *Therapist Suppresses Pt.'s Negative Self Representations*, captures the therapist's personal and emotional responses to Ms. M, her control of the interaction with the patient, and the assumption of a didactic, challenging, and authoritative role. The cluster includes what is presumably Ms. M's reaction to this stance, that is, difficulty in understanding her therapist, and feelings of being misunderstood. The other two factors were named *Psychodynamic Technique* and *Patient Dysphoric Affect*. Factor scales were constructed by averaging the relevant PQS items for each of the four clusters (see Jones et al. 1993b for details concerning the statistical analysis). The items that best define two of the factors relevant to this discussion, *Therapist Neutral Acceptance* and *Therapist Suppresses Pt.'s Negative Self Representations* are listed in Table 8–4.

Factor scores for the treatment hours were correlated with Ms. M's scores on the SCL-90-R, which was administered at regular intervals over the course of the therapy. Therapist Neutral Acceptance was positively correlated with higher levels of patient-reported symptoms ($.31$, $p < .05$), while Therapist Suppresses Pt.'s Negative Self Representations was associated with lower symptom levels ($-.33$, $p < .05$). Results of the time-series analysis testing the relationship between the four process dimensions and symptom change (GSI score) showed that lower levels of Therapist Neutral Acceptance lead to symptom improvement.

At first glance this may seem to be a puzzling finding. However, further study of the case showed that the therapist was not less accepting of Ms. M, but rather less accepting of her self-punitive attitudes and her negative self representations (Fretter 1995, Pole and Jones 1998). This phenomenon is captured in the interaction structure in which the therapist challenges and suppresses the patient's

TABLE 8–4. Interaction Structures in Ms. M's Therapy

Therapist Neutral Acceptance

Q 18 Therapist conveys a sense of nonjudgmental acceptance.

Q 3 Therapist's remarks are aimed at facilitating patient speech.

Q 28 Therapist accurately perceives the therapeutic process.

Q 6 Therapist is sensitive to the patient's feelings, attuned to the patient; empathic.

Q 93 Therapist is neutral.

Q 31 Therapist asks for more information or elaboration.

Q 46 Therapist communicates with patient in a clear, coherent style.

Therapist Suppresses Pt.'s Negative Self Representations

Q 24 Therapist's own emotional conflicts intrude into the relationship.

Q 37 Therapist behaves in a teacher-like (didactic) manner.

Q 77 Therapist is tactless.

Q 17 Therapist actively exerts control over the interaction (e.g., structuring, and/or introducing new topics).

Q 51 Therapist condescends to or patronizes the patient

Q 5 Patient has difficulty understanding the therapist's comments.

Q 99 Therapist challenges the patient's view (vs. validates patient's perceptions).

Q 14 Patient does not feel understood by therapist.

negative self representations. This repetitive interaction was often initiated by the therapist's neutral silence. When the therapist was silent, the patient became more self-critical and self-punitive in her attitude, and was beset by feelings of inadequacy and low self-esteem. In response, the therapist then began to talk a good deal, and openly argued against Ms. M's self-perception as, for example, an inadequate or self-indulgent mother or spouse, by presenting evidence to the contrary. The patient's negative self representations intensified during therapy sessions unless the therapist took an active role in combating them. For example, the therapist demonstrated, in both attitude and action, that Ms. M's abilities were not harmful to others, and argued strongly that Ms. M should cultivate her talents.

In the following verbatim illustration of the Therapist Suppressing Pt.'s Negative Self Representations interaction structure, the patient has just been talking about her sense that she is not contributing enough to family life and that she has been too self-indulgent by coming to therapy and taking tennis lessons.

Therapist: Why do you think that your husband stays in this relationship? If it's so lopsided? And that you're getting too much and he's giving too much?

Patient: I don't know. I suppose in the back of my mind there's a fear that one day he'll wake up and see that. He just hasn't noticed it.

T: Yeah. He just married you, but he's already on his way to realizing he made a big mistake.

P: (*laugh*) Yeah. That's true, that's true. I don't know.

T: You've had the same feelings here, you know—that you're not going to contribute enough to the therapy. You're not paying enough. You're not talking enough. You're not depressed enough.

P: (*laugh*) Yeah, that's right.

T: I think that this attitude of your not giving, not doing enough just really follows you. That's what led you to saying you need to be more generous with yourself. In some of the early sessions you were talking about wanting to really develop your specialness and really be creative and let yourself go and grow in the way that you know you can, that you're blocked from doing.

P: Uh-huh.

T: And you told of the special times you've had so far, and you would talk about them in a very belittling way, right? "Oh yeah, I was very popular for these two years but I was just a pretty face, but it was just high school." You thought you were tooting your own horn.

P: Yeah.

T: You thought that this was real bragging.

P: Uh-huh.

T: And that's where we got to this concept of being more generous with yourself, about allowing yourself to feel more deserving of your relationship with your husband, for example.

P: Uh-huh. Yeah. I suppose that's right.

T: It's the idea that you don't deserve this. You're not doing enough.

P: Yeah. I think that's right. I try to remember because now, when I look back, it's sort of a funny thing. I wish I could put myself back two or three or five or seven or ten years ago and see if I said the same stuff. Because when I look back two, three, five, seven, ten, fifteen years ago, I carried way more than my share of the burden. I wonder if I still felt like I wasn't, I just don't know. I just don't. I would be curious to know. I just don't.

T: I'm sure that that's correct.

P: Think so?

T: Oh, from what you've told us about your marriage to your first husband and your totally squelching all of your ambitions and abilities and skills and recognition, you know, so as supposedly not to threaten him. So that he wouldn't feel threatened. You didn't allow yourself that.

P: Yeah. Yeah. It's really quite a change that my life has taken in the last few years. I mean people say, "God, you know it's easier if you have to make a transition to where your life is easier and you have less problems that you have to overcome." In a way, and that makes sense. I mean that's a logical (*laugh*) thing to think. But you know, in a way, it just seems like to me it would be easier just to go the other way, (*laugh*) to . . .

T: . . . work yourself to death rather than . . .

P: Yeah.

T: . . . feeling guilty about not doing enough.

P: Just do it. Just get busy and do this stuff yourself. That's right. In a way it just seems like there's less conflict there (*laugh*) anyway. I don't know. I don't know. I don't know what to say. . . . It's just really much more difficult for me.

T: Mm-hmm.

P: I don't know.

T: You know the stories you wrote, they're just wonderful.

P: You liked them?

T: Loved them. They were just great. I think they are a good example of your lack of generosity with yourself. I mean, you're a wonderful writer. They're great stories. They're wonderfully written.

P: Oh. Thank you.

T: You know, you can't put them down. I mean they are full of emotion and values and a lot about life.

P: Great.

T: And you are a really good writer.

P: Thank you.

T: And you came in and told me, "I have no skills, I'm just no good," you know.

P: Yeah.

T: You have real talent here and a real ability that could develop and go further. You could really enjoy and feel really good about it. So I wonder why this "Pooh, pooh, oh, I'm terrible." Why all of that?

During the beginning phase of the therapy, our Q-sort data show that the therapist was more nonjudgmental, facilitative, and neutral, and that Ms. M's depressive affect during the therapy sessions seems to have gradually "pulled" the therapist toward a more authoritative and emotionally reactive and involved posture. This change in the nature of the process was predictive of Ms. M's gradual reduction in symptom level. The therapist held a particular hypothesis about pathogenesis in Ms. M organized around the notion of "survivor guilt" (Weiss and Sampson 1986). Central to this formulation was the traumatic death of Ms. M's brother in a swimming accident when she was 7, and her mother's subsequent depression of many years' duration. Ms. M came to believe that her mother would have preferred her death to that of her brother. The therapist became convinced that Ms. M had in fact never been appropriately prized, encouraged, and acknowledged by either of her parents. Ms. M's therapist developed a clearly articulated formulation that guided her intervention strategy. Nevertheless, the intensity of Ms. M's negative self representations and related depressed mood determined at least in part *when* the therapist became more forcefully challenging. This repetitive interaction is captured in the Therapist Suppressing Pt.'s Negative Self Representations factor. The content of the Q-items that constitute this interaction structure includes items capturing the therapist's countertransference reactions, and the active, challenging, didactic role she assumed. The therapist actively fought against Ms. M's negative self representations when Ms. M attempted to actualize her earlier experiences and role relationships, real or fantasied.

We have been able to empirically demonstrate the presence of interaction structures in all the cases we have studied. They can also be routinely observed in clinical practice. The interaction structure construct has much in common with already familiar theoretical and technical terms such as analyzing the transference in the *here and now* and *working through.* However, it provides an empirical underpinning for aspects of these concepts. Moreover, it also includes the two-person, intersubjective component of therapeutic action. Interaction structure refers to how the patient's character pathology, conflicts, and symptoms express themselves in the relationship with the therapist, and how the therapist becomes involved with the patient in what might be called a symptomatic way. These patterns of interaction are the observable behavioral and emotional components of the transference-countertransference.

Interaction structures can play a mutative role through several modes. In the case of Ms. A, mutually influencing interactions facilitated her ability to experience and represent certain mental states. Insight, self-knowledge, and the capacity for self-reflection developed in the context of a relationship with a therapist who endeavored to understand Ms. A's mind through the medium of their interaction, an understanding conveyed through interpretation. The case of Mr. B represents an instance in which a significant repetitive therapist–patient interaction remained uninterpreted, not understood, and outside of explicit awareness, blocking greater self-knowledge in the patient, obstructing progress, and leading to therapeutic stalemate. The third case, Ms. M, seems to represent another mode of therapeutic action, one in which unacknowledged interaction structures do not prevent at least certain kinds of patient change. In the case of Ms. M, the focus of the therapist's interpretive activity was outside the transference, for example, on the patient's relationship with her mother, husband, and other family members, and on her guilt and self-punitive attitude. The patient gained insight into her conflicts, and a capacity for self-reflection. Uninterpreted, unconscious interaction patterns may have contributed to Ms. M's change by creating opportunities for the modification of problematic mental representations of self and others in ways that remained at least partially outside of consciousness.

Our findings also have implications for process-outcome research strategies by underscoring the complex nature of causal relations in psychotherapy. Our data suggest that while there may be similarities in interaction structures across patients, there are key differences as well. It is unlikely that a particular therapist action (transference interpretations or seemingly supportive interventions), or even certain kinds of processes, invariably signify something fixed for all patients. The subjective meaning of observable processes will vary across therapist–patient dyads. If differing causal links between process and outcome can be identified in just a few cases, multiplying such effects many times over in studies of samples of patients and therapists could easily account for the difficulty in identifying significant process-outcome correlations in conventional studies relying on samples of therapists and patients. A focus on the variability within the therapy dyad is the very core of process research.

How Can the Interaction Structure Construct
Help the Therapist?

Interaction structures are the observable, enacted, and emotionally experienced component of mental representations of self and other in the therapy situation. These patterns of interaction do not represent all that is dynamically unconscious. They are the manifest, behavioral aspect of the transference-countertransference. The construct is clinically useful in a number of respects. Interaction structures capture the behavioral and emotional surface. Repetitive patterns of interaction can be observed directly by therapist and patient; they are accessible, and their presence can be confirmed consensually. They are particularly useful in providing for exploration clinical data that are alive and have a sense of immediacy. Grounding an exploration of the patient's mental life on interaction structures that can be felt and observed helps avoid an overly intellectualized consideration of what the patient is doing, and why. It also reduces the need to rely on inferences about the patient's motives and intentions that are sometimes difficult to verify.

Since these interaction patterns can be observed and mutually verified by therapist and patient, using them as a starting point for exploration reduces the problems associated with the therapist's authoritative role, such as idealizations of the therapist, patient compliance, and reliance on the therapist's authority, knowledge, and wisdom. The therapist is less induced to take the role of "the one who knows" what is going on in the patient's mind, and the solution to the patient's problems. Recognizing interaction patterns is also helpful in clinical supervision. In fact, the clinical supervisor, who has the benefit of the perspective associated with less countertransference, will often identify interactions structures more easily than the therapist, who may be in the grip of countertransference feelings.

An important mode of therapeutic action is the recognition and understanding of these interaction patterns by therapist and patient. Patient change is the result of relatively specific repetitive patterns that facilitate the psychological processes that enable patients to experience and represent certain mental states, and to have knowledge of their own intentionality. Specific forms of experiences with the therapist are necessary for the patient to develop a sense of subjectivity, agency, and self-knowledge. An underlying premise is that recognition, interpretation, and understanding of the meanings of these interaction patterns is an important component of the change process.

Uninterpreted, unacknowledged interaction structures can serve a defensive function and, as with Mr. B, can be the source of stalemates in therapy. However, even as they function defensively, uninterpreted interaction patterns can also serve a supportive function, as was the case in Mr. S's first treatment (see Chapter 1), and help to relieve anxiety and depressive symptoms. Uninterpreted, unacknowledged interaction structures are at least in part unconsciously enacted by both therapist and patient. In fact, many supportive interventions, especially those that are undertaken without careful thought, mask transference–countertransference interaction patterns.

The presence of interaction structures that remain uninterpreted and outside of awareness do not necessarily obstruct patient change. Some therapies, for a variety of reasons, do not focus on the transference–countertransference. Patients must strongly resist awareness of their reactions to the therapist, or the therapist, for countertransference reasons, is less able to take up transference reactions in a skillful and useful way. In such instances, some kinds of patient change can occur through other modes of therapeutic action. Insight and capacity for self-reflection can be gained by work outside of the transference-countertransference. Ms. M, for example, developed insight into the source of her depression, which she did not at all connect with her brother's death at the beginning of therapy. She also acquired a much greater capacity to think about herself and to know her own motives and wishes. Nevertheless, the extratransferential focus of the treatment did not allow Ms. M to gain insight into her own aggression and hostility, making her vulnerable to recurrent depression.

The interaction structure construct, and its associated theory of therapeutic action, is based on empirical research. In the last decades, a clinically and theoretically vigorous psychoanalysis has generated a rich and diverse set of theories about the nature of the change process. Already established drive-structural, ego psychological, and neo-Kleinian points of view have been joined by newer self psychological, relational, and intersubjective perspectives. A real difficulty has been how to determine the validity, and usefulness, of these alternate, sometimes competing perspectives. The traditional methods of resolving theoretical disputes in psychoanalysis have been discussion and debate, the slow accumulation of clinical experience with certain approaches, and continued development of theory. These methods of resolving scientific problems can be very usefully augmented by empirical research. This work shows that systematic empirical inquiry is able not only to confirm psychoanalytic ideas, but can also lead to new integrations.

The theoretical ferment within psychoanalysis is occurring during a time when the scientific status of psychoanalysis is being questioned by an array of critics, from philosophy of science to biological psychiatry and nonanalytic therapists who wish to promote their own methods of intervention. In this context, the need to ground analytic theories about the change process in research has assumed real urgency. It is hoped this work will fortify clinicians' conviction about the value and validity of psychoanalytic approaches to treatment. Although analytic clinicians often concede the need for research, some have not seen how the very serious difficulties in capturing empirically and quantifying subtle and complex clinical and theoretical constructs can be overcome. Perhaps this work will, as well, foster the recognition that psychoanalytic research can be conducted in ways that are clinically and theoretically meaningful.

Notes

1. The Beck Depression Inventory is a twenty-one-item self-report designed to assess current syndromal depression. Subjects are instructed to complete each item in terms of how they have felt over the preceding week. The BDI has shown good concurrent validity when compared with psychiatric ratings of depression in both clinical populations and college student populations (Bumberry et al. 1978).

2. The Symptom Checklist 90-R is a multidimensional self-report inventory of symptoms that has demonstrated both good reliability and sensitivity to change in psychotherapy, and is a widely used symptom change measure.

3. The Automatic Thoughts Questionnaire is a thirty-item self-report instrument designed to measure the frequency and intensity of negative thoughts about the self, which cognitive-behavioral theorists posit to be an etiologic source of depression. The ATQ has become one of the most widely used outcome measures in cognitive/behavioral research.

4. The Minnesota Multiphasic Personality Inventory can be used to identify a wide range of clinical syndromes; particularly relevant

for this study is scale 2 (Depression), a sixty-item true-false inventory embedded within the larger 550-item measure. Scale 2 of the MMPI is at least as sensitive a measure of change in depression as any of the other instruments, and is far less susceptible to response sets and dissimulation.

5. The Social Adjustment Scale is a forty-two-question self-report instrument that measures either instrumental or expressive role performance over the past two weeks in six major areas of functioning: work as a wage earner, housewife, or student; social and leisure activities; relationship with extended family; marital role as a spouse; parental role; and membership in the family unit. The instrument has demonstrated strong discriminant validity as well as adequate internal consistency and test-retest stability.

6. The Inventory of Interpersonal Problems is a 127-item measure designed to identify interpersonal sources of distress. Instructions ask the respondent to consider each problem on the list and, in a format similar to that of the SCL-90-R, to rate how distressing that problem has been on a scale ranging from 0 (not at all) to 4 (extremely). Horowitz and colleagues (1988) have found that while both the IIP and symptom measures are sensitive to change early in treatment, only the IIP continues to be change sensitive at later stages of treatment.

7. Gottman and Ringland (1981) have developed a statistical approach that formally tests this logic. Their bivariate time-series analysis is designed to determine whether one series of scores (e.g., on an outcome measure) may be predicted from the history of another series of scores (e.g., collaborative exploration) controlling for autocorrelation within the first series. Predicting one series from the history of the other is called cross-regression, while predicting a series from its own history is called autoregression. Four regression equations (models) are built for each series. The models differ with respect to the number of autoregressive and cross-regressive terms that they contain. The number of terms in a model corresponds to the number of lags (i.e., the number of data points into the future that are used in the regression equation). Likelihood ratio tests are then employed to discover which model best describes the series with the minimum number of terms. The unidirectionality of influence is then tested by

transposing the predicted and predicting series and repeating the procedure (see Jones and Price 1998, Pole and Jones 1998 for details of the statistical analyses). Scores on the process factors for each Q-sorted treatment hour and GSI scores were subjected to a time-series analysis to determine if one series was partially predictable from another. This analysis demonstrated whether shifts in the process factors, or interaction structures, influenced changes on patients' symptom scores.

Appendix

The Psychotherapy Process
Q-set (PQS) Coding Manual

The purpose of the 100 items of the Psychotherapy Process Q-set is to provide a basic language for the description and classification of therapy process. The PQS is intended to be largely neutral with respect to any particular theory of therapy, and should permit the portrayal of a wide range of therapeutic interactions. The use of a standard language and rating procedure provides the means for systematically characterizing therapist–patient interaction. Rather than focusing on small segments of patient or therapist communications, raters Q-sort entire therapy sessions, allowing judges a greater opportunity to capture events of importance, and providing them with the possibility of rating assimilated or digested impressions of therapy process. The general purpose of the instrument is to provide a meaningful index of the therapeutic process that may be used in comparative analyses or studied in relation to pre- and posttherapy assessments.

The procedure is relatively simple. After studying the process data, and arriving at some formulation of the material, look through the 100 cards. You are to sort these statements into a row of *nine* categories, placing at one end of the row those cards you believe to be the *most characteristic* with respect to your understanding of the material and, at the other end, those cards you believe to be *most uncharacteristic* with reference to your reading of the data. A con-

venient method of sorting is to first form three stacks of
cards—those items deemed characteristic being placed on
one side, those items deemed uncharacteristic being placed
on the other side, and those cards remaining falling in
between. No attention need be paid to the number of
cards falling into each of these three groupings at this time.
When the three piles of cards have been assembled, they
can be further divided, this time into their proper proportions. The number of cards to be placed in each category
are listed below:

Category	No. of Cards	Label of category
9	5	Extremely characteristic or salient
8	8	Quite characteristic or salient
7	12	Fairly characteristic or salient
6	16	Somewhat characteristic or salient
5	18	Relatively neutral or unimpor-tant
4	16	Somewhat uncharacteristic or negatively salient
3	12	Fairly uncharacteristic or nega-tively salient
2	8	Quite uncharacteristic or nega-tively salient
1	5	Extremely uncharacteristic or negatively salient

You may feel some discomfort at the constraints imposed upon you by the Q-sort items and the sorting procedure. As is true of other systems of content analysis, the
Q-sort is designed to reduce complex interaction to man-

ageable proportions, and to achieve research economy. No instrument of this kind perfectly fits or captures all therapeutic interactions. It should also be noted that assignment of a fixed number of cards to each category has been shown empirically to be a more valuable procedure than the situation in which a clinician can assign any number of cards to a category. The Q-items themselves represent a good deal of thought and psychometric analysis. While not all characteristics or events of a particular therapy can be expressed by the extremeness of placement of certain of the statements, they can almost always be captured by a conjunction of two or more of the items. The intent of the Q-sort is to allow the description of dimensions of psychotherapy process by means of a suitable placement of items and the ultimate configuration of multiple items that is consequently constructed.

The Q-sort comprises three types of items:

1. items describing patient attitude and behavior or experience;
2. items reflecting the therapist actions and attitudes;
3. items attempting to capture the nature of the interaction of the dyad, or the climate or atmosphere of the encounter.

The definitions, or descriptions, of the items in this manual and the examples provided, are intended to minimize potentially varying interpretations of the items. It should be carefully studied. Judges are asked to take the position of a "generalized other," that is, an observer who views the interaction between the patient and the therapist from the outside. In placing each item ask yourself: Is this attitude, behavior, or experience clearly present (or absent)? If the evidence is not compelling, ask yourself: To what extent is it present or absent? Search for *specific* evidence. Try to be as open-minded and objective as possible. Avoid, for example, judgments of whether a particular therapist activity is effective or ineffective, or desirable or undesirable from a particular theoretical position. Be aware of preconceived ideas you may have about "ideal" therapeutic interactions. In particular, try not to be affected by your personal reactions to either therapist or patient; for example, avoid the tendency for your ratings to be influenced by whether you would like to have this person as your therapist, or by how you might react to the patient if you were the therapist.

Raters are sometimes uncertain as to whether a particular item should be placed in the *relatively neutral* or *unimportant* category, or in one of the categories reflecting that it is *uncharacteristic* of the hour. An item should be placed in the *neutral* category when it is truly irrelevant or inconsequential in relation to the interaction. A more extreme placement of the item in the *uncharacteristic* direction signals that absence of a particular behavior or experience is remarkable and should be captured in the Q-sort description of the hour. In other words, an event whose absence would be important to mark in order to achieve a more complete description of the hour can be captured by an item placement in an uncharacteristic rather than neutral category. Many items have specific instructions about this in their definitions. Raters may occasionally feel that there is insufficient evidence to make a judgment of this kind (as well as to make other kinds of item placements) with good confidence. However, extensive work has already demonstrated that with patience and care, high interrater reliability of Q-descriptions can be achieved.

Item 1: **Patient verbalizes negative feelings (e.g., criticism, hostility) toward therapist (vs. makes approving or admiring remarks).**

Place toward *characteristic* end if patient verbalizes feelings of criticism, dislike, envy, scorn, anger, or antagonism toward therapist, e.g., patient rebukes therapist for failing to provide enough direction in the therapy.

Place toward *uncharacteristic* direction if patient expresses positive or friendly feelings about therapist, e.g., makes what appear to be complimentary remarks to therapist.

Item 2: **Therapist draws attention to patient's nonverbal behavior, e.g., body posture, gestures.**

Place toward *characteristic* end if therapist draws attention to patient's nonverbal behavior, such as facial expressions, blushes, laughter, throat clearing, or body movements, e.g., therapist points out that although patient says s/he is angry, the patient is smiling.

Place toward *uncharacteristic* end if there is little or no focus on nonverbal behavior.

Item 3: **Therapist's remarks are aimed at facilitating patient speech.**

Place toward *characteristic* end if therapist's responses or behavior indicate that he or she is listening to the client and encouraging him or her to continue, such as mm-hmm, yeah, sure, right, and the like.

Place toward *uncharacteristic* end if therapist does not respond in such a manner as to facilitate patient talk (item does *not* refer to questions, exploratory comments).

N.B. Rate item based on the therapist's intent, regardless of the actual effect on the facilitation of patient speech.

Item 4: The patient's treatment goals are discussed.

Place toward *characteristic* end if there is talk about what the patient wishes to achieve as a result of therapy. These wishes or goals may refer to personal or "inner" changes (e.g., "I started therapy in order to get over my depressions") or change in life circumstances ("I wonder if therapy will result in my getting married").

Place toward *uncharacteristic* end if there is no reference or allusion by therapist or patient to the possible consequences of the therapy.

Item 5: Patient has difficulty understanding the therapist's comments.

Place toward *characteristic* end if patient seems confused by therapist's comments. This may be defensive or a result of therapist's lack of clarity, e.g., patient repeatedly says "What?" or otherwise indicates that s/he doesn't know what the therapist means.

Place toward *uncharacteristic* end if patient readily comprehends therapist's comments.

Item 6: Therapist is sensitive to the patient's feelings, attuned to the patient; empathic.

Place toward *characteristic* end if therapist displays the ability to sense the patient's "private world" as if it was his or her own; if the therapist is sensitive to the patient's feelings and can communicate this understanding in a way that seems attuned to the patient, e.g., therapist makes a statement that indicates an understanding of how the patient felt in a certain situation.

Place toward *uncharacteristic* end if therapist does not seem to have a sensitive understanding of patient's feelings or experience.

Item 7: Patient is anxious or tense (vs. calm and relaxed).

Place toward *characteristic* end if patient manifests tenseness or anxiety or worry. This may be demonstrated by direct statements, e.g., "I feel nervous today," or indirectly by stammers, stuttering, etc., or other behavioral indicators.

Place toward *uncharacteristic* end if patient appears calm or relaxed or conveys a sense of ease.

Item 8: Patient is concerned or conflicted about his or her dependence on the therapist (vs. comfortable with dependency, or wanting dependency).

Place toward *characteristic* end if patient appears concerned about or uncomfortable with dependency, e.g., shows a need to withdraw from the therapist, or in some manner reveals a concern about becoming dependent on the therapy.

Place toward *uncharacteristic* end if patient appears comfortable with being dependent. This may take the form of expressions of helplessness; or the patient may appear either comfortable or gratified by a dependent relationship with the therapist.

Rate as *neutral* if patient experiences a sense of relative independence in the therapy relationship.

Item 9: Therapist is distant, aloof (vs. responsive and effectively involved).

Place toward *characteristic* direction if therapist's stance toward the patient is cool, formal, and detached, or marked by emotional retreat or withdrawal.

Place toward *uncharacteristic* end if therapist is genuinely responsive and affectively involved.

Item 10: Patient seeks greater intimacy with the therapist.

Rate as *characteristic* if patient appears to either wish or attempt to transform the therapy relationship into a more social or personal and intimate relationship, e.g., patient expresses concern about the therapist; or attempts to gain knowledge of the therapist's personal life.

Place in *uncharacteristic* direction if patient does not appear to seek greater closeness with the therapist.

Item 11: Sexual feelings and experiences are discussed.

Place toward *characteristic* end if the patient's sexuality is discussed. This can take the form of a discussion of sexual problems, or the patient's sexual feelings or fantasies or actual sexual experiences, e.g., patient talks of wanting to have sex with a romantic partner more frequently.

Place toward *uncharacteristic* end if patient does not discuss sexual or erotic material.

Item 12: Silences occur during the hour.

Place toward *characteristic* end if there are many periods of silence or significant pauses during the hour, or a few extended periods of silence.

Place in *uncharacteristic* direction if there are few silences.

N.B. Brief pauses in speech should not be rated as silences unless they are very frequent, or longer than several seconds.

Item 13: Patient is animated or excited.

Place toward *characteristic* end if patient directly expresses, or behaviorally displays, a feeling of excitation or appears aroused in some way, e.g., patient becomes animated in response to therapist's interpretation.

Place toward *uncharacteristic* end if patient appears bored, dull, or lifeless.

Item 14: Patient does not feel understood by therapist.

Place toward *characteristic* end if patient expresses concern about, or conveys the feeling of being misunderstood, or assumes that the therapist cannot understand, e.g., a widow doubts the therapist's ability to understand her plight since he has never been in her situation.

Place toward *uncharacteristic* end if patient somehow conveys the sense that the therapist understands his or her experience or feelings, e.g., patient comments, in response to therapist's remarks, "Yes, that's exactly what I mean."

Item 15: Patient does not initiate topics; is passive.

Place toward *characteristic* end if patient does not initiate topics for discussion, bring up problems, or otherwise fails to assume some responsibility for the hour, e.g., patient states that s/he doesn't know what to talk about.

Place toward *uncharacteristic* end if patient is willing to break silences, or supplies topics either spontaneously or in response to therapist's probes, and actively pursues or elaborates them.

Item 16: There is discussion of body functions, physical symptoms, or health.

Place toward *characteristic* direction if discussion emphasizes somatic concerns or physical symptoms, e.g., patient may complain of fatigue or illness, or of having headaches, menstrual pains, poor appetite, and the like.

Place toward *uncharacteristic* end if physical complaints are not an important topic of discussion.

Item 17: Therapist actively exerts control over the interaction (e.g., structuring, and/or introducing new topics).

Place toward *characteristic* end if therapist intervenes frequently. Do not rate on the basis of perceptiveness or appropriateness of interventions, e.g., rate as very characteristic if therapist is so active that s/he frequently interrupts or intervenes to ask questions or make a point, or provides a good deal of direction during the hour.

Place toward *uncharacteristic* direction if therapist intervenes relatively infrequently, and makes little effort to structure the interaction; or if therapist tends to follow the lead of patient, e.g., allowing patient to introduce main topics and helping patient to follow his or her train of thought.

Item 18: Therapist conveys a sense of nonjudgmental acceptance. (N.B. Placement toward uncharacteristic end indicates disapproval, lack of acceptance.)

Place toward *characteristic* end if therapist refrains from overt or subtle negative judgments of the patient; "unacceptable" or problematic behavior of the patient may be explored while conveying the sense that the patient is worthy. Therapist displays unconditional acceptance.

Place toward *uncharacteristic* end if therapist's comments or tone of voice convey criticism, a lack of acceptance. A more extreme placement indicates therapist communicates that patient's character or personality is somehow displeasing, objectionable, or disturbed.

Item 19: There is an erotic quality to the therapy relationship.

Place toward *characteristic* end if the therapy relationship seems somehow sexualized. This could range from the presence of a warm, erotically tinged relationship to coy, or seductive behavior on the part of the patient, to overtly stated wishes for sexual gratification, e.g., patient talks of sexual experiences in such a way as to invite the sexual interests of the therapist.

Place toward *uncharacteristic* end if therapy relationship seems basically unsexualized; a more extreme placement in this direction indicates that patient or therapist avoid topics or behavior that might be viewed as betraying a sexual interest; or that there is an attempt to suppress erotic feeling.

Item 20: Patient is provocative, tests limits of the therapy relationship. (N.B. Placement toward uncharacteristic end implies patient behaves in a compliant manner.)

Place toward *characteristic* end if patient seems to behave in a manner aimed at provoking an emotional response in the therapist, e.g., patient may invite rejection by the therapist by behaving in a way that might anger him or her, or by violating one or another aspect of the therapy contract.

Place toward *uncharacteristic* end if patient is particularly compliant or deferential, or seems to be playing the role of the "good patient" as a way of courting the therapist.

Item 21: Therapist self-discloses.

Place toward *characteristic* end if therapist reveals personal information, or personal reactions to the patient, e.g., therapist tells patient where he or she grew up, or tells the patient "I find you a very likable person."

Place toward *uncharacteristic* end if therapist refrains from such self-disclosure. More extreme placement in this direction indicates therapist does not self-disclose even when patient exerts pressure for therapist to do so, e.g., therapist does not directly answer the question when patient asks whether the therapist is married.

Item 22: Therapist focuses on patient's feelings of guilt.

Place toward *characteristic* end if therapist focuses on, or somehow draws attention to, patient's guilty feelings particularly when there is an intent to help alleviate such feelings, e.g., therapist remarks that patient appears to feel guilty when she occasionally does not respond to one of her daughter's incessant requests for help.

Place toward *uncharacteristic* end if therapist does not emphasize patient's feelings of guilt.

Item 23: Dialogue has a specific focus.

Place toward *characteristic* end if interaction is kept to a single or a few primary foci, e.g., the foremost topic of the hour is the patient's feeling that throughout the course of his life, and in many different ways, he has failed to live up to his father's expectations of him.

Place toward *uncharacteristic* end if multiple topics are discussed or if dialogue seems somewhat diffuse.

Item 24: Therapist's own emotional conflicts intrude into the relationship.

Place toward *characteristic* end if therapist appears to respond to the patient in a somehow ineffective or inappropriate way, and when this response does not stem solely from the therapy encounter, but conceivably derives from the therapist's own emotional or psychological conflicts, i.e., countertransference reaction, e.g., therapist seems to steer away from certain affects that the patient expresses or needs to express.

Place toward *uncharacteristic* end if therapist's personal emotional responses do not intrude in the therapy relationship inappropriately.

Item 25: Patient has difficulty beginning the hour.

Place toward *characteristic* end if patient manifests discomfort or awkwardness in the initial moments or minutes of the session, e.g., after a lengthy silence, the patient says, "Well, I don't know what to talk about today."

Place in *uncharacteristic* direction if patient begins hour directly without lengthy pauses or prompting questions from the therapist.

Item 26: Patient experiences discomforting or troublesome (painful) affect.

Place toward *characteristic* end if patient expresses feelings of shame, guilt, fear, or sadness while the session is in progress. Extremeness of placement indicates the intensity of the affect.

Place toward *uncharacteristic* direction indicates the patient does not express such troublesome feelings, or expresses feelings of comfort or contentment.

Item 27: Therapist gives explicit advice and guidance (vs. defers even when pressed to do so).

Place toward *characteristic* end if therapist gives explicit advice or makes particular suggestions which patient is then free to accept or ignore, e.g., therapist says, "You know, you might find it helpful to consult a lawyer about how to handle your inheritance." Or therapist might guide patient to consider a range of options and to explore each alternative, e.g., therapist may point out possibilities the patient overlooks and direct patient to explore possible consequences of each line of action.

Place toward *uncharacteristic* end if therapist refrains from giving advice; extreme placement in this direction indicates that the therapist does not supply such guidance despite pressure from the patient to do so.

Item 28: Therapist accurately perceives the therapeutic process.

Place toward *characteristic* end if the therapist seems to accurately perceive the patient's experience of the therapy relationship. This should be inferred from the therapist's comments, interventions, or general stance toward the patient. Judgment should be independent of the type of therapy (i.e., cognitive-behavioral, psychoanalytic) being conducted; rater should attempt an assessment from the perspective of the kind of therapy represented.

Place toward *uncharacteristic* end if the therapist appears in some manner to misperceive the patient's emotional state, the intent of his or her speech, the nature of the interaction between them, or to misformulate the problem.

Item 29: Patient talks of wanting to be separate or distant.

Place toward *characteristic* direction if patient talks about wanting greater distance or a sense of independence from someone (excludes therapist), e.g., states wish to finally be free of his or her parents' influence.

Place toward *uncharacteristic* direction if patient does not talk of wanting to be separate, independent, or detached.

Item 30: Discussion centers on cognitive themes, i.e., about ideas or belief systems.

Place toward *characteristic* end if dialogue emphasizes particular conscious ideational themes, beliefs, or constructs used to appraise others, the self or the world, e.g., therapist suggests they look more closely at a patient's idea or belief that unless he accomplishes everything he attempts perfectly, he is worthless.

Place toward *uncharacteristic* end if there is little or no discussion of such ideas or constructs.

Item 31: Therapist asks for more information or elaboration.

Place toward *characteristic* end if the therapist asks questions designed to elicit information, or presses the patient for a more detailed description of an occurrence, e.g., therapist asks about the patient's personal history, or inquires what thoughts went through the patient's mind when she met an acquaintance by chance on the street.

Place toward *uncharacteristic* end if therapist does not actively elicit information.

Item 32: Patient achieves a new understanding or insight.

Place toward *characteristic* end if a new perspective, or new connection or attitude, or warded-off content emerges during the course of the hour, e.g., following the therapist's remark, the patient appears thoughtful and says, "I think that's true. I had never really thought about the situation that way before."

Place toward *uncharacteristic* end if no evidently new insight or awareness emerges during the hour.

Item 33: Patient talks of feelings about being close to or needing someone.

Place toward *characteristic* end if patient talks about being, or wanting to be, close or intimate with someone (excluding therapist), e.g., patient states he is lonely, and would like to be with someone.

Place toward *uncharacteristic* direction if patient does not make statements about wanting to be close and intimate.

Item 34: Patient blames others, or external forces, for difficulties.

Place toward *characteristic* end if patient tends to externalize, blaming others or chance events for difficulties, e.g., patient claims his or her problems with work stem from bad luck with employers.

Place toward *uncharacteristic* end if patient tends to assume responsibility for his or her problems, e.g., noting that unhappiness in romantic relationships may be the result of choosing unsuitable partners.

Item 35: Self-image is a focus of discussion.

Place toward *characteristic* end if a topic of discussion is patient's concept, or feelings, attitudes, and perceptions of self whether positive or negative, e.g., patient talks of how it is sometimes difficult for her to stand up for herself because she then experiences herself as being too aggressive.

Place toward *uncharacteristic* end if images of the self play little or no part in the dialogue.

Item 36: Therapist points out patient's use of defensive maneuvers, e.g., undoing, denial.

Place toward *characteristic* end if a major topic is the control operations used by the patient to ward off awareness of threatening information or feelings, e.g., the therapist points out how the patient is compelled to profess love for his father directly after having made critical remarks about him.

Place toward *uncharacteristic* end if this sort of interpretation of defenses plays little or no role during the hour.

Item 37: Therapist behaves in a teacher-like (didactic) manner.

Place toward *characteristic* end if therapist's attitude or stance toward patient is like that of a teacher to a student. This can be judged independently of content, i.e., therapist can impart information or make suggestions without behaving in a didactic or teacherly way; alternatively interpretations could be offered in the form of instruction.

Place toward *uncharacteristic* direction if therapist does not assume a tutor-like role in relation to the patient.

Item 38: There is discussion of specific activities or tasks for the patient to attempt outside of session.

Place toward *characteristic* end if there is discussion of a particular activity the patient might attempt outside of therapy, such as testing the validity of a particular belief or behaving differently than she might typically do, or reading books, e.g., there is talk about the patient facing a feared situation or object that she usually avoids.

Place toward *uncharacteristic* if there is no talk about the patient attempting particular actions of this sort outside of therapy.

Item 39: There is a competitive quality to the relationship.

Place toward *characteristic* end if either patient or therapist seems competitive with the other. This may take the form of boasting, "one-upping," or putting the other down, e.g., the patient suggests that therapists live a cloistered life while s/he is out living and working in the real world.

Place toward *uncharacteristic* end if there is little or no feeling of competitiveness between patient and therapist.

Item 40: Therapist makes interpretations referring to actual people in the patient's life. (N.B. Placement toward uncharacteristic end indicates therapist makes general or impersonal interpretations.)

Place toward *characteristic* end if therapist's interpretations refer to particular people the patient knows, e.g., therapist says, "You felt hurt and angry when your mother criticized you."

Placement of the item in the *uncharacteristic* direction signifies that interpretations do not refer to particular people, or refer to other aspects of the patient's life, e.g., therapist comments, "You seem to be inclined to withdraw when others become close."

Item 41: Patient's aspirations or ambitions are topics of discussion.

Place toward *characteristic* end if patient talks about life projects, goals, or wishes for success or status, e.g., patient talks about her hopes to become a lawyer and earn a substantial income.

Place toward *uncharacteristic* end if patient shows or talks about a constriction of future expectations in the discussion of realistic plans or wishful thinking.

Item 42: Patient rejects (vs. accepts) therapists comments and observations.

Place toward *characteristic* end if patient typically disagrees with or ignores therapist's suggestions, observations, or interpretations, e.g., after the therapist made a major interpretation, the patient casually remarked that s/he didn't think that was quite it.

Placement toward *uncharacteristic* direction indicates that patient tends to agree with therapist's remarks.

Item 43: Therapist suggests the meaning of others' behavior.

Place toward *characteristic* direction if therapist attempts to interpret the meaning of the behavior of people in the patient's life, e.g., the therapist suggests that the patient's romantic partner has problems with intimacy.

Place toward *uncharacteristic* end if therapist does not make comments about the meaning of the behavior of others.

Item 44: Patient feels wary or suspicious (vs. trusting and secure).

Place toward *characteristic* end if patient appears wary, distrustful, or suspicious of the therapist, e.g., patient wonders whether the therapist really likes him or her, or if there is another, hidden meaning in the therapist's remarks.

Place toward *uncharacteristic* end if patient seems to be trusting and unsuspicious.

Item 45: Therapist adopts supportive stance.

Place toward *characteristic* end if therapist assumes a supportive, advocate-like posture toward the patient. This may take the form of approval of something the patient has done, or encouraging, for example, the patient's self-assertion. Or the therapist may agree with the patient's positive self-statement, or emphasize the patient's strengths, e.g., "You did this in the past, and you can do it again."

Place toward *uncharacteristic* direction if therapist tends not to assume a supportive role of this sort.

Item 46: Therapist communicates with patient in a clear, coherent style.

Place toward *characteristic* end if therapist's language is unambiguous, direct, and readily comprehensible. Rate as very characteristic if therapist's verbal style is evocative, and marked by a freshness of words and phrasing.

Place toward *uncharacteristic* end if therapist's language is diffuse, overly abstract, jargon-laden, or stereotypic.

Item 47: When the interaction with the patient is difficult, the therapist accommodates in an effort to improve relations.

Place toward *characteristic* end if therapist appears willing and open to compromise and accommodation when disagreement occurs, or when conflicts arise in the dyad, e.g., when the patient becomes annoyed with the therapist, he or she makes some effort to mollify the patient.

Place toward *uncharacteristic* end if therapist does not exert an effort to improve matters when the interaction becomes difficult.

Item 48: The therapist encourages independence of action or opinion in the patient.

Place toward *characteristic* end if therapist urges patient to think for him or herself and to take action based on what he or she thinks best, e.g., therapist notes that he has now heard from the patient what her mother and colleagues think she should do, but it's not clear what she wants or thinks.

Place toward *uncharacteristic* direction if therapist does not introduce the issue of independence or initiative as a topic of discussion.

Item 49: The patient experiences ambivalent or conflicted feelings about the therapist.

Place toward *characteristic* end if patient expresses mixed feeling about the therapist or if the patient's overt verbalizations about the therapist are incongruent with the tone of his or her behavior or general manner, or if there seems to be some displacement of feelings, e.g., the patient cheerfully agrees with the therapist's suggestion but then goes on to express hostility toward people who tell him or her what to do.

Place toward *uncharacteristic* end if there is little expression of patient ambivalence toward therapist.

Item 50: Therapist draws attention to feelings regarded by the patient as unacceptable (e.g., anger, envy, or excitement).

Place toward *characteristic* direction if therapist comments upon or emphasizes feelings that are considered wrong, inappropriate, or dangerous by the patient, e.g., therapist remarks that patient sometimes feels a jealous hatred of his more successful brother.

Place toward *uncharacteristic* end if therapist tends not to emphasize feeling reactions that the patient finds difficult to recognize or accept.

Item 51: Therapist condescends to or patronizes the patient.

Place toward *characteristic* end if therapist seems condescending toward patient, treating him or her as if less intelligent, accomplished, or sophisticated. This may be inferred from the manner in which therapist delivers comments, or offers advice.

Place toward *uncharacteristic* direction if therapist conveys by his or her manner, tone of voice, or comments, that s/he does not assume an attitude of superiority.

Item 52: Patient relies upon therapist to solve his/her problems.

Place toward *characteristic* end if patient appears to present problems to the therapist in a manner that suggests a hope or expectation that the therapist will offer specific suggestions or advice in the way of a solution, e.g., patient states uncertainty as to whether or not to break up with a romantic partner and asks the therapist what to do. Note that the appeal for a solution need not be explicitly stated but may be implied by the manner in which the patient discusses the problem.

Place toward *uncharacteristic* end if patient does not appear explicitly or implicitly to rely on the therapist to solve problems.

Item 53: Patient is concerned about what therapist thinks of him or her.

Place toward *characteristic* end if patient seems concerned with what the therapist might think of his or her behavior, or is concerned about being judged, e.g., the patient might comment, "You are probably thinking that was a stupid thing to do." Rater may also infer this from patient behavior, e.g., patient boasts of accomplishments in order to favorably impress the therapist.

Place toward *uncharacteristic* if patient does not seem concerned with the kind of impression s/he is creating, or appears unworried about being judged by therapist.

Item 54: Patient is clear and organized in self-expression.

Place toward *characteristic* direction if patient expresses him- or herself in a manner that is easily understandable, and relatively clear and fluent.

Placement in *uncharacteristic* direction is indicative of rambling, frequent digression, or vagueness. This can sometimes be judged by the rater's inability to readily follow the connections between topics the patient discusses.

Item 55: Patient conveys positive expectations about therapy.

Place toward *characteristic* end if patient expresses the hope or expectation that therapy will be of help. A more extreme placement in this direction indicates that the patient expresses unrealistically positive expectations, i.e., therapy will solve all of his or her problems and will be a protection against future difficulties, e.g., client may convey hope that therapy will provide quick results.

Place toward *uncharacteristic* end if patient expresses criticisms of therapy, e.g., conveys a sense of disappointment that therapy is not more effective or gratifying. A more extreme placement indicates patient expresses skepticism, pessimism, or disillusionment about what can be accomplished in therapy.

Item 56: Patient discusses experiences as if distant from his or her feelings. (N.B. Rate as neutral if affect and import are apparent but modulated.)

Refer to patient's attitude toward the material spoken, how much s/he appears to care about it, as well as how much overt affective expression there is. Place toward *characteristic* end if patient displays little concern or feeling, and is generally flat, impersonal, or halfheartedly indifferent (tension may or may not be apparent).

Rate as *uncharacteristic* if affect and import are apparent, but well modulated and balanced by cooler material. Place toward *very uncharacteristic* end if patient expresses sharp affect, or outbursts of emotion, and deeply felt concern.

Item 57: Therapist explains rationale behind his or her technique or approach to treatment.

Place toward *characteristic* end if therapist explains some aspect of the therapy to the patient, or answers questions about the treatment process, e.g., therapist may reply in response to a direct question or request by the patient that s/he prefers not to answer immediately, since this would provide a better opportunity to explore thoughts or feelings associated with the question. This item is also intended to capture the therapist suggesting the patient use, or instructing the patient about, certain therapy techniques, e.g., therapist suggests that patient try to focus on her feelings, or close her eyes and attempt to imagine a scene, or to hold a conversation in fantasy with someone during the hour.

Place toward *uncharaceristic* end if little or no effort is made by therapist to explain the rationale behind some aspect of the treatment even if there is pressure, or there may be some usefulness, in doing so.

Item 58: Patient resists examining thoughts, reactions, or motivations related to problems.

Place toward *characteristic* end if patient is reluctant to examine his or her own role in perpetuating problems, e.g., by balking, avoiding, blocking, or repeatedly changing the subject whenever a particular topic is introduced.

Place toward *uncharacteristic* end if patient actively contemplates, or is able to pursue, trains of thought that might be emotionally stressful or unsettling.

Item 59: Patient feels inadequate and inferior (vs. effective and superior).

Place toward *characteristic* end if patient expresses feelings of inadequacy, inferiority, or ineffectiveness, e.g., patient states that nothing he attempts really turns out the way he hopes it will.

Place toward *uncharacteristic* direction if patient expresses a sense of effectiveness, superiority, or even triumph, e.g., recounts personal achievements, or claims attention for a personal attribute or skill.

Item 60: Patient has cathartic experience. (N.B. Rate as uncharacteristic if emotional expression is not followed by a sense of relief.)

Place toward *characteristic* direction if patient gains relief by giving vent to suppressed or pent-up feeling, e.g., patient cries intensely over the death of a parent, and then tells the therapist he feels better as a result of getting these feelings out.

Place toward *uncharacteristic* end if the experience of strong affect is not followed by a sense of relaxation or relief.

Rate as *neutral* if cathartic experience plays little or no role in the hour.

Item 61: Patient feels shy and embarrassed (vs. unselfconscious and assured).

Place toward *characteristic* end if patient appears shy, embarrassed, or not self-assured, or at the extreme, humiliated or mortified.

Place toward *uncharacteristic* end if patient appears unselfconscious, assured, or certain of him- or herself.

Item 62: Therapist identifies a recurrent theme in the patient's experience or conduct.

Place toward *characteristic* end if therapist points out a recurrent pattern in the patient's life experience or behavior, e.g., therapist notes that patient repeatedly offers herself to sexual partners on a platter, thereby inviting shabby treatment.

Place toward *uncharacteristic* end if therapist does not identify such a theme or recurrent pattern.

Item 63: Patient's interpersonal relationships are a major theme.

Place toward *characteristic* end if a major focus of discussion is the patient's social or work relationships, or personal emotional involvements *(excludes* discussion of therapy relationship [see Item 98] and *excludes* discussion of love or romantic relationships [see Item 64]), e.g., patient discusses at some length his or her distress over conflicts with a boss.

Place toward *uncharacteristic* direction if a good portion of the hour is devoted to discussion of matters that are not directly connected to relationships, e.g., the patient's compulsion to work, or drive to achieve, or his/her preoccupation with food and eating.

N.B. Item does not refer to discussion of relationships in the distant past. (See Item 91, Memories or reconstructions of infancy and childhood are topics of discussion.)

Item 64: Love or romantic relationships are a topic of discussion.

Place toward *characteristic* end if romantic or love relationships are talked about during the hour, e.g., patient talks about feelings toward a romantic partner.

Place toward *uncharacteristic* direction if love relationships do not emerge as a topic.

N.B. This item refers to the *quality* of the relationship as opposed to marital status, e.g., discussion of a marital relationship that does not involve love or romance would *not* be rated in the characteristic direction.

Item 65: Therapist clarifies, restates, or rephrases patient's communication.

Place toward *characteristic* end if one aspect of the therapist's activity is restating or rephrasing the patient's affective tone, statements, or ideas in a somewhat more recognizable form in order to somehow render their meaning more evident, e.g., therapist remarks, "What you seem to be saying is that you're worried about what therapy will be like."

Place toward *uncharacteristic* end if this kind of clarifying activity is seldom used by the therapist during the hour.

Item 66: Therapist is directly reassuring. (N.B. Place in uncharacteristic direction if therapist tends to refrain from providing direct reassurance.)

Place toward *characteristic* end if therapist attempts to directly allay patient's anxieties, and instills the hope that matters will improve, e.g., therapist tells patient there is no reason for worry, he's sure the problem can be solved.

Place toward *uncharacteristic* end if therapist tends to refrain from providing direct reassurance of this kind when pressed to do so.

Item 67: Therapist interprets warded-off or unconscious wishes, feelings, or ideas.

Place toward *characteristic* end if therapist draws the patient's attention to feelings, thoughts, or im-

pulses that may not have been clearly in awareness. Rater must attempt to infer the quality of
mental content (i.e., the extent to which it is in
awareness) from the context of the hour (*exclude*
interpretation of defensive maneuvers; see Item
36).

Place in *uncharacteristic* direction if therapist focuses on material that appears to be clearly in the
conscious awareness of the patient.

Item 68: Real vs. fantasized meanings of experiences are actively differentiated.

Place toward *characteristic* end if therapist or patient notes differences between patient's fantasies
about an occurrence and the objective reality, e.g.,
therapist points out that although the patient may
have harbored death wishes toward the deceased,
he did not, in reality, cause his heart attack. Distortions and erroneous assumptions should also
be included, e.g., therapist asks where patient got
that idea when he repeatedly described the world
as dangerous.

Place toward *uncharacteristic* direction if little of
the activity of the therapy hour is concerned with
distortions of reality.

Item 69: Patient's current or recent life situation is empha-sized in discussion.

Place toward *characteristic* end if patient or therapist emphasizes very recent or current life events,
e.g., patient talks about depression over a spouse's
recent death.

Place toward *uncharacteristic* direction if discussion of current life situation was not an important aspect of the hour.

Item 70: Patient struggles to control feelings or impulses.

Place toward *characteristic* end when patient attempts to manage or control strong emotions or impulses, e.g., patient fights to hold back tears while obviously distressed.

Place toward *uncharacteristic* end if patient does not appear to make an effort to control, restrain, or mitigate feelings s/he is experiencing, or has little or no difficulty achieving control over them.

Item 71: Patient is self-accusatory; expresses shame or guilt.

Place toward *characteristic* end if patient expresses self-blame, shame, or guilt, e.g., patient claims that if s/he had paid more attention to a spouse's low moods, the spouse might not have committed suicide.

Place toward *uncharacteristic* direction if patient does not make statements reflecting self-blame, a sense of shame, or pangs of conscience.

Item 72: Patient understands the nature of therapy and what is expected.

Placement toward *characteristic* end reflects the extent to which the patient appears to comprehend what is expected of him or her in the situation and what will happen in therapy.

Placement toward *uncharacteristic* end suggests that the patient is uncertain or confused or misunderstands his or her role in therapy and what is expected in the situation.

Item 73: The patient is committed to the work of therapy.

Place toward *characteristic* end if patient seems committed to the work of therapy. May include willingness to make sacrifices to continue the endeavor, in terms of time, money, or inconvenience; may also include genuine desire to understand more about himself in spite of the psychological discomfort this may entail, e.g., a patient is so interested in beginning treatment that he is willing to give up a weekly golf game to keep therapy appointments.

Place toward *uncharacteristic* end if patient seems ambivalent about therapy, or unwilling to tolerate the emotional hardships that therapy might entail. May be expressed in terms of complaints about the expense of therapy, scheduling conflicts, or statements of doubt about the effectiveness of treatment, or uncertainty about wanting to change.

Item 74: Humor is used.

Place toward *characteristic* end if therapist or patient display humor during the course of the hour. This may appear as a defense/coping mechanism in the patient; or the therapist may use wit or irony to make a point or to facilitate development of a working relationship with the patient, e.g., patient demonstrates an ability to laugh at herself or her predicament.

Place toward *uncharacteristic* direction if the interaction appears grave, austere, or somber.

Item 75: Interruptions or breaks in the treatment, or termination of therapy, are discussed.

Place toward *characteristic* end if either patient or therapist talks of interruptions or breaks in the treatment, e.g., for vacations or illness, or of ending therapy. Includes all references to treatment interruptions or termination, i.e., whether it is wished for, feared, or threatened.

Place in *uncharacteristic* direction if discussion of interruptions in the treatment, or termination, seems to be avoided, e.g., an upcoming lengthy break in the treatment due to summer vacation is mentioned in passing, but neither patient nor therapist pursues topic.

Rate as *neutral* if no reference to interruptions in treatment, or termination, is made.

Item 76: Therapist suggests that patient accept responsibility for his or her problems.

Place toward *characteristic* direction if therapist attempts to convey to the patient that he must take some action, or change somehow, if his or her difficulties are to improve, e.g., therapist comments, "Let's look at what you may have done to elicit that response (from another person)."

Place toward *uncharacteristic* end if therapist's actions are in general not aimed at persuading patient to assume greater responsibility, or if the therapist suggests the patient already assumes too much responsibility.

Item 77: Therapist is tactless.

Place toward *characteristic* end if therapist's comments seem to be phrased in ways likely to be perceived by the patient as hurtful or derogatory. This lack of tact or sensitivity may not be a result of therapist's annoyance or irritation, but rather a result of lack of technique, polish, or verbal facility.

Place toward *uncharacteristic* end if therapist's comments reflect kindliness, consideration, or carefulness.

Item 78: Patient seeks therapist's approval, affection, or sympathy.

Place toward *characteristic* end if patient behaves in a manner that appears designed to make therapist like him or her, or to gain attention or reassurance.

Place toward *uncharacteristic* direction if patient does not behave in this fashion.

Item 79: Therapist comments on changes in patient's mood or affect.

Place toward *characteristic* end if therapist makes frequent or salient comments about shifts in the patient's mood or quality of experience, e.g., therapist notes that in response to his comments, patient has shifted from a "devil may care" attitude to feeling hurt but working more seriously on his problems.

Place toward *uncharacteristic* end if therapist tends not to comment on changes in patient's states of mind during the hour.

Item 80: Therapist presents an experience or event in a different perspective.

Place toward *characteristic* end if therapist restates what the patient has described in such a way that the patient is likely to look at the situation differently ("reframing" or "cognitive restructuring"). A new (and usually more positive) meaning is given to the same content, e.g., after patient berates herself for having started an ugly quarrel with a romantic partner, therapist says, "Perhaps this is your way of expressing what you need in that relationship." In rating this item, a particular event or experience that has been reframed should be identified.

Place in *uncharacteristic* direction if this does not constitute an important aspect of the therapist's activity during the hour.

Item 81: Therapist emphasizes patient's feelings in order to help him or her experience them more deeply.

Place toward *characteristic* end if therapist stresses the emotional content of what the patient has described in order to encourage the experience of affect, e.g., therapist suggests that the interaction the patient has just described in a storytelling manner probably made him feel quite angry.

Place toward *uncharacteristic* direction if therapist does not emphasize the experience or affect or appears interested in patient's objectified descriptions.

Item 82: The patient's behavior during the hour is reformulated by the therapist in a way not explicitly recognized previously.

Place toward *characteristic* end if therapist makes frequent or a few salient comments about the patient's behavior during the hour in a way that appears to shed new light on it, e.g., therapist suggests that the patient's late arrival for the hour may have a meaning, or therapist notes that whenever patient begins to talk about emotional topics, he quickly shifts to another focus.

Place toward *uncharacteristic* end if therapist tends not to reformulate the patient's in-therapy behavior.

Item 83: Patient is demanding.

Place toward *characteristic* end if patient makes more than the "average" number of demands or requests of the therapist or pressures therapist to meet a request, e.g., patient requests evening appointments, medication, or requests more structure or more activity on therapist's part.

Place toward *uncharacteristic* end if patient is reluctant or hesitant to make usual or appropriate requests of the therapist, e.g., fails to ask for another appointment despite a schedule conflict with another, very important event.

Item 84: Patient expresses angry or aggressive feelings.

Place toward *characteristic* end if patient expresses resentment, anger, bitterness, hatred, or aggression (*excludes* such feelings directed at therapist; see Item 1).

Place in *uncharacteristic* direction if the expression of such feelings does not occur, or if patient expresses feelings of affection or love.

Item 85: Therapist encourages patient to try new ways of behaving with others.

Place toward *characteristic* end if therapist suggests alternative ways of relating to people, e.g., therapist asks patient what he thinks might happen if he were to be more direct in telling his mother how it affects him when she nags. More extreme placement implies that the therapist actively coaches patient on how to interact with others, or rehearses new ways of behaving with others.

Place toward *uncharacteristic* end if therapist tends not to make suggestions about how to relate to others.

Item 86: Therapist is confident or self-assured (vs. uncertain or defensive).

Place toward *characteristic* end if therapist appears confident, sure, and nondefensive.

Rate as *uncharacteristic* if therapist appears uncertain, embarrassed, or at a loss.

Item 87: Patient is controlling.

Place in *characteristic* direction if patient exercises a restraining or directing influence in the hour, e.g., patient dominates the interaction with compulsive talking, or interrupts the therapist frequently.

Place in *uncharacteristic* direction if patient does not control the interaction, working with therapist in a more collaborative fashion.

Item 88: Patient brings up significant issues and material.

Placement in *characteristic* direction indicates that rater judges that what the patient brings up and talks about during the hour is importantly related to patient's psychological conflicts, or are topics of real concern.

Place toward *uncharacteristic* end if discussion seems unrelated to or somehow removed from issues of central concern.

Item 89: Therapist acts to strengthen defenses.

Place toward *characteristic* end if therapist's stance is characterized by a calm, attentive compliance intended to avoid upsetting the patient's emotional balance or if he or she actively intervenes to help patient avoid or suppress disturbing ideas or feelings.

Place in *uncharacteristic* direction if therapist does not act to shore up defenses or suppress troublesome thoughts or feelings.

Item 90: Patient's dreams or fantasies are discussed.

Place toward *characteristic* end if a topic of discussion is dream content or fantasy material (daydreams or night dreams), e.g., patient and therapist explore the possible meanings of a dream the patient had the night before starting therapy.

Place toward *uncharacteristic* end if there is little or no discussion of dreams or fantasy during the hour.

Item 91: Memories or reconstructions of infancy and childhood are topics of discussion.

Place toward *characteristic* end if some part of the hour is taken up by a discussion of childhood or memories of early years of life.

Place in *uncharacteristic* direction if little or no time is devoted to a discussion of these topics.

Item 92: Patient's feelings or perceptions are linked to situations or behavior of the past.

Place toward *characteristic* end if several links or salient connections are made between the patient's current emotional experience or perception of events with those of the past, e.g., therapist points out (or patient realizes) that current fears of abandonment are derived from the loss of a parent during childhood.

Place toward *uncharacteristic* end if current and past experiences are discussed, but not linked overtly.

Place toward *neutral* category if these subjects are discussed very little or not at all.

Item 93: Therapist is neutral.

Place toward *characteristic* end if therapist tends to refrain from stating opinions or views of topics patient discusses. Therapist assumes role of neutral commentator, and the patient's view of matters is made preeminent in the dialogue, e.g., therapist asks how it would be for the patient if she, as the therapist, approved of his expressing his anger, and subsequently inquires how it would be for him if she disapproved.

Place toward *uncharacteristic* direction if therapist expresses opinions, or takes positions either explicitly or by implication, e.g., therapist tells patient that it is very important that he learn how to express his anger, or comments that the relationship the patient is in right now is not a very good one, and that she should consider getting out of it.

N.B. Neutrality is not synonymous with passivity. The therapist can be active and still maintain a neutral stance.

Item 94: Patient feels sad or depressed (vs. joyous or cheerful).

Place toward *characteristic* end if patient's mood seems melancholy, sad, or depressed.

Place toward *uncharacteristic* end if patient appears delighted or joyful or somehow conveys a mood of well-being or happiness.

Item 95: Patient feels helped.

Place toward *characteristic* end if patient somehow indicates a sense of feeling helped, relieved, or encouraged.

Placement *uncharacteristic* direction indicates that patient feels discouraged with the way therapy is progressing, or frustrated, or checked. (N.B. Item does *not* refer to events outside of therapy.)

Item 96: There is discussion of scheduling of hours, or fees.

Place toward *characteristic* end if therapist and patient discuss the scheduling or rescheduling (times, dates, etc.) of a therapy hour, or if there is discussion of the amount of fee, time of payment, and the like.

Place toward *uncharacteristic* direction if these topics are not taken up.

Item 97: Patient is introspective, readily explores inner thoughts and feelings.

Place toward *characteristic* end if patient appears unguarded, and relatively unblocked. In this instance the patient pushes beyond ordinary constraints, cautions, hesitancies, or feelings of delicateness in exploring and examining thoughts and feelings.

Place *in uncharacteristic* direction if patient's discourse appears hesitant or inhibited, shows constraint, reserve, or a stiffening of control, and does not appear loose, free, or unchecked.

Item 98: The therapy relationship is a focus of discussion.

Place toward *characteristic* end if therapy relationship is discussed, e.g., therapist calls attention to features of the interaction or interpersonal process between the patient and him or herself.

Place toward *uncharacteristic* end if therapist or patient does not comment on the nature of transactions between them, i.e., focuses on content.

Item 99: Therapist challenges the patient's view (vs. validates the patient's perceptions).

Place in *characteristic* end if therapist somehow raises a question about the patient's view of an experience or an event, e.g., therapist might say "How is that so?" or "I wonder about that," or simply utter an "Oh?" This item does *not* refer to interpretations or reframing in the sense of providing a new or different meaning to the patient's discourse, but instead refers simply to raising a question about the patient's viewpoint in some way.

Place in *uncharacteristic* direction if therapist somehow conveys a sense of agreement, concurrence with, or substantiation of the patient's perspective, e.g., therapist may say, "I think you're quite right about that" or "You seem to have a good deal of insight into that."

Item 100: Therapist draws connections between the therapeutic relationship and other relationships.

Place toward *characteristic* end if therapist makes several or a few salient comments linking the patient's feelings about the therapist and feelings toward other significant individuals in his or her life. Includes current relationships, and past or present relationships with parents (transference/parent link), e.g., therapist remarks that she thinks the patient is sometimes afraid she will criticize her just as her mother does.

Place toward *uncharacteristic* end if therapist's activity during the hour includes no or few attempts to link the interpersonal aspects of therapy with experiences in other relationships.

References

Ablon, J. S., and Jones, E. E. (1998). How expert clinicians' prototypes of an ideal treatment correlate with outcome in psychodynamic and cognitive-behavioral therapy. *Psychotherapy Research* 8:71–83.
———. (1999). Psychotherapy process in the National Institute of Mental Health Treatment of Depression Collaborative Research Program. *Journal of Consulting and Clinical Psychology* 67:64–75.
Abrams, S. (1990). The psychoanalytic process: the developmental and the integrative. *Psychoanalytic Quarterly* 59:650–677.
Alexander, F., and French, T. M. (1946). *Psychoanalytic Therapy: Principles and Applications.* New York: Ronald Press.
American Psychiatric Association (1994). *Diagnostic and Statistical Manual of Mental Disorders*, 4th ed. Washington, DC: APA.
Arlow, J. A. (1969). Fantasy, memory, and reality testing. *Psychoanalytic Quarterly* 38:28–51.
Beck, A. T., Ward, C. H., Mendelson, M., et al. (1961). An inventory for measuring depression. *Archives of General Psychiatry* 4:561–571.
Benjamin, L. S. (1993). *Interpersonal Diagnosis and Treatment of Personality Disorders.* New York: Guilford.
Block, J. (1961/1978). *The Q-Sort Method in Personality Assessment and Psychiatric Research.* Springfield, IL: Charles C Thomas.
Blum, H. P. (1980). The value of reconstruction in adult psychoanalysis. *International Journal of Psycho-Analysis* 61:39–54.
Boesky, D. (1990). The psychoanalytic process and its components. *Psychoanalytic Quarterly* 59:550–584.
Brenneis, C. B. (1997). *Recovered Memories of Trauma: Transferring the Present to the Past.* Madison, CT: International Universities Press.

Brenner, C. (1974). Depression, anxiety and affect theory. *International Journal of Psycho-Analysis* 55:25–32.

———. (1982). *The Mind in Conflict*. New York: International Universities Press.

Breuer, J., and Freud, S. (1893). Studies on hysteria. *Standard Edition* 2:1–305.

Bumberry, W., Oliver, J. M., and McClure, J. N. (1978). Validation of the Beck Depression Inventory in a university population using psychiatric estimate as a criterion. *Journal of Consulting and Clinical Psychology* 46:150–155.

Caston, J. (1993). Mannequins in the labyrinth and the couch-lab intersect. *Journal of the American Psychoanalytic Association* 41:51–65.

Cavell, M. (1993). *The Psychoanalytic Mind*. Cambridge: Harvard University Press.

———. (1998). Triangulation, one's own mind and objectivity. *International Journal of Psycho-Analysis* 79:449–467.

Chassan, J. B. (1979). *Research Design in Clinical Psychology and Psychiatry*, 2nd ed. New York: Wiley.

Chused, J. S. (1991). The evocative power of enactments. *Journal of the American Psychoanalytic Association* 39:615–639.

Crits-Christoph, P., and Connolly, M. B. (1998). Empirical basis of supportive-expressive therapy. In *Empirical Studies of the Therapeutic Hour*, ed. R. F. Bornstein and J. M. Masling, pp. 109–151. Washington, DC: American Psychological Association.

Dahlstrom, W. G., and Welsh, G. S., eds. (1960). *An MMPI Handbook*. Minneapolis: University of Minnesota Press.

Derogatis, L. R., Lipman, R. S., Rickels, K., et al. (1974). The Hopkins Symptom Checklist (HSCL): a self-report symptom inventory. *Behavioral Science* 19:1–15.

Elkin, I., Shea, T. M., Watkins, J. T., et al. (1989). National Institute of Mental Health Treatment of Depression Collaborative Research Program. *Archives of General Psychiatry* 46:971–982.

Endicott, J., and Spitzer, R. L. (1977). A diagnostic interview: the schedule for affective disorders and schizophrenia. *Archives of General Psychiatry* 35:837–844.

Feldman, M. (1997). The dynamics of reassurance. In *The Contemporary Kleinians of London*, ed. R. Schafer, pp. 321–343. Madison, CT: International Universities Press.

Fenichel, O. (1941). Problems of psychoanalytic technique. *Psychoanalytic Quarterly* 7:421–442.

Ferenczi, S. (1932). *The Clinical Diary of Sandor Ferenczi*, ed. J. Dupont. Cambridge: Harvard University Press.

Fonagy, P., Moran, G. S., Edgcumbe, R., et al. (1993a). The role of mental representations and mental processes in therapeutic action. *Psychoanalytic Study of the Child* 48:9–48. New Haven, CT: Yale University Press.

Fonagy, P., Moran, G. S., and Target, M. (1993b). Aggression and the psychological self. *International Journal of Psycho-Analysis* 74:471–485.

Fonagy, P., and Target, M. (1996). Predictors of outcome in child psychoanalysis: a retrospective study of 763 cases at the Anna Freud Centre. *Journal of the American Psychoanalytic Association* 44:27–77.

———. (1997). Perspectives on the recovered memories debate. In *Recovered Memories of Abuse: True or False?*, ed. J. Sandler and P. Fonagy, pp. 183–216. Madison, CT: International Universities Press.

Fretter, P. B. (1995) A control-mastery case formulation of a successful treatment for major depression. *In Session: Psychotherapy in Practice* 1:3–17.

Freud, A. (1946). *The Ego and the Mechanisms of Defense*, trans. C. Baines. New York: International Universities Press.

Freud, S. (1912). The dynamics of transference. *Standard Edition* 12:97–108.

———. (1917). Mourning and melancholia. *Standard Edition* 14:237–259.

———. (1921). Group psychology and the analysis of the ego. *Standard Edition* 18:67–143.

———. (1926a). The question of lay analysis. *Standard Edition* 20:183–258.

———. (1926b). Inhibitions, symptoms and anxiety. *Standard Edition* 20:77–175.

———. (1937). Constructions in analysis. *Standard Edition* 23:257–269.

Gabbard, G. (1997). A reconsideration of objectivity in the analyst. *International Journal of Psycho-Analysis* 78:15–26.

Gill, M. (1954). Psychoanalysis and exploratory psychotherapy. *Journal of the American Psychoanalytic Association* 2:771–797.

———. (1982). *Analysis of Transference*. New York: International Universities Press.

Glover, E. (1931). The therapeutic effect of inexact interpretation: a contribution to the theory of suggestion. *International Journal of Psycho-Analysis* 12:397–411.

Gopnik, A. (1998). Man goes to see a doctor. *The New Yorker,* August 24 and 31, pp. 114–121.

Gottman, J. M. (1981). *Time Series Analysis.* New York: Cambridge University Press.

Gottman, J. M., and Ringland, J. (1981). The analysis of dominance and bidirectionality in social development. *Child Development* 52:393–412.

Gray, P. (1994). *The Ego and the Analysis of Defense.* Northvale, NJ: Jason Aronson.

Green, A. (1996). What kind of research for psychoanalysis? *International Psycho-Analysis* 5:8–9.

Greenson, R. R. (1967). *The Technique and Practice of Psychoanalysis,* vol. 1. New York: International Universities Press.

Grünbaum, A. (1984). *The Foundations of Psychoanalysis: A Philosophical Critique.* Berkeley, CA: University of California Press.

Hamilton, M. (1967). Development of a rating scale for primary depressive illness. *British Journal of Social and Clinical Psychology* 6:278–296.

Hollon, S. D., and Kendall, P. C. (1980). Cognitive self-statements in depression: development of an automatic thoughts questionnaire. *Cognitive Therapy and Research* 4:383–395.

Hornstein, G. A. (1992). The return of the repressed: psychology's problematic relations with psychoanalysis, 1909–1960. *American Psychologist* 47:254–263.

Horowitz, L. M., and Rosenberg, S. E. (1994). The consensual response psychodynamic formulation: part I. Method and research results. *Psychotherapy Research* 3/4:222–233.

Horowitz, L. M., Rosenberg, S. E., Baer, B. A., et al. (1988). The inventory of interpersonal problems: psychometric properties and clinical application. *Journal of Consulting and Clinical Psychology* 56:885–892.

Jacobson, N. S., and Truax, P. (1991). Clinical significance: a statistical approach to defining meaningful change in psychotherapy research. *Journal of Consulting and Clinical Psychology* 41:51–65.

Jones, E. E. (1993). How will psychoanalysis study itself? *Journal of the American Psychoanalytic Association* 41:91–108.

———. (1998). Depression: intervention as assessment. In *Making Di-*

agnosis Meaningful, ed. J. W. Baron, pp. 267–297. Washington, DC: American Psychological Association.

Jones, E. E., Cumming, J. D., and Horowitz, M. J. (1988). Another look at the nonspecific hypothesis of therapeutic effectiveness. *Journal of Consulting and Clinical Psychology* 56:48–55.

Jones, E. E., Ghannam, J., Nigg, J. T., and Dyer, J. F. P. (1993). A paradigm for single case research: the time series study of a long-term psychotherapy for depression. *Journal of Consulting and Clinical Psychology* 61:381–394.

Jones, E. E., Hall, S. A., and Parke, L. A. (1991). The process of change: the Berkeley Psychotherapy Research Group. In *Psychotherapy Research: An International Review of Programmatic Studies*, ed. L. Beutler and M. Crago, pp. 99–106. Washington, DC: American Psychological Association.

Jones, E. E., and Price, P. B. (1998). Interaction structure and change in psychoanalytic psychotherapy. In *Empirical Studies of the Therapeutic Hour*, ed. R. Bornstein and J. Masling, pp. 27–62. Washington, DC: American Psychological Association.

Jones, E. E., and Pulos, S. M. (1993). Comparing the process in psychodynamic and cognitive-behavioral therapies. *Journal of Consulting and Clinical Psychology* 61:985–1015.

Jones, E. E., and Windholz, M. (1990). The psychoanalytic case study: toward a method for systematic inquiry. *Journal of the American Psychoanalytic Association* 38:985–1015.

Joseph, B. (1996). *Uses of the past by patient and analyst in the psychoanalytic process*. Paper presented to the San Francisco Psychoanalytic Institute, November.

Kernberg, O. (1975). *Borderline Conditions and Pathological Narcissism*. New York: Jason Aronson.

———. (1980). *Internal and External Reality*. New York: Jason Aronson.

———. (1988). Psychic structure and structural change: an ego-psychology object relations theory viewpoint. *Journal of the American Psychoanalytic Association* 36:315–337.

Klein, M. (1935). A contribution to the psychogenesis of manic-depressive states. *International Journal of Psycho-Analysis* 16:145–174.

Kohut, H. (1971). *The Analysis of the Self*. New York: International Universities Press.

———. (1984). *How Does Analysis Cure?* New York: International Universities Press.

Kris, E. (1956). The recovery of childhood memories in psychoanalysis. *Psychoanalytic Study of the Child* 11:54–88. New York: International Universities Press.

Loewald, H. P. (1960). On the therapeutic action of psychoanalysis. *International Journal of Psycho-Analysis* 41:16–33.

Loftus, E. F. (1993). The reality of repressed memory. *American Psychologist* 48:518–537.

Luborsky, L. (1953). Intra-individual repetitive measurements (P-technique) on understanding symptom structure and psychotherapeutic change. In *Psychotherapy: Theory and Research*, ed. O. H. Mowrer, pp. 389–413. New York: Ronald Press.

———. (1967). Momentary forgetting during psychotherapy and psychoanalysis: a theory and research method. In *Motives and Thought: Psychoanalytic Essays in Honor of David Rappaport*, ed. R. R. Holt, pp. 177–217. New York: International Universities Press.

———. (1995). The first trial of the P technique in psychotherapy research—a still lively legacy. *Journal of Consulting and Clinical Psychology* 63:6–14.

Luborsky, L., and Crits-Christoph, P. (1998). *Understanding Transference: The Core Conflictual Relationship Theme Method*, 2nd ed. Washington, DC: American Psychological Association.

Main, M. (1993). Discourse, prediction, and recent studies in attachment: implications for psychoanalysis. *Journal of the American Psychoanalytic Association* 41:209–244.

Malan, D. H. (1976). *The Frontier of Brief Psychotherapy*. New York: Plenum.

Mayes, L., and Spence, D. (1994). Understanding therapeutic action in the analytic situation: a second look at the developmental metaphor. *Journal of the American Psychoanalytic Association* 42:789–817.

McLaughlin, J. T. (1981). Transference, psychic reality, and countertransference. *Psychoanalytic Quarterly* 50:639–664.

———. (1991). Clinical and theoretical aspects of enactment. *Journal of the American Psychoanalytic Association* 39:595–639.

McWilliams, N. (1998). Relationship, subjectivity, and inference in diagnosis. In *Making Diagnosis Meaningful*, ed. J. W. Barron, pp. 197–226. Washington, DC: American Psychological Association.

Millon, T. (1991). Classification in psychopathology: rationale, alternatives, and standards. *Journal of Abnormal Psychology* 100:245–261.

Mitchell, S. A. (1993). *Hope and Dread in Psychoanalysis.* New York: Basic Books.

Modell, A. (1976). "The holding environment" and the therapeutic action of psychoanalysis. *Journal of the American Psychoanalytic Association* 24:285–308.

Morton, J. (1997). Cognitive perspectives on recovered memories. In *Recovered Memories of Abuse: True or False?*, ed. J. Sandler and P. Fonagy, pp. 39–63. Madison, CT: International Universities Press.

Murray, J. F. (1995). On object, transference, and two-person psychology: a critique of the new seduction theory. *Psychoanalytic Psychology* 12:31–41.

Ogden, T. (1994). *Subjects of Analysis.* Northvale, NJ: Jason Aronson.

Pole, N., and Jones, E. E. (1998). The talking cure revisited: content analysis of a two-year psychodynamic psychotherapy. *Psychotherapy Research* 8:171–189.

Racker, H. (1968). *Transference and Countertransference.* New York: International Universities Press.

Reich, W. (1933). *Character-analysis.* New York: Orgone Institute Press.

Renik, O. (1993). Analytic interaction: conceptualizing technique in light of the analyst's irreducible subjectivity. *Psychoanalytic Quarterly* 62:553–571.

Sandler, J. (1976). Countertransference and role-responsiveness. *International Review of Psycho-Analysis* 3:43–47.

Sandler, J., and Fonagy, P., eds. (1997). *Recovered Memories of Abuse: True or False?* Madison, CT: International Universities Press.

Schafer, R. (1976). *A New Language for Psychoanalysis.* New Haven, CT: Yale University Press.

———. (1983). *The Analytic Attitude.* New York: Basic Books.

———. (1997). Introduction: The Contemporary Kleinians of London. In *The Contemporary Kleinians of London*, ed. R. Schafer, pp. 1–25. Madison, CT: International Universities Press.

Schlesinger, H. J. (1988). A historical overview of conceptions of the mode of therapeutic action of psychoanalytic psychotherapy. In *How Does Treatment Help?*, ed. A. Rothstein, pp. 7–27. New York: International Universities Press.

Seligman, M. E. (1995). The effectiveness of psychotherapy. *American Psychologist* 50:965–974.

Shea, M. T., Elkin, I., Imber, S. D., et al. (1992). Course of depressive symptoms over follow-up: findings from the National Institute of

Mental Health Treatment of Depression Collaborative Research Program. *Archives of General Psychiatry* 49:782–787.

Spence, D. (1982). *Narrative Truth and Historical Truth: Meaning and Interpretation in Psychoanalysis.* New York: W. W. Norton.

Spence, D., Dahl, H., and Jones, E. E. (1993). Impact of interpretation on associative freedom. *Journal of Consulting and Clinical Psychology* 61:395–402.

Spezzano, C. (1993). *Affect in Psychoanalysis: A Clinical Synthesis.* New York: Analytic Press.

Spitzer, R. L., Endicott, J., and Robins, E. (1979). *Research Diagnostic Criteria (RDC) for a selected group of functional disorders,* 3rd ed. New York: Biometric Research, New York State Psychiatric Institute.

Strachey, J. (1934). The nature of therapeutic action in psychoanalysis. *International Journal of Psycho-Analysis* 15:127–159.

Strupp, H. (1998). Negative process: its impact on research, training, and practice. In *Empirical Studies of the Therapeutic Hour,* ed. R. F. Bornstein and J. M. Masling, pp. 1–26. Washington, DC: American Psychological Association.

Sugarman, A., and Wilson, A. (1995). Introduction to the special section: contemporary structural analysts critique relational theories. *Psychoanalytic Psychology* 12:1–8.

Target, M. (1998). The recovered memories controversy. *International Journal of Psycho-Analysis* 79:1015–1028.

Viederman, M. (1995). The reconstruction of a repressed sexual molestation fifty years later. *Journal of the American Psychoanalytic Association* 43:1169–1195.

Wallerstein, R. (1986). *Forty-two Lives in Treatment.* New York: Guilford.

Weiss, J. (1993). *How Psychotherapy Works.* New York: Guilford.

Weiss, J., and Sampson, H. (1986). *The Psychoanalytic Process.* New York: Guilford.

Weissman, M. M., Prusoff, B. M., Thompson, W. D., et al. (1978). Social adjustment by self-report in a community sample and in psychiatric outpatients. *Journal of Nervous and Mental Disease* 166:317–326.

Westen, D. (1990). Towards a revised theory of borderline object relations: contributions of empirical research. *International Journal of Psycho-Analysis* 71:661–694.

Wetzler, S. (1985). The historical truth of psychoanalytic reconstructions. *International Review of Psycho-Analysis* 12:187–197.

Williams, L. (1994). Recall of childhood trauma: a prospective study of women's memories of child sexual abuse. *Journal of Consulting and Clinical Psychology* 62:1167–1176.

Williams, M. (1987). Reconstruction of early seduction and its after effects. *Journal of the American Psychoanalytic Association* 35:145–163.

Wilson, M. (1993). *DSM-III* and the transformation of American psychiatry: a history. *American Journal of Psychiatry* 150:399–410.

Winnicott, D. W. (1965). *The Maturational Processes and the Facilitating Environment.* New York: International Universities Press.

Wolff, P. H. (1996). The irrelevance of infant observation for psychoanalysis. *Journal of the American Psychoanalytic Association* 44:369–392.

World Health Organization (1989). *Mental Disorders: 10th Revision of the International Classification of Diseases (ICD-10).* Geneva, Switzerland: WHO.

Credits

The author gratefully acknowledges permission to reprint material from the following sources.

Chapter 1: "Modes of Therapeutic Action" in *International Journal of Psycho-Analysis* 78:1135–1150. Copyright © 1997 Institute of Psychoanalysis.

Chapter 2: "Depression: Invention as Assessment" in *Making Diagnosis Meaningful: Enhancing Evaluation and Treatment of Psychological Disorders*, ed. J. Barron, pp. 267–297. Copyright © 1998 American Psychological Association.

Chapter 7: "How Will Psychoanalysis Study Itself?" in *Journal of the American Psychoanalytic Association* 41:91–108. Copyright © 1993 International Universities Press.

Chapter 8: "A Paradigm for Single-Case Research: The Time Series Study of a Long-Term Psychotherapy for Depression" in *Journal of Consulting and Clinical Psychology* 61:381–394. Copyright © 1993 American Psychological Association. "Interaction Structure and Change in Psychoanalytic Therapy" in *Empirical Studies of the Therapeutic Hour*, ed. R. Bornstein and J. Masling, pp. 27–62. Copyright © 1998 American Psychological Association.

Index

Resistance. *See also* Defenses
  confrontation, 125
  counterresistance concept,
      126–127
  interpretation of, 129–134
Rosenberg, S. E., 54

Sampson, H., 13, 25, 259, 266,
      305
Sandler, J., 14, 16, 108
Schafer, R., 122–123, 125,
      126
Schlesinger, H. J., 14
Self-knowledge. *See* Knowledge
Self-reflection, 79–117. *See also*
      Memory
  clarification, 91–95
  confrontation, 95–98
  memory, 101–117
    childhood trauma,
        107–112
    contemporary approaches,
        112–117
    generally, 101–107
    overview, 81–82
    questioning, 82–91
    theme identification, 98–100
Seligman, M. E., 254
Sexual abuse, childhood,
      memory of, self-reflection,
      107–112
Shea, M. T., 220
Single-case research
  causalilty and generalizability,
      264–269
  Psychotherapy Process Q-set
      (PQS), 261–264
Spence, D., 13, 25, 98, 103,
      265
Spezzano, C., 51
Spitzer, R. L., 278

Static approaches, evaluation
      for psychotherapy, 40–42
Strachey, J., 10, 11, 241
Strupp, H., 206–207
Subjectivity, countertransfer-
      ence and, 165–174
Sugarman, A., 15
Suggestion, modes of action,
      9–12
Supportive approaches, 209–
      249
  described, 212–222
  guilt sharing, 241–245
  interaction structures and,
      227–232
  interpersonal influences,
      222–227
  interventions, use of, 233–
      235
  overview, 211–212
  re-education and reality
      testing, 235–241
  reassurance, 245–249
Supportive interaction struc-
      ture, research case studies,
      297–308. *See also* Research
      case studies

Target, M., 9, 109, 114, 117
Theme identification, self-
      reflection, 98–100
Theory
  change, xii
  psychoanalytic therapy, xiv–
      xv
Therapeutic alliance
  Psychotherapy Process Q-set
      (PQS), 260
  transference, 162
Therapeutic relationship,
      modes of action, 3–4

About the Author

Enrico Jones, Ph.D., is Professor of Psychology at the University of California, Berkeley, and former head of its Psychology Clinic and Director of its Clinical Psychology Training Program. He founded the Berkeley Psychotherapy Research Project, which for the past two decades has generated psychoanalytically informed empirical research. Dr. Jones is also a member of the faculty of the San Francisco Psychoanalytic Institute and a practicing psychoanalyst in Berkeley.